THIS IS MY COUNTRY

This is my Country

A Personal Blend of the Purest Scotch
by W. GORDON SMITH

Illustrations by Barbara Brown

SOUVENIR PRESS

First published 1976 by Souvenir Press Ltd,
43 Great Russell Street, London WC1B 3PA
and simultaneously in Canada by

Methuen Publications,
Agincourt, Ontario

ISBN 0 285 622374

Printed in Great Britain by
Ebenezer Baylis and Son Ltd,
The Trinity Press, Worcester, and London

Designed by Christopher Scott

Contents

"Tell me about Scotland and yourself," said the Princess. "Tell me your stories and sing me your songs."

The Prince sulked and looked at the floor.

"There is too much to tell," he said.

"I have time enough to listen," she said. "A thousand years if need be."

"That may not be enough," he muttered into his chest.

"And you know that I have an open mind and a warm heart," she said, laying a jewelled hand on his sleeve.

The Prince raised his head.

"I fear you will need both," he said, and began his story.

THE BYDAND MYTHS

Scotland

This is my country,
The land that begat me,
These windy spaces
Are surely my own.
And those who here toil
In the sweat of their faces
Are flesh of my flesh,
And bone of my bone.

Alexander Gray

She saw a sun on a summer sky,
And clouds of amber sailing bye;
A lovely land beneath her lay,
And that land had glens and mountains gray;
And that land had vallies and hoary piles;
And marlèd seas, and a thousand isles;
Its fields were speckled, its forests green,
And its lakes were all of a dazzling sheen,
Like magic mirrors, where slumbering lay
The sun and the sky and the cloudlet gray;
Which heaved and trembled and gently swung,
On every shore they seemed to be hung;
For there they were seen on their downward plain
A thousand times and a thousand again;
In winding lake and placid firth,
Little peaceful heavens in the bosom of earth.

Kilmeny sighed and seemed to grieve,
For she found her heart to that land did cleave;
She saw the corn wave on the vale,
She saw the plaid and the broad claymore,
And the brows that the badge of freedom bore;
And she thought she had seen the land before.

James Hogg

Dear Mr Street:

There you were, reading American "Variety" at 32,000 feet (which serves you right) when you came across a friendly review of my play "Jock". By the time your aircraft had touched down at Heathrow you had already resolved to persuade me to write a book based on the same theme as the play – an attempt to explain why the Scots are what they are. Then we met in London to discuss the project. We talked about this kind of anthology and that, but chiefly about football and I came home with a publisher's advance in my pocket and no clear ideas about my book or what you all wanted from me. Many months have come and gone, a second deadline approacheth, and I am no nearer fulfilling my commission. I say all this now because another football season is almost upon us and its excitements and traumas will not be conducive to work. Could you ask around on my behalf and find out just exactly what you all want for your money.

Dear Mr Smith:

As your agent in this project I want the book to catch the spirit and the mood of your country. As a mere Sassenach and Arsenal supporter, surely you don't expect me to tell you how to do this; you succeeded with your play so surely you can do it again. People don't read plays, but sometimes they can be induced to read books. Assuming, of course, that the books get written.
P.S. I have business in Frankfurt next week. Hope to see some good football – if you know what I mean.

Dear Mr Street:

The faintly disguised sneer about our football standards is beneath
even Scottish contempt. So, it's Frankfurt is it? While I burn the midnight (North Sea) oil? You should go armed, like Robert Louis Stevenson, with a Burns translation:

"Now that I have got my German Burns, I lean a good deal upon
him for opening a conversation, and read a few translations to every
yawning audience that I can gather. I am grown most insufferably
national, you see. I fancy it is a punishment for my want of it at
ordinary times.

> Mein Herz ist im Hochland, mein Herz ist nicht hier.
> Mein Herz ist im Hochland im grünen Revier.
> Im grünen Reviere zu jagen das Reh;
> Mein Herz ist im Hochland, wo immer ich geh.

"There is one thing that burthens me a good deal in my patriotic
garrulage, and that is the black ignorance in which I grope about
everything, as, for example, when I gave yesterday a full and, I fancy,
a startlingly incorrect account of Scotch education to a very stolid
German on a garden bench: he sat and perspired under it, however,
with much composure. I am generally glad enough to fall back again,
after these political interludes, upon Burns, toddy, and the Highlands."

Two points before we go furth of that hundred-year-old letter from
Frankfurt to Edinburgh: the *Concise Oxford Dictionary* says:

> "the Scotch themselves usu. prefer the form Scottish, also used
> by the English esp. in dignified style or context, or Scots rare in
> Engl. use exc. in compliment to Scotch hearers . . ."

Yes, we prefer it, and yes, keep coming with the compliments. And
Stevenson, contrary to any wishes he may have had in the matter, is
usually called Robert Louis, French-style, by the Scots, and not Lewis,
Scots-style, as he was baptised.

The mirror which you have asked me to hold aloft to catch the
reflection of a nation remains cloudy and ghosted with images of Burns
and toddy, heathery haggises and wee bandy men. All the grist is
gathered at the mill but the wheel will not turn. I worry about the
book's architecture, its shape and form and contours. I fear I may even
have to return the advance – actually give the money back, thereby
shattering another illusion about the Scots.

If you can give me a clue, any guidance at all, about the book – how much of it should be anthology, how much autobiographical anecdote, how much bedside rather than coffee table? – perhaps, just maybe, I could thread the needle and stitch all these orphan pieces together.

P.S. The ultimate Scottish international team would be:- Knox; Wallace, Bruce; Burns, Montrose, Dunbar; Adam, Napier, Smith, Telford and Stewart. Absolute certainty of salvation in goal; tigerish tackling and devilish cunning at full back; a centre back of legendary courage and dash; two earthily honest wing halves who are robust yet sweetly constructive; and an old-fashioned forward line of five attackers, blending wit, craft and creativity, linking superbly, and full of running. By the way, the left-winger can be Charles Edward, Lachie, or Jackie – they could all shift a bit when the going was good or bad. God, as usual, would have the whistle.

Dear Gordon Smith: FRANKFURT

Please get on with it! I am merely the middle-man, but I should warn you that you and your publisher, though racially different, are saddled with similar mythologies. So be certain that if you don't deliver soon he will not wait upon your conscience before demanding his money back. And please don't belabour me about your brief. Why should I know how you should put the book together? Some time ago I was commissioned to compile an anthology about football and freely admit I have been hoping that you could suggest a new form to me.

Frankfurt is wet and sticky but a haven of tranquillity compared to the World Cup when the place overflowed with foul-mouthed, drunken Scots. Did I ever tell you about the gentleman from a place called Pumpherston who burst into my bedroom at 4 a.m. and insisted that I drink the health of his team with what he called, "the Tartan Treble" – a mixture, apparently, of pilsner, hair lacquer, and industrial anti-freeze?

P.S. I have the whistle.

Early Lessons

There was very little amusement in the room but a Scotchman to hate. Some people you must have observed have a most unpleasant effect upon you when you see them speaking in profile – this Scotchman is the most accomplished fellow in this way I ever met with. The effect was complete. It went down like a dose of bitters, and I hope will improve my digestion. At Taylor's too, there was a Scotchman – not quite so bad for he was as clean as he could get himself.

John Keats

The Hills of Home

After illicit love and flaring drunkenness, nothing appeals so much
to Scotch sentiment as having been born in the gutter.

T. W. H. Crosland

I don't remember realising that I was Scottish.

There was a yah-yah English family in the street, a freckled Irish
boy who waggled his porky ears in the class, and a black Jamaican
teacher with big breasts. A pickled walnut under a pink turban peddled
brushes and rugs round the doors. Every so often a man with a beret
and wet cigarette in the corner of his face pushed a bicycle, trousered
with onions, up our steep hill. An Egyptian doctor and his family moved
into the neighbourhood for a time, ate sheep's brains, and left.

I remember realising that *they* were different. They were the people
from beyond "multitudinous seas incarnadine" whose souls were being
saved by my Sunday School pennies.

Some differences were inescapable. At school Roman Catholics and
Jews and the son of a militant atheist excused themselves from religious
instruction on the grounds of dogma, disbelief or biology, and the
eternal damnation which they could not escape in the next world held
no terrors for them in this world as they played silent pontoon or fur-
tively explored each other's pubescent sexuality at the back of the class.

The known world stopped at the end of the street. The only tramcar,
a number 24, happened to operate in a secure circle, so that no matter
where one got on, one was always returned. All round in the distance
there were hills that one could always see, and beyond those in the
north, we were told, rose the Highlands. And we could see the sea, or
the wide river estuary that waved and foamed like the sea and rolled out
across the deeps to Norway.

On St Patrick's day, for reasons that were never explained, we rolled
newspapers into hard balls and trapped them in twine. Swinging them
round our heads we cornered an adversary and demanded of him:
"Scotch or Irish?" The law of Edinburgh averages being what it is we
assaulted twenty friends to every foe and I remember volunteering to
be Irish on more than one occasion simply to make some playground
massacre more interesting. It was no different from tossing a coin to see
who should be Geronimo and who Tom Mix in our vivid daily re-
constructions of the North American genocide.

We were not rich enough to have a radio or a gramophone and the
piano that propped up a parlour wall was sold when we took in a lodger
and I (given a fatuous alternative) chose swimming lessons rather than
the dubious delights of learning to play "Für Elise". I knew other
people had radios because my father owned a battery charger and, as an

unlikely sideline to his shoemaking business, he replenished accumulators for the going rate. My contribution to the family business, which was never more than twenty-four hours away from bankruptcy, was to deliver these greasy glass jars, bubbling from the charge, their smelly acids hissing and spitting and biting my bare legs as I hurried them back to their magical connections.

I suppose we bought a daily newspaper, and I was soon delivering them by the hundred, but I have no memory of seeing one, let alone reading one, in the house. A lady to whom I delivered accumulators, shoes, newspapers, and subsequently milk, who sometimes rewarded me with a downy peach from her greenhouse, used to iron *The Scotsman* so that it was as crisp and crackly as the toast on her husband's breakfast table. She was very different.

The cinema had shown the first talking picture the year I was born yet I was still to catch my first glimpse of the silvery screen. The city supported half-a-dozen theatres and two great football clubs yet I did not even know of their existence. Enough of my youth remained for me to mis-spend it in billiards saloons.

We lived at the end of a terraced block of four new houses, two up, two down, kitchenette and bathroom, girt by funereal laurels, smug on top of a hill, with a quacking farm steading only five hundred yards away and a green field across a burn across the road. My mother's sisters and brothers, my bombazined and serged aunts and uncles, came to us for a bath. My father's relatives probably had baths of their own or, like the old-fashioned miners, believed that too much washing weakened the back.

Apart from going to work and school and church and Sunday School we did nothing. Absolutely nothing. If there was a world beyond my world it was conjured out of dreams and nameless fears and nightmares, summoned by sermons, given uncertain shape by painted pictures of Palestine and dark etchings depicting darker deeds in school history books.

I assumed then, as I do now, that as a race we began in the alluvial mud and crawled out of the sea, that a cold wet haar enveloped the land until one day the boiling lava and the creeping glacier collided with each other and Scotland emerged out of a shroud of steam. Something like that. Something awful like that.

Other people went to parties, had holidays, travelled in trains, knew the next episode of Flash Gordon, saw tries scored at Murrayfield, were Episcopalians, answered the telephone, knew what steak tasted like, and said fuck as if it were spelt with a "ph".

We lived above our station and I, for one, felt it. But I could inhale at the age of eight, was a packet-a-day man by the time I was nine, and on the "you show me yours and I'll show you mine" basis I had acted as master of ceremonies at many a puppy-show.

At eleven my chief claim to attention and notoriety was my knowledge of a formula, consisting of iodine crystals and ammonia, for a mild but startling explosive, so sensitive that it could be detonated by a clumsy fly. I am still fascinated by explosions and loud reports but would not blow up any living thing, not even a fly.

By the age of eleven, without knowing it, I had begun to recognise general differences and to make myself different, and sensed for the first time that we Scots were a race apart, inhabiting a separate landscape. I was not told this, nor did I overhear it when the state of the world was discussed, as it was, in my presence. Certainly it was not stressed in school where my bourgeois teachers put almost hysterical emphasis on daily prayers for King and Empire.

Books made all the difference. The civil servant down the road could hear Hilversum, Athlone and Luxemburg on his super-heterodyne receiver. One of the two car-owners in the entire community drove all the way to France and back. The lady through the wall became even more unhinged, bought a new harmonium, and night after night accompanied her quavering soprano voice through the entire works of Moody and Sankey. But I had access to books.

There was *The Coral Island* and *Treasure Island*, *Virginibus Puerisque* and *Travels with a Donkey in the Cevennes*, *Kidnapped* and *Father and Son*, *The Life and Letters of John Donne*, Shakespeare, Goethe, an atlas of the world, and *An Illustrated History of the Great War*.

I read everything and understood very little. Pecking here and there like a demented hen I pierced the black boredom of my childhood. I terrorised librarians, and to this day recall that palpable stab at the heart when I was told there was no Sherlock Holmes story which I had not read. Dixon Hawk, Sexton Blake, Father Brown, Poirot, Marlowe, Wimsey and Carella have all proved to be inadequate suitors for those thwarted innocent affections.

It was said of me then that I would stand on my head to read the labels on a passing suitcase. I gobbled up text like ice-cream in voracious gulps and swallows, savouring little, digesting nothing. Once in a while, with even greater greed, I relished something so much that I teased and spun it out, licking it like a lollipop, making it last the night. Such a book was in Sir Walter Scott's mind when he entered up his journal on May 24, 1827.

A good thought came in my head to write stories for little Johnie Lockhard... I am persuaded both children and the lower class of readers hate books which are written *down* to their capacity and love those that are more composed for their elders and betters. I will make if possible a book that a child will understand yet a man will feel some temptation to peruse should he chance to take it up. It will require however a simplicity of stile not quite my own. The Grand and interesting consists in ideas not in words. A clever thing of this kind will have a run.

The "clever thing" became Scott's child's history of Scotland, *Tales of a Grandfather*. It was part of his incredible struggle during the last six years of his life to pay off debts of over £120,000. By most literary standards and by any historical yardstick it is a bad book, a well-intentioned pot-boiler, yet it is not too much to say that it changed the course of my life.

Our edition in the bookcase by the window was red and fat and sumptuous, gilt-edged, half-bound in morocco, and studded with full-colour plates of men in armour, waving plumes, tilted lances, caparisoned chargers, and cleaving claymores. A label announced that it had been awarded to my father "for composition" at St Bernard's School, Dean Park Street, Edinburgh.

> For that is the mark of the Scot of all classes: that he stands in an attitude towards the past unthinkable to Englishmen, and remembers and cherishes the memory of his forbears, good or bad; and there burns alive in him a sense of identity with the dead even to the twentieth generation.
>
> *Robert Louis Stevenson*

Within a week of going to secondary school the flames were fanned by *The Lay of the Last Minstrel*, Scott's vast narrative Borders poem. It is seldom read now, even in schools, and I suffered the same fidgety anguish as my fellows throughout most of its tedious length, but we had a Boadicea of an English mistress – "Ma" Castles to us – whose dramatic delivery would have rivalled Mrs Siddons' at her best. She impaled us on her voice, bored holes in us with her eyes, and with her arms sawing the air spat such scorn at us that I remember every shiver of it to this day:

> Breathes there the man with soul so dead,
>   Who never to himself hath said,
>   This is my own, my native land!
> Whose heart hath ne'er within him burn'd,
> As home his footsteps he hath turn'd
>   From wandering on a foreign strand!
> If such there breathe, go, mark him well;
> For him no Minstrel raptures swell;
> High though his titles, proud his name,
> Boundless his wealth as wish can claim;
> Despite those titles, power, and pelf,
> The wretch, concentred all in self,
> Living, shall forfeit fair renown,

And, doubly dying, shall go down
To the vile dust, from whence he sprung,
Unwept, unhonour'd, and unsung.

She waved Scott's words like banners before our eyes.

The secret sympathy,
    The silver link, the silken tie,
Which heart to heart, and mind to mind,
    In body and in soul can bind.

March, march, Ettrick and Teviotdale,
Why the deil dinna ye march forward in order?
March, march, Eskdale and Liddesdale,
All the Blue Bonnets are bound for the Border.
    Many a banner spread
    Flutters above your head,
Many a crest that is famous in story.
    Mount and make ready then,
    Sons of the mountain glen,
Fight for the Queen and the old Scottish glory.

Come from the hills where your hirsels are grazing,
Come from the glen of the buck and the roe;
Come to the crag where the beacon is blazing,
Come with the buckler, the lance, and the bow.
    Trumpets are sounding,
    War-steeds are bounding,
Stand to your arms then, and march in good order;
    England shall many a day
    Tell of the bloody fray,
When the Blue Bonnets come over the Border.

An army of heroes, no longer pasteboard cut-outs or wispy drawings, marched through our minds. We saw William Wallace, greatest of all Scottish patriots, dragged to the gallows at Tyburn, hanged by the neck for two minutes, cut down alive, castrated, disembowelled, his entrails burnt before his eyes, beheaded, then quartered. We saw his head piked on Smithfield Bridge and the crows pick out his eyes. And we saw Robert the Bruce take a terrible revenge at Bannockburn.

The English cover all the earth this hot June day. Their knights charge at the first halloo. They ford the burn and mount the rise and there, before them, outnumbered three to one, the Scots, with their patriot king on a small grey pony. The English knight, de Bohun, black-armoured and crimson-plumed, spurs his heaving charger, tilts his lance, and thunders across the plain. The king talks with his men. He pretends that he cannot feel the earth shake under de Bohun's charger. The tip of the lance is but a few feet from him when, at the last moment, he pulls his pony aside. The charger comes on, and on, and with one blow of his battleaxe the Bruce smashes de Bohun's head to pulp. Lord Robert was king that day. "I have broken the haft of my good battleaxe," was all he said. And the brains of de Bohun spilled out on the ground.

Jock

The hair bristled on our scalps and our spines arched with a savage joy. She could wring our hearts, too, particularly when it came to great disasters like Flodden. She would begin with a solemn catalogue of the dead, tolling the words like a funeral bell . . .

thirteen earls, the Bishop of St Andrews, barons, knights, the provosts of cities and burghs, lairds, farmers, and *twelve thousand men* . . .

then, as if she could command her own phantom piper to moan the lament behind her, she led us sadly into "The Flowers o' the Forest".

Dule and wae for the order sent our lads to the Border!
    The English, for aince, by guile wan the day;
The Flowers o' the Forest, that foucht aye the foremost,
    The prime o' our land are cauld in the clay.

We hear nae mair lilting at our yowe-milking;
    Women and bairns are heartless and wae,
Sighing and moaning on ilka green loaning,
    The Flowers o' the Forest are a' wede away.

Jean Elliot

It was terrible. Sweet Mary, Mither o' God, I canna tell you how terrible it was. I saw the king staund high in his stirrups. I saw him spy the Earl o' Surrey inside a ring o' English spears, an' I saw him chairge like a' the dugs o' hell was at his tail. I saw four, five, six, *seven* arrows whummel intae the king. I saw yin o' his hands hingin' tae his airm by only a slither o' skin. I saw yin swing fae a billhook bring his life's bluid pumpin' oot o' his neck. An' when he was only the length o' a lance awa' fae the Earl o' Surrey, I saw him fall.

Jock

He [James IV] is not a good captain because he begins to fight before he has given his orders . . . he does not think it right to begin any warlike undertaking without being himself the first in danger. His deeds are as good as his words. For this reason, and because he is a very humane prince, he is much loved. He loves war so much, that I fear, judging from the provocation he receives, the peace will not last long.

Pedro di Ayala [1498]

This elderly lady, dragged out of retirement because the young teachers were off to war, not only presented us with the past, she challenged us with it, dared us to ignore it, and commanded our allegiance to the old vows and testaments:

For, as long as but ane hundred of us remain alive, never will we on any conditions be brought under English rule. It is in truth not for glory, nor riches, nor honours that we are fighting, but for freedom – for that alone, which no honest man gives up but with life itself.

from the Declaration of Arbroath
[1320]

Behind it all, however, something else gleamed and sparkled. She was like an atheist singing hymns. She loved the old battle tunes and the majesty of the words, but could never resist bringing us down with a bump, switching suddenly from romance to reality.

The Jinxed Jameses

I won't go into the tedious business about how the Stewarts started. The top lot became kings, and a right shower they turned out to be . . . well, I'll have to qualify that. Robert II, the first of them, was 54 when he became king, and it's a wonder he wasn't dead at 34. He was Robert the Steward, affectionately known as Old Bleary Eyes. He had at least eight bastard sons and God knows how many legitimate and semi-legitimate children of one legitimate and another semi-legitimate marriage . . . Surely I don't have to explain the bleary eyes . . .

We don't have to waste any breath on his son, Robert III, who at least had the honesty to describe himself as "the most miserable of men and the worst of kings." He was even wrong about that!

The Jameses were cursed. The first four of them, all young men, died violent deaths. For 200 years only children succeeded to the throne.

James I was a beautiful man – tall, strong, and athletic. He was a poet and musician, and the first kingly king since Robert the Bruce. Few men have had such a curse of envious cousins, few kings more contenders for their crowns. In the sanctuary of the Blackfriars in Perth, in 1437, a trap was sprung. Nine daggers cut the king to shreds as he was dragged out of his hiding-place – an outlet of the royal privy. There was a terrible irony about that privy outlet. The king's escape was thwarted because he had ordered that the escape hole in the outer wall of the house should be covered over. It had claimed too many royal tennis balls.

James II stood too close to one of his new cannons at the seige of Roxburgh Castle and it blew up in his face. So that was the end of him.

The nobles defeated James III at the Battle of Sauchieburn in 1488. He fled the field but fell off his horse. He asked a woman to fetch him a priest, which she did, and the king asked the priest for absolution. The priest administered the last rites with a dagger.

James IV got his lot at Flodden, after the wedding of the Thistle and the Rose and the signing of a treaty that was meant to ensure "a good, real, sincere, true, entire, and firm peace to endure for ever."

James V wasn't quite two when his father died at Flodden. By the time he was twenty he'd peddled his pedigree round all the Courts in Europe and settled for a wee French wife. He brought her home – where the climate killed the lassie – then sent to France for a replacement. A widow, Mary of Guise, arrived with a large dowry and a broad mind. She needed both. Jamie the Fifth had expensive tastes and many mistresses. He fathered at least nine bastards to different fancy women and died at the age of thirty – of very natural causes! One of the last things he heard in this world was that his wife had given birth to a daughter, who was to become Mary Queen of Scots, and the whole world knows what happened to her. Elizabeth affected great grief and said it was all a terrible mistake, and James VI, Mary's son, footered and fumbled for the right words, but even in the death of his mother he saw political advantage.

Jamie the Saxt, the wisest fool in Christendom, and Jamie the

24

Saxt, I've got to admit, was probably a queer. The Stewarts are no more proof against that predilection than any other. He certainly behaved like it when he gave his queen the boot and found a lot of fairies at the bottom of the royal garden. On the other hand – and notice how the democratic processes are beginning to work already – the best evidence for his homosexuality seems to be that alone among the Jameses he had no mistresses. So maybe he just didn't fancy it all that much.

When Lizzie snuffed it – and she took her time about it, didn't she? – he moved off down the road with all his goods and chattels. London gluttony eventually got the better of him and he ate himself to death on a diet of melons and strawberries. He left behind some bad poetry, pamphlets condemning smoking and witchcraft, and a reputation in the Highlands as an evil, murdering, black-hearted, bandy-legged sot. And, believe me, that's a polite translation from the Gaelic.

Jock

"Ma" Castles reached her romantic apogee – and, by definition, therefore had her feet farthest from the ground – with Prince Charles Edward Louis Philip Casimir Stuart, the Chevalier or Young Pretender (as she called him) or Bonny Prince Shortbried (as I invariably think of him).

> Royal Charlie's now awa'
> Safely o'er the friendly main,
> Mony a heart will break in twa
> Should he no' come back again.
> Will ye no' come back again,
> Will ye no' come back again,
> Better lo'ed you'll never be,
> Will ye no' come back again?

The old song, sung slowly and sweetly and not bastardised into a maudlin bellow, can still stir the heart. Like the haunting alchemy of the "Canadian Boat Song", the authorship of which several books have failed to settle:

> From the lone shieling of the misty island
> Mountains divide us, and the waste of seas –
> Yet still the blood is strong, the heart is Highland,
> And we in dreams behold the Hebrides.

And if, in our adolescent ignorance and insensitivity, we failed to respond to such arcane pleasure, she would rally us with:

> A battle there was that I saw, man,
> And we ran, and they ran,
> And they ran, and we ran,
> And *we* ran, and they ran awa', man.

Or she would indulge our natural instincts for braggadocio, an Italian word invented by an Englishman and a poor synonym for "gallus", an instantly-available Scottish word, still used, and meaning "deserving the gallows":

> Pity me, without hands three,
> Two for the pipes and a sword hand free.

It must now be apparent that this latter-day Jean Brodie was at best entertaining, at worst dangerous.

> If a man were permitted to make all the ballads, he need not care who should make the laws of a nation . . .

. . . she would chant at us, quoting another of her patriot heroes, Andrew Fletcher of Saltoun.

Ballads are the anthems of revolution and the hymns of martyrs. The citizens of mainland Britain – including Scotland – cannot understand this about the Irish. Perhaps one can never fully comprehend the latent power of a song which commemorates epic deeds or brave men until one has sat in the parlour of an Irish pub, hands linked with total strangers, every voice – including one's own – raised in passionate chorus. Thus the Kevin Barrys, Robert Emmets and Father Murphys of that tortured land by dying gained immortality and, by one of the oldest processes in the world, live more abundantly in the folk memory of a race.

"Ma" Castles, in her own way, led our singing. She would have applauded the Greek revolutionary Theodorakis who, knowing that his songs were adrenalin to the cause, devised a novel way to send them out into the waiting world while the military junta kept him under house arrest. His young son was allowed to go to school every day through the cordon of guards, but was always liable to be searched. So when Theodorakis had composed some new ballads he recorded them on magnetic tape, fashioned the tightly-rolled tape into buttons, and the songs were carried out to the revolutionaries on his son's coat.

The Scottish National Party have no good songs that I have heard sung. As a nation we have the second-best national songs in the world, yet no national anthem acceptable to the hundreds of thousands who annually give a resounding raspberry to "God Save the Queen" at Hampden. Even "Scotland the Brave" is an Irish tune.

Scotland's revolutionary ballads dried up after the Jacobite cause ended at Culloden. The songs of that period, many of them by political necessity euphemistic and symbolic, survive because the most melodic of them suited the sentimental music-hall singers and their successors on television.

The recent revival of interest in traditional folk music has resuscitated such great songs as "Such a Parcel of Rogues in a Nation", for which Robert Burns is given some of the credit.

> Fareweel to a' our Scottish fame,
>   Fareweel our ancient glory!
> Fareweel ev'n to the Scottish name,
>   Sae famed in martial story!
> Now Sark rins o'er the Solway sands,
>   An' Tweed rins to the ocean,
> To mark where England's province stands –
>   Such a parcel of rogues in a nation!
>
> What force or guile could not subdue
>   Thro' many warlike ages
> Is wrought now by a coward few
>   For hireling traitor's wages,
> The English steel we could disdain,
>   Secure in valour's station;
> But English gold has been our bane –
>   Such a parcel of rogues in a nation!
>
> O, would, or I had seen the day
>   That Treason thus could sell us,
> My auld grey head had lien in clay
>   Wi' Bruce and loyal Wallace!
> But pith and power, till my last hour
>   I'll mak this declaration:
> "We're bought and sold for English gold" –
>   Such a parcel of rogues in a nation!

A few years ago I wrote a song, "Come by the Hills", and it is probably very much in the mainstream of contemporary Scottish songs – a gentle ballad, melodic, wistful, with that flawless Scottish virtue, pride.

27

The Moira Andersons of this world sing it sweetly and sincerely. The last verse is:

> Come by the hills to the land where legends remain,
> Where glories of old stir the heart and may yet come again,
> Where the past has been lost and the future has still to be won,
> And the cares of tomorrow must wait till this day is done.

I switched on television one night and found a hairy Irishman in a beery folk cellar belting out that verse as if it were a last call to arms. And I realised that my undistinguished song and his even less distinguished performance spoke a simple truth. For the Scots the romantic past has indeed been lost, we publicly mourn it almost every day in one irrational way or another, and the future, notwithstanding oil revenues and the prospects of some form of self-government, is not so important that it is worth going to war about. For the Irish, even more emotionally romantic than ourselves, every injustice, every lost cause of the past has been mounted as another rung on the ladder towards some glorious tomorrow.

When the "Ma" Castles of this world fire young hearts with nationalist ardour it is for lost castles, splendid debacles, scattered chieftains, dead kings, hollow heroes, treachery, murder, squalor, disease and poverty.

At least, that is what our history teachers told us. "Ma" Castles' subject was the English language.

Dear Mortimer Street:

Pinning down our national character is a bit like trying to trap mercury with a bent fork. Plundering my bookshelves I've found so many epigrams and epithets that maybe you should consider marketing a South British desk calendar with a daily dose of anti-Scottish abuse.

Dear Gordon Smith:

I had no idea your national emblem so accurately represented your national failing. Why are you all so prickly?

By the way, is it true that in some of the minor Scottish leagues they still wear pit-boots with reinforced steel toe-caps for cup-ties away from home? The question is a mere morsel of serious research for my football anthology.

About the abuse, wasn't it your Robbie who said something about "seeing ourselves as others see us"? Or was that Shakespeare?

A People's Character

The Scots cannot endure to hear their country or Countrymen spoken against.

John Ray

Mirror, Mirror on the Wall

I think being Scottish makes you very specific, you have a particular kind of distortion, like some kind of prism and the light that comes through gets reflected in a special way. The difficulty is to use the degree of distortion and yet not end up in a cul-de-sac. Ideally the distortion should lead you back out to where everybody else is because everybody else must have had something like the same kind of things happening to them. I don't think being Scottish is either an enormous disadvantage or an enormous advantage, but I do think being Scottish is a very specific kind of existential event. I think I'm very Scottish and I'm discovering each day how much more Scottish I am. As the variety of apparent choices in life open up to me, I realise how few of them are real choices. I just go on doing the things I always did and these things seem to be governed by my origins.

Alan Sharp

I have been trying all my life to like Scotchmen, and am obliged to desist from the experiment in despair.

Charles Lamb

You've forgotten the grandest moral attribute of a Scotsman, Maggie, that he'll do nothing which might damage his career.

J. M. Barrie

In all my travels I never met with any one Scotchman but what was a man of sense. I believe everybody of that country that has any, leaves it as fast as they can.

Thomas Lodge

Metaphysical Lovers

It requires a surgical operation to get a joke well into a Scotch understanding. Their only idea of it, or rather that inferior variety of this electric talent which prevails occasionally in the North, and which, under the name of WUT, is so infinitely distressing to people of good taste, is laughing immoderately at stated intervals. They are so imbued with metaphysics that they even make love metaphysically. I overheard a young lady of my acquaintance, at a dance in Edinburgh, exclaim, in a sudden pause of the music, "What you say, my Lord, is very true of love in the *aibstract*, but – " Here the fiddlers began fiddling furiously, and the rest was lost. No nation has so large a stock of benevolence of heart: if you meet with an accident, half Edinburgh immediately flocks to your door to inquire after your *pure* hand or your *pure* foot, and with a degree of interest that convinces you their whole hearts are in the inquiry. You find they usually arrange their dishes at dinner by the points of the compass; "Sandy, put the gigot of mutton to the south, and move the singet sheep's head a wee bit to the nor-wast." If you knock at the door, you hear a shrill female voice from the fifth flat shriek out, "Wha's chapping at the door?" which is presently opened by a lassie with short petticoats, bare legs, and thick ankles. My Scotch servants bargained they were not to have salmon more than three times a week, and always pulled off their stockings, in spite of my repeated objurgations, the moment my back was turned. Their temper stands anything but an attack on their climate. They would have you even believe they can ripen fruit; and, to be candid, I must own in remarkably warm summers I have tasted peaches that made most excellent pickles; and it is upon record that at the siege of Perth, on one occasion, the ammunition failing, their nectarines made admirable cannon balls. Even the enlightened mind of Jeffrey cannot shake off the illusion that myrtles flourished at Craig Cook. In vain I have represented to him that they are of the genus *Carduus*, and pointed out their prickly peculiarities. In vain I have reminded him that I have seen hackney coaches drawn by four horses in the winter, on account of the snow; that I had rescued a man blown flat against my door by the violence of the winds, and black in the face; that even the experienced Scotch fowls did not venture to cross the streets, but sidled along, tails aloft, without venturing to encounter the gale. Jeffrey sticks to his myrtle illusions, and treats my attacks with as much contempt as if I had been a wild visionary, who had never breathed his caller air, nor lived and suffered under the rigour of his climate, nor spent five years in discussing metaphysics and medicine in that garret of the earth – that knuckle-end of England – that land of Calvin, oatcakes, and sulphur.

Sydney Smith

Among ourselves, the Scotch, as a nation, are particularly disagreeable. They hate every appearance of comfort themselves and refuse it to others. Their climate, their religion, and their habits are equally averse to pleasure. Their manners are either distinguished by a fawning sycophance (to gain their own ends, and conceal their natural defects), that makes one sick; or by a morose, unbending callousness, that makes one shudder.

William Hazlitt

The humid and penetrating atmosphere of Scotland had for sometime affected me in a very disagreeable manner, notwithstanding the active life I led. I found that the mists, the frequent rains, the change of winds, the sharpness of the air, and the absence of the sun plunged me into an involuntary melancholy, which I should not long have been able to support.

Faujas de Saint-Fond

After an interminable journey, changing at Inverness, then going west to Achnasheen through a formless, sodden landscape, the shapes of the hills muffled by a purplish fuzz of heather, we motored along the banks of Loch Maree, and finally arrived at Poolewe, where the river Ewe, flowing from Loch Maree, enters a tidal loch. Pool House, which we rented furnished, was panelled with shiny pitch pine; the walls were hung with engravings of Highland cattle after Peter Graham, the chairs were covered with hideous cretonnes and the threadbare carpet was full of holes. The only book in the house was Queen Victoria's *Leaves from Our Journal in the Highlands*. This kind of dilapidated simplicity is said by sensitive people to have great charm, but it had none for me. . . . If I had been an imaginative child I might have consoled myself with the fantasy of being in my native land. "Breathes there the man with soul so dead?" Well, I am sorry to say there does. I am, and always have been, completely devoid of genealogical piety. The right of a family tree is as distasteful to me as a VAT form. Endless bogs, not an acre of cultivated land, persistent rain, followed by swarms of midges – it did not need the villainous landlords of leftist mythology to drive people away from this melancholy, unproductive coast line.

Kenneth Clark

In This Wonderland . . .

. . . in Orkney, their Ews bring forth two Lambs a piece; that in the Northermost of Shetland Islands, about the Summer Solstice, there is no Night; that in the Park of Cumbernaule are White Kine and Oxen;

that at Slanes there is a putrifying water in a Cove; that at Aberdeen is a Vitriolin Well, that they say is excellent to dissolve the Stone, and expel Sand from the Reins and Bladder, and good for the Colick, being drunk in July &c. These prodigious wonders in one Countrey are admirable, but these are not half of them. Loughness never freezes; in Lough Lommond are fishes without fins: and 2dly the Waters thereof rage in great waves without wind in calm weather: and thridly and lastly, Therein is a floating Island. In Kyle is a deaf Rock 12 foot every way, yet a Gun discharged on one side of it, shall not be heard to the other. In another place is a Rocking-stone of a reasonable bigness, that if a Man push it with his finger, it will move very lightly, but if he address his whole force, it availeth nothing; with many more marvels of a like nature, which I wou'd rather believe than go thither to disprove.

The Observator's New Trip to Scotland [1708]

You Scots . . . are such a mixture of the practical and the emotional that you escape out of an Englishman's hand like a trout.

J. M. Barrie

It is never difficult to distinguish between a Scotsman with a grievance and a ray of sunshine.

P. G. Wodehouse

There are few more impressive sights in the world than a Scotsman on the make.

J. M. Barrie

An Englishman is a man who lives on an island in the North Sea governed by Scotsmen.

Phillip Guedella

All Things Good

The Scottish towns are like none which I ever saw, either in England, Wales, or Ireland: there is such an air of antiquity in them all, and such a peculiar oddness in their manner of building. But we were most surprised at the entertainment we met with in every place, so far different from common report. We had all things good, cheap, in great abundance, and remarkably well dressed.

John Wesley

On the whole, I must say, I think the time we spent there was six weeks of the *densest* happiness I have ever met with in any part of my life; and the agreeable and instructive society there in such plenty has left so pleasing an impression on my memory, that, did not strong connections draw me elsewhere, I believe Scotland would be the country I should choose to spend the remainder of my days in.

Benjamin Franklin

The Scots are as diligent, as industrious, as apt for Labour and Business, and as capable of it, when they are abroad, as any People in the World; and why should they not be so at Home? and, if they had Encouragement, no doubt they would.

Daniel Defoe

None Such

Last Sunday my review of *Twelfth Night* amazingly stated that Sir Toby Belch is usually played as a "Scottish oaf". He is not. There are no Scottish oafs. It should have read, "sottish oaf".

Harold Hobson
(*Sunday Times*, 16.2.75)

The Scotch are proverbially poor and proud, we know they can remedy their poverty when they set about it. No one is sorry for them.

William Hazlitt

Treacherous Scotland, to no interest true.

John Dryden

A greedy, dark, degenerate place of Sin
For th' Universe to shoot her Rubbish in ...
Pimps, Bullies, Traitors, Robbers, 'tis all one,
Scotland, like wide-jaw'd Hell, refuses none.

A Trip Lately to Scotland
[1705]

The vile Scots ...

Petrarch

The tediousness of these people is certainly provoking. I wonder if
they ever tire one another!

Charles Lamb

Scotland has had many an ill picture drawn for her in the world; and
as she has been represented in False Draughts, no wonder the Injurys
she suffered are intolerable. All the Spies sent hither have carry'd back
an ill Report of the Land, and fill'd the World with weak Banters and
Clamour at they know not what.

Daniel Defoe [himself a spy]

The Bowels of Vesuvius

The chief national characteristics of the Scotch are constancy and
unwearied perseverance. These qualities have made that dreary and
barren land a home of prosperity, a flourishing paradise. Those who
see with envy that Scotchmen go anywhere, take to anything, are always
and everywhere happy, are in the habit of saying that you may bury a
Scotchman in the bowels of Vesuvius and he will find a way out. It is
meant for irony, but it is the greatest compliment that can be paid to
a nation.

Lajos Kossuth

A land of meanness, sophistry and lust.

Lord Byron

The English are polite and considerate. Other peoples are more polite. Others are more considerate. But none combines the two things so well, so generously and so naturally. I am making a pilgrimage to London by tonight's train. I hope to meet several Englishmen. None of them will, I think, really understand me or my nation and he will have no idea at all of our innermost thoughts, of what we reverence or to what we aspire. But I shall be disagreeably surprised if anybody treads on my toes deliberately or punches my vaccination mark. If he does he will certainly have Scots blood in his veins.

James Bridie

Scotsmen proceed everywhere; and wherever they are found, they are esteemed for their probity and honour, and are characterized by an energy which knows not how to yield, and a determination which is invincible.

Rev. Charles Rogers

It has been the bane of Scottish literature and disgrace of her antiquities, that we have manifested an eager propensity to believe without inquiry.

Sir Walter Scott

Limbo of Vanities

... So flushed and riotous can the Scottish mind become over a commercial prospect that it sometimes sends native caution by the board, and a man's really fine idea becomes an empty balloon to carry him off to the limbo of vanities.

There is a megalomaniac in every parish in Scotland ... in every district, almost, you may find a poor creature who for thirty years has cherished a great scheme by which means to revolutionise the world's commerce, and amass a fortune in monstrous degree. He is generally to be seen shivering at the Cross, and (if you are a nippy man) you shout carelessly in going by, "Good morning, Tamson; how's the scheme?" And he would be very willing to tell you if only you would listen. "Man," he will cry eagerly behind you, "if I only had anither wee

39

wheel in my invention – she would do, the besom! I'll süne have her ready noo."

Poor Tamson!

George Douglas Brown

There are singular contradictions in the Scottish character; hardness and tenderness seem to meet and mingle in equal proportions, the sarcastic and the reverential perpetually striving for mastery; how they rejoice if they are able to espy something in a train or chain of reasoning through which they can pierce! – and, on the other hand, they become most delightfully unreasonable, and bow themselves down before some single and solitary touch of truly affectionate eloquence; they are unable to resist it, and they have no desire to attempt to do so.

Speculative hard-headedness unites in the national character with a sublime and lofty enthusiasm concerning things altogether remote and intangible.

Paxton Hood

Scotch Love

A married couple in the parish of Farnell had lived together happily for several years. One evening, when they were seated at their fireside, a mouse chanced to run across the floor. "There's a moosie," said the wife, "it cam frae below the bed." "Na," said the husband, "it cam oot below the kist [chest]." The parties began to debate the point, a keen argument ensued, and angry words passed on both sides. The controversy was resumed in the morning, and continued with increasing violence from day to day, till the wife left the house and returned to her friends. The couple lived apart for twelve years, when, on the intercession of friends, they became reconciled. They resumed house-keeping together, and during five years the voice of discord was unheard. At length the wife ventured to refer to the cause of their long estrangement. "Wasn't it very absurd, dear John," said she, "that we should have separated about sic a trifle as a moosie comin' frae below the bed?" "I tell ye that it cam oot below the kist, woman," said the husband sharply. "It didna do that, John," retorted the wife, "I mind see'n 't, as if 'twere yesterday, comin' frae under the bed." The husband started to his feet and vehemently maintained that his wife was speaking falsely. The spirit of discord was again evoked. The parties separated, and were never reunited.

Rev. Charles Rogers

Il y a beaucoup d'amour dans la classe des paysans en Ecosse.

Stendhal

State of the Nation, 1698

There are at this day in Scotland – besides a great many poor families very meanly provided for by the church-boxes, with others who, by living on bad food, fall into various diseases – *two hundred thousand people begging from door to door*. These are not only no way advantageous, but a very grievous burden to so poor a country. And though the number of them be perhaps double to what it was formerly, by reason of this present great distress, yet in all times there have been about one hundred thousand of those vagabonds, who have lived without any regard or subjection either to the laws of the land, or even those of God and nature. No magistrate could ever be informed, or discover, which way one in a hundred of these wretches died, or that ever they were baptised. Many murders have been discovered among them; and they are not only a most unspeakable oppression to poor tenants – who, if they give not bread, or some kind of provision, to perhaps forty such villains in one day, are sure to be insulted by them – but they rob many poor people who live in houses distant from any neighbourhood. In years of plenty, many thousands of them meet together in the mountains, where they feast and riot for many days; and at country-weddings, markets, burials, and the like public occasions, they are to be seen, both men and women, perpetually drunk, cursing, blaspheming, and fighting together. These are such outrageous disorders, that it were better for the nation they were sold to the galleys or West Indies, than that they should continue any longer to be a burden and curse upon us.

Andrew Fletcher of Saltoun

Every Sunday a collection is made in the different congregations for the sick and necessitous, as poor's rates are unknown in Scotland; but as the natives can practice the lesson of being content with little, or are

41

possessed of such a spirit of independence, that they will not submit to the disgrace of asking alms without urgent necessity, the small pittance thus gathered weekly, and placed under the distribution of the minister and elders, has hitherto been found sufficient for every purpose of regular charity. Thus in a country where the greatest number are poor, there are yet very few beggars.

Thomas Pennant [1769]

Light Fantastic

I took the opportunity of going several times to the subscription balls given every three weeks at Montrose by the local lairds. I never saw a very large company, but it was perfectly chosen and really brilliant. The Scottish dance or *reel* is extremely difficult for a foreigner to follow; the time is so fast and so different from the French country-dances, that very few can master it, but the natives dance it very gracefully and nimbly.

The Chevalier de Latocnaye

One cannot but be conscious of an underlying melancholy in Scots-women. This melancholy is peculiarly attractive in the ball-room, where it gives a singular piquancy to the enthusiasm and earnestness that they put into their national dances.

Stendhal

Their Women are, if possible, yet worse than the Men, and carry no Temptations, but what have at Hand suitable Antidotes . . . Their Voice is like Thunder, and will as effectually sowre all the Milk in a Dairy, or Beer in a Cellar, as forty Drums beating a Preparative. It is a very Common Thing for a Woman of Quality to say to her Footman, "Andrew, take a fast Gripe of my A——, and help me over the Stile . . ." They pretend to be descended from one Madam Scota, Daughter to King Pharoah; but the best Proof, they give of it, is their Bringing two of the Plagues of Egypt along with them, *viz*, Lice and the Itch; which they have intailed on their Posterity ever since.

Scotland Characterised [1701]

The Occasion of the Itch

Every street shows the nastiness of the Inhabitants, the excrements lye in heaps, and there is not above one house of Office in the Town, which may not improperly be call'd a house of Office itself. In a Morning the Scent was so offensive, that we were forc't to hold our Noses as we past the streets, and take care where we trod for fear of disobliging our shoes, and to walk in the middle at night, for fear of an accident to our heads. The Lodgings are as nasty as the streets, and wash't so seldom, that the dirt is thick eno' to be par'd off with a Shovell. Every room is well scented with a close stoole, and the Master Mistress and Servants lye on a flour, like so many Swine in a Hogsty; This with the rest of their sluttishness is no doubt the occasion of the Itch, which is so common amongst them. We had the best lodgings we could get, for which we paid 31.5s. Scots, being about 10d. a night English, and yet we went thro' the Master's Bed chamber and the Kitchin and dark Entry, to our room which look't into a place they call the close, full of Nastinesse, 'tis a common thing for a Man or woman to go into these closes at all times of the day, to ease nature. We were mightily afraid of the Itch the first night, which made us keep on our white thread Stockins, and gloves, but we had the good fortune to escape it.

Joseph Taylor [1705]

Shy of the Water

The fishermen would not be mentioned but for their remarkable laziness . . . until they are driven out by the last necessity, they will not meddle with salt water. At low ebb, when their boats lie off at a considerable distance from the shore, for want of depth of water, the women tuck up their garments to an indecent height, and wade to the vessels, where they receive their loads of fish for the market; and when the whole cargo is brought to land they take the fishermen upon their backs, and bring them on shore in the same manner.

Edward Burt

We are wonderful patient haters for conscience sake up here in the North.

Robert Louis Stevenson

43

Oft have I heard thee mourn the wretched lot of the poor, mean, despis'd, insulted Scot.

Charles Churchill

Patriot in Exile

If the gratitude which I owe as a man and as a patriot to the people of Great Britain in general allowed me to make any distinction between different places according to the duration of the kindness I received, I should have to say that in Scotland I felt as if in a second home, and that I was received as a son, and never repudiated.

Lajos Kossuth

Mr Arthur Lee mentioned some Scotch who had taken possession of a barren part of America, and wondered why they should choose it. Johnson: "Why, Sir, all barrenness is comparative. The *Scotch* would not know it to be barren." Boswell: "You have now been in Scotland, Sir, and say if you did not see meat and drink enough there." Johnson: "Why yes, Sir; meat and drink enough to give the inhabitants sufficient strength to run away from home."

James Boswell

Verbal Inflation

A pedling shopkeeper, that sells a pennyworth of thread, is a *merchant*, the person who is sent for that thread has received a *commission*, and bringing it to the sender is making a *report*. A bill to let you know there is a single room to be let, is called a *placard*, the doors are *ports*, an enclosed field of two acres is a *park*, and the wife of a laird of fifteen pounds a year is a *lady*, and treated with – your *ladyship*.

Edward Burt

Put no faith in aught that bears the name of music while you are in Scotland, he said; you have not a fiddler in France who would not make a Rossini at Edinburgh.

Amedée Pichot

Our neighbour nation will say of us, poor Scotland! beggarly Scotland! scabbed Scotland! Lousy Scotland! yes, but Covenanted Scotland! that makes amends for all.

Robert Calder

Shining Away

The Scots are not easy in conversation. They are more anxious to shine than to please. Everyone wishes to be thought wise, and you shall often see a stupid fellow entrench himself in gravity and preserve a profound silence, from the selfish fear of exposing his ignorance, or risking the little share of reputation he may possess. But see this man in another company where he knows he is surrounded by those more stupid than himself, he shines away and engrosses the whole conversation. His hearers hate him for his superiority; yet they are contented he should shine, rather than that they should run the risk of discomfiture by opposing him. In all companies, where there is an obvious diversity of talent, is to be observed this submission of inferior to superior ability; and when persons of equal colloquial abilities are thrown together, their discourse is rather disputation than conversation. An excessive frigidity is the consequence of the want of the frankness, which with us is the heart and soul of social enjoyment. A cautious reserve appears to pervade the breast of every Scotsman; he answers a question as if he were undergoing a cross-examination; the mysterious habit grows upon him, till he makes a secret of things which it would do him no manner of harm although all the world knew them.

An Edinburgh gentleman, who has all the open straightforwardness of English manner, said to me the other day, "I cannot endure the selfish reserve of my countrymen. They become tolerable only when they are half tipsy."

An English Commercial Traveller [1815]

45

Aberdeen Archetype

Fleming, my landlord, let an upper storey to lodgers in order to better his condition. He was an industrious creature, and did all he could to procure a livelihood. His wife was the very model of an Aberdeenshire woman in three particulars – she spoke to perfection the vile lingo of her country, she was an inveterate smoker, and her loquacity was interminable.

Donald Sage

She put about a pound of tea into a tolerably large-sized pot, with nearly a gallon of "burn" water, and seasoned the whole as she would any other stew, with a reasonable proportion of butter, pepper, and salt! When served up at the breakfast table, however, the sauce only was administered, the leaves being reserved for future decoctions.

Donald Sage

Bring Out Your Dead

In time of pestilence the discipline had been sharp and sudden, and what we now call "stamping out contagion" was carried on with deadly rigour. The officials, in their gowns of grey, with a white St Andrew's cross on back and breast, and a white cloth carried before them on a staff, perambulated the city, adding the terror of man's justice to the fear of God's visitation. The dead they buried on the Borough Muir; the living who had concealed the sickness were drowned, if they were women, in the Quarry Holes, and if they were men, were hanged and gibbeted at their own doors; and wherever the evil had passed, furniture was destroyed and houses closed. And the most bogeyish part of the story is about such houses. Two generations back they still stood dark and empty; people avoided them as they passed by; the boldest schoolboy only shouted through the keyhole and made off;

for within, it was supposed, the plague lay ambushed like a basilisk, ready to flow forth and spread blain and pustule through the city. What a terrible next-door neighbour for superstitious citizens! A rat scampering within would send a shudder through the stoutest heart. Here, if you like, was a sanitary parable, addressed by our uncleanly forefathers to their own neglect.

Robert Louis Stevenson

The Scottish peasantry were wont to take great pride in a stock of home-made linen . . . some pieces were kept with singular care, such as were of a particular texture or as being the manufacture of a beloved mother. But, above all, there was *one* called "the weel-hained web" – that was the dead linen, reserved for winding-sheets. That was consecrated, and there were usually several ready-made robes of the same stuff to dress the body ere the blood was cold, "for," said a gudewife, "there's a number of us yet to bury . . ." None but friends knew anything about this attire, and their exhibition and history are only confided to favourites, or at a time when hearts are interchanging their secret thoughts. On such occasions you would observe the eye filled with tears, started by mournful recollections or anticipations, and all conversation conducted in whispers, as if a dread being were present and hallowing the elements before them.

Paxton Hood

47

Weights and Measures

I shall give you a notable instance of precaution used by some of them against the tailor's purloining.

This is to buy everything that goes to the making of a suit of clothes, even to the stay-tape and thread; and when they are to be delivered out, they are, all together, weighed before the tailor's face.

And when he brings home the suit, it is again put into the scale with the shreds of every sort, and it is expected the whole shall answer the original weight.

Edward Burt

Basic Bowls

The bowls were played by rolling or throwing a cannon ball, and he who could with the fewest strokes send it beyond a mark at the further end of the link, was declared the victor. A man being on one occasion killed while playing at this game, the magistrates caused it to be discontinued.

E. J. Guthrie [1885]

Knobs and Knockers

The Lord Justice-Clerk's house was provided with a *pin* or *risp*, instead of the more modern convenience – a knocker. The Scottish ballads, in numberless passages, make reference to this article; no hero in those compositions ever comes to his mistress's door but he *tirles at the pin*. What, then, was a pin? It was a small slip or bar of iron, starting out from the door vertically, serrated on the side towards the door, and provided with a small ring, which, being drawn roughly along the serrations or nicks, produced a harsh and grating sound, to summon the servant to open. Another term for the article was a *crow* . . . Hardly one specimen of the pin, crow, or ringle now survives in the Old Town. They were almost all disused many years ago, when knockers were generally substituted as more stylish . . . Pins were, upon the whole, considered very inoffensive, decent, old-fashioned things, being made of a modest metal, and making little show upon a door; knockers were thought upstart, prominent, brazen-faced articles, and received the full share of odium always conferred by Scotsmen of the old school upon tasteful improvements. Every drunken fellow, in reeling home at night, thought it good sport to carry off all the knockers that came in his way; and as drunken gentlemen were very numerous, many acts of violence were committed, and sometimes a whole stair was found stripped of its knockers in the morning . . . Knockers were frequently used as missile weapons by the bucks of that day against the Town-guard; and the morning sun sometimes saw the High Street strewed with them . . . Mrs Campbell remembered residing in an Old Town house, which was one night disturbed in the most intolerable manner by a drunken party at the knocker. In the morning the greater part of it was found to be gone; and it was besides discovered, to the horror of the inmates, that part of a finger was left sticking in the fragments, with the appearance of having been forcibly wrenched from the hand.

Robert Chambers

The sturdy Armstrongs,
The trusty Boyds,
The greedy Campbells,
The dirty Dalrymples,
The lying Dicks,
The famous Dicksons,
The lucky Duffs,
The bauld Frasers,
The gallant Grahams,
The haughty Hamiltons,

The handsome Hays,
The muckle-backit Hendersons,
The jingling Jardines,
The gentle Johnstones,
The angry Kerrs,
The light Lindsays,
The black Macraes,
The wild Macraws,
The brave Macdonalds,
The fiery Macintoshes,
The proud Macneils,
The false Monteiths,
The manly Morrisons,
The gentle Neilsons,
The bauld Rutherfords,
The saucy Scotts,
The proud Setons,
The puddling Somervilles,
The worthy Watsons.

Dear Mortimer Street:

I've got my shoes and socks off and I'm paddling about at the edge of the sea. Is this the kind of thing you want? It's deep and dark out there and the cross-currents are dangerous for all but the strongest of swimmers. Read, digest, and let me know what you think.

Dear Gordon Smith:

So far, so-so. It's too soon to say, but keep it up, anyway.

One of your refugees, who runs the sandwich bar (he calls them "sangwidges") at the end of the street and grows marijuana in his window-boxes, tells me that the first football you played up there was with your enemies' heads. Is this true?

By the way, do you think you will ever find an adequate replacement for Billy Bremner? He was such a lion of a man, an inspiration and a wonder. I don't care what he did, why must you always squabble so much amongst yourselves?

Swinging Kilts

I suppose we are what we are because of the climate, or Calvinism, or some racial inheritance – or even Dr Gregory's mixture. We're damned thrawn, loyal to the point of lunacy, lousy lovers, clumsy, suicidally arrogant, socially graceless.

Jock

And Ranting Reeds

Our greatest compliment to anything is to say: "It's no' bad." And it's like drawing teeth to get that much. Tell us about some magnificent human achievement and we'll say: "Him? Christ, I kent his faither." The tartan admass. The lumpen prolemactariat. The hodden grey of the football terracing. The bunneted intellectual. Us. We're the tribe who sent Moses back up the hill for the eleventh Commandment, and when he came down with the tablet it said: "Thou shalt resist all change."

Have you ever wondered about our international image? Is it our courage, our honesty, our capacity for hard work, our independent spirit, our humanity? Ask them in Bahrein or Calabria or Chittagong. They'll tell you the same story. About a Scotsman, Englishman, Irishman and a Jew. They'd all got on in the world and hadn't seen each other for ten years. They decided on a reunion. They'd have the biggest dinner of their lives at the Cafe Royal in Regent Street. They had the lot! Eight courses. Three different wines. Brandy. Cigars. And the waiter was hovering about with the bill. Eighty-six pounds! He wasn't very sure who he should deliver it to or the reception he'd get, but a Scottish voice shouted out, "Here, gie it tae me, for God's sake." And the headlines the next morning said: JEWISH VENT-RILOQUIST BATTERED TO DEATH.

Jock

My mother who had been a serving lass in a middle-class house, said the Scots were "a wee bit special". Our eggs had two yolks. She never set her feet outside Scotland, but England was special, too, because that was where the king lived, and Mr Churchill, and that couldn't be too bad, could it?

My father occasionally scorned the English, deploring their ignorance of Scotland, particularly their mispronunciation of place-names and distorted views of Scottish history, but then my father was a very scornful man when he was my age.

The minister never tired of telling us that we were *of the chosen*, and that seemed special enough, but he confused me by referring to the Jews as *the chosen people*. Did that mean we were one of the Lost Tribes of Israel? He was the sort of man who spoke in italics and capital letters. The opposite of the *chosen* were, of course, the *damned*, therefore the English were damned.

My Auntie Liz, who lived up the same tenement stair in the Lawn-market that Boswell once lived up, was very Scottish.

Much may be made of a Scotchman if he be caught young.

BOSWELL: I do indeed come from Scotland, but I cannot help it . . .

JOHNSON: That, Sir, I find, is what a very great many of your countrymen cannot help.

Norway, too, has noble wild prospects: and Lapland is remarkable for prodigious noble prospects. But, Sir, let me tell you, the noblest prospect which a Scotchman ever sees, is the high road that leads him to England.

Sir, it is not so much to be lamented that Old England is lost, as that the Scotch have found it.

Seeing Scotland, Madam, is only seeing a worse England.

Oats – A grain, which in England is generally given to horses, but in Scotland supports the people.

Samuel Johnson

My Auntie Liz lived so close to Edinburgh Castle that one felt she could raise the drawbridge simply by leaning out of her front-room windows. Tackety-boots clattered past all day. Hooves sparked on the granite setts. Skirling pipes and a rattle of drums heralded another parade, and bayonets flashed in the sun. Looking down on it the swinging tartan seemed like an endless conveyor belt of stained glass.

That's the garrison beating retreat. You can always tell when it's retreat. Sounds more like a charge. The drummers hurry on the pipers, and the pipers skirl as fast as their bags'll blaw, just so's the one lot can beat the others to the pubs.

Jock

I cannot out of our armie furnish yow with a sober fiddler; there is a fellow here plays exceeding well, but he is intollerably given to drink; nor have we many of these people. Our armie hes few or none that carie not armes. We are sadder and graver than ordinarie soldiers, only we are well provided of pypers; I have one for every company in my regiment, and I think they are as good as drummers.

Lord Lothian [*1641*]

Tune of the Heroes

To those who know not the pipes, the feel of the bag in the oxter is a gaiety lost. The sweet round curve is like a girl's waist; it is friendly and warm in the crook of the elbow and against a man's side, and to press it is to bring laughing or tears ... The march came first to the chanter – the old tune, the fine tune that Kintail has heard before, when the wild men in their red tartan came over hill and moor; the tune with the river in it, the fast river and the courageous that kens not stop nor tarry, that runs round rock and over fall with a good humour, yet no mood for anything but the way before it. The tune of the heroes, the tune of the pinelands and the broad straths, the tune that the eagles of Loch Duich crack their beaks together when they hear, and the crows of that countryside would as soon listen to as the squeal of their babies.

Neil Munro

Lord of the Dance

The great war-pipes of Caledonia. A sheep's bladder, some ebony tubes, a bit of silver, carved ivory, a tassel or two, and a fringe of tartan. And terror in the hearts of the enemy. The greatest laxative in the world. To have an army led by a piper is like going into a cup final two goals up. Nero did not fiddle while Rome burned. He sat back and skirled a tune or two on the *tibia utricularis*. And, of course, they couldn't hear the fire alarm for the noise he was making.

A musical instrument that became a weapon of war. A weapon of war that became Lord of the Dance. To play the pipes well is to belong to the most exclusive and privileged and *thirsty* Mafia in the world.

> Nae instrument, however sweet,
> Can wi' the Highland pipes compete;
> For tho' its notes are only nine,
> It's warbling voice is so divine
> That when evoked with skill and art
> It moves all feelings of the heart,
> And Rage and Love, and Joy and Grief
> Thro' it find utterance and relief.

Jock

Thwarted Lovers

In Kintyre, Islay, Colonsay, Mull, and Cape Wrath they tell a story about a piper. Always he is thwarted in love. Always he pipes himself into a deep cave in search of hell. Always he is accompanied by his dog. The piper never returns. The dog always returns. Always badly burned.

The Bydand Myths

Pibroch for Luck

I passed a piper in the street as I went to the Dean's and could not help giving him a shilling to play "Pibroch a Donuil Dhu" for luck's sake.
    What a child I am!

Sir Walter Scott

There's meat and music here, as the fox said when he stole the bagpipes.

Traditional

Phantom Piper

There was a legend long current in Glasgow, that about a hundred years ago [1780], as a citizen was passing at midnight through the churchyard which surrounds the Cathedral, he saw a neighbour of his own, lately buried, rise out of his grave, and dance a jig with the devil, who played the air called "Whistle o'er the lave o't", upon the bagpipe, which struck the whole city with so much horror, that the town-drummer was sent through the streets next morning, to forbid any one to play, sing, or whistle, the nefarious tune in question.

Charles Kirkpatrick Sharpe

Citation

To George Clarke, piper of the 71st, as a mark of the Society's approbation of his spirited and laudable conduct at the Battle of Vimiera, in continuing to play upon his pipes to animate the men after being himself severely wounded.

Inscription by Highland Society
on set of ornamental bagpipes.

The Sutherlands

We advanced through the village and came in front of the Secundrabagh, when a murderous fire was opened on us from the windows and flat roof of a two-storied building in the centre of the garden ... The Punjabis dashed over the mud wall shouting the war-cry of the Sikhs ... led by their two European officers, who were both shot down before they had gone a few yards. This staggered the Sikhs and they halted. As soon as Sir Colin saw them waver, he turned to Colonel Ewart, who

59

was in command of the seven companies of the 93rd and said, "Colonel Ewart, bring on the tartan – let my own lads at them." Before the Command could be repeated or the buglers had time to sound the advance, the whole seven companies, like one man, leaped over the wall with such a yell of pent-up rage as I had never heard before or since. It was not a cheer, but a concentrated yell of rage and ferocity that made the echoes ring again, and it must have struck terror into the defenders for they actually ceased firing, and we could see them through the breach rushing from the outside wall to take shelter . . . Here I must not omit to pay a tribute of respect to the memory of Pipe-Major John McLeod, who with seven pipers . . . struck up the Highland charge, called by some "The Haughs of Cromdale", and by others, "On Wi' the Tartan" – the famous charge of the Great Montrose when he led his Highlanders so often to victory. When all was over and Sir Colin complimented the pipe-major on the way he had played, John said, "I thought the boys would fecht better wi' the national music to cheer them."

Forbes Mitchell

As to the bagpipes, they positively put me to the rack.

Amedée Pichot

A Cure for Cramp

The most extraordinary recipe was that of my Highland piper, John Bruce, who spent a whole Sunday in selecting twelve stones from twelve *south-running* streams, with the purpose that I should sleep upon them, and be whole. I caused him to be told that the recipe was infallible, but that it was absolutely necessary to success that the stones should be wrapped up in the petticoat of a widow who had never wished to marry again; upon which the piper renounced all hope of completing the charm.

Sir Walter Scott

The Piper of Sloane Street

Thanks to the War Office, we know the name of the piper who played the Second Kincardineshires through the breach at El Berba. His name, as everybody has heard, is Captain Hugh MacCallum, although how a captain and adjutant came to be acting as a piper at the moment of the advance is a matter between the Army authorities and Hugh himself.

I daresay we'll hear the inside story in good time, but I knew most of it a week or two before the official announcement. A newsreel man who was flown home with his films gave me most of the details, even to the name of the tune with which Hugh piped the men through on the skirts of the barrage.

Mind, you, I wouldn't say Hugh was a classic piper, but I knew him of old as a determined one. He proved it the night I met him, a summer or two before the war, walking down Sloane Street in his sun-bleached kilt, with his second-best set of pipes under his arm.

"Well, Hugh," I said, as we stopped. "Has it come to this – playing in the streets?"

"Just so," he admitted, grimly enough. "But there's no disgrace in it . . . and I'm not playing for pennies." Then he told me about Jean Carmichael.

Jean Carmichael was a girl with red hair who came from Roseburgh in Angus – Hugh's own town. She had a job in London, and the two had met there again and become friendly – although it was all too clear that the friendship was somewhat warmer on Hugh's side than it was on Jean's. The pair of them had the independent mind, so that I wasn't surprised to hear the latest chapter – that Hugh had put the big question to her that day, and she had turned him down.

"Well, well!" said I. "That's a pity" – (wondering if it was, for I knew the temper of both of them) – and I added, "You'll just have to try again another day."

"Try again!" he said. "That's just what I'm on my way to do – this very night," and he slapped the pipes so that the big drone grunted into the eye of an urchin who was peering up it.

Hugh's plan was simple. He was going along to serenade Jean below the window of her little room in Coronation Court, a block of flats somewhere behind Sloane Street. The tune he would play was one composed by himself, called "The Girl With Red Hair!" It was a brisk march, composed by way of salute to Jean – and this was part of the trouble. The girl thought that piping and other Scottish excesses were out of place in London, and Hugh, patient but uncompromising, had tried many times to correct this heresy. Quite apart from the matter of his courtship he felt he had a responsibility to guide a countrywoman back to straight thinking on this point.

"So," he told me, "I'm going to play to her every evening for an hour until she makes up her mind to have me – pipes and all . . . I tell

61

you what," he said, "you can come along and see that none of these London bobbies tries to stop me. There's nothing like a good go at the pipes for making me want to punch somebody on the jaw – especially if he's got the kind of accent they use hereabouts."

Hugh was never an easy man to argue with, but I murmured something about when in Rome doing as the Romans do. I was pointing out that perhaps the folk of Coronation Court weren't so keen on piping that they could take an hour of it every night on the doorstep, when Hugh interrupted me with –

"That'll do you! There's only one person in London I allow to talk like that, and we're on our way to cure her. Come on!"

Outside the great façade of the block of flats, Hugh pointed out the drawn curtains of Jean's window on the corner of the second floor, and explained how his musical assault was going to work in the name of romance. He would walk up and down the pavement outside, night after night, until some night the curtains would part and Jean, in womanly submission, would be standing there signalling her acceptance of the MacCallum point of view. Hugh saw the solution as simply as that. His importunity would wear her down and leave no regrets. And if it happened late or early it was all the same to him, for, as he pointed out to me, he was always getting the exercise.

"So keep your eye on that window, boy," he told me. "And tell me when she appears, just in case I happen to be marching the other way."

With that he swung his pipes on his shoulder, blew them up with a tuning touch or two to the drones, and was off along the pavement to the tune of "The Girl With Red Hair."

Coronation Court took it very well to begin with. Curtains fluttered as the tenants started to lean out on the sills, laughing and listening. But there was no stir at Jean's window. Groups of people stopped, some of them for many minutes. Some of the enterprising ones volunteered cries of "Hook!" and gave brief impersonations of Scotch comedians. A dog which sat down in the road to wail a primitive accompaniment was ushered by me into Pont Street. Cars swerved as they passed and sometimes stopped a block or two away to listen.

The tune was a fine swaggering four-part march, with a very sweet cut back to the simple melody in the second variation of the fourth part. With the sustained playing, the reeds were going like bells, and the street between the buildings was roaring with noise. But in an hour there was time to play it fifty-four times, and that's plenty of times even for the best of tunes. Hugh stopped dead on the hour – a most methodical fellow – and the silence burst on Kensington like thunder.

"Well, it's always a start," said Hugh, as we walked to Knightsbridge Station.

The second night went much the same, and most of the next night too, although towards the end of this third session one or two men came singly down to the door of the flats and gestured to me, diffidently, appearing to enquire if I were responsible for the affair. "Doing it for a bet," I shouted to each of them in a friendly way, and they went off nodding agreeably. Only one of them appeared unsatisfied – a little bald man from the ground floor. On the fourth night we had just arrived when he darted out like a terrier, and as he ran round the corner of the block past me I heard him say something about getting a policeman.

I took a chance on tactics here by setting off round the other side of the block and down the opposite street. I was the lucky one. When I found the policeman he was leaning up against a mews-doorway, keeping time to the distant piping with a pencil on his whistle chain. He looked like an ally. He might even be a piper himself . . . so I said,

"You're listening to the pipes?"

"Yess, yess . . . I wass indeed," he agreed, in a voice two counties north-west of my own. "Man – but he's got a sweet finger . . . tell me, though, why is he always playing the one tune?"

Gladly I told him – I told him the whole story, and he laughed until some of Hugh's audience started to move round to the side street where we were, thinking they were missing something.

"All right! Leave it to me," said the policeman finally (he was a Ross-shire man, of course), "I'll keep out of the way of the wee bald fellow. He'll be wanting to bring an action for breach of the peace maybe. God! But it's a funny district, this!" He wouldn't hear my thanks, but his parting advice was – "Just tell your piper to hurry now. They'll likely be shifting me back to the Mile End Road at the end of this month."

I spent the rest of that playing session having a talk with the resident manager of the flats. He could have made difficulties if anybody could. But it turned out that his grandmother had been a MacPherson and he saw the point of everything. His office was on the ground floor at the front. Raising his voice so that I could still hear him every time Hugh strode past the window, the manager admitted that he wished Hugh luck. He proposed that his men should start in the morning to dismantle the water system in the bald man's room, in the search for a plumbing fault. The telephone, also, might go out of order. You could never be sure of phones nowadays. In fact, this tenant might be made to feel that he wanted to move. This was a most useful interview. As I left the manager's room, the bald man himself came bursting in, back from his vain search for a policeman. He seemed to have a complaint for the manager.

The talk reminded me of one other leak in the defence wall, and when we got out of the train at Knightsbridge on the fifth night I went into a phone box and rang the exchange supervisors. This needed some careful negotiation. I told them, when I got through, that I wanted to send a telephone message to someone in the north. Was there anybody there who understood Gaelic? I knew, you see, that I could explain this thing better in Gaelic, and anyway it would need a special temperament to do what I wanted done. Well, there was a Gaelic speaker.

"Hold on a moment," said the person to whom I spoke first, "you want Miss MacIntosh."

Presently I heard the chime of harps, disguised as a girl's voice, saying that she knew Gaelic. And didn't she! It took me a few minutes to tell the story, in the best Gaelic I could muster. When I was done there floated over the wires to me laughter that sounded like fairy music. As a result of it all, I won't say that official business suffered, nor that the safety of the country was imperilled, but I will say that for a number of days something happened to any telephone calls in that district as soon as the word "bagpipes" was mentioned. Her name was Flora.

You know, all that Hugh had to do during this time was to play, and Coronation Court heard "The Girl With Red Hair," nine hundred and twenty-three times. I think I can fairly say that my job was more strenuous than Hugh's. Almost every night, as I dodged through the neighbourhood heading off some fresh interference, the pleading voice of the policeman would reach me from some doorway –

"By God! isn't your piper taking his time . . . and that wee Baldy hunting me off my feet."

I tramped round all the police stations, and then the divisional stations, and then went to headquarters, finding here a sergeant, there an inspector or a superintendent, who was either a piper or an ally. But this was keeping only a move ahead of our enemy, who was also making the rounds. At each point he was being nobly obstructed, but not for long. When the bald man's complaint battered its way up to the higher levels I found at Scotland Yard a deputy assistant commissioner whom I knew, and he parried brilliantly for a week. But all this time Jean's curtain never stirred, and I came, a little despairing, to the eighteenth night.

The crowds were a little bigger that night. Off Hugh went, up and down, and he hadn't covered much ground when the sort of thing happened that you can't believe even when you see it. The corner window opened and Jean leaned out skirling –

"Run, you big black devil, run!"

At the same time a Black Maria bounced round the corner – she had seen it from the other window – but Hugh had thrown down the pipes and leaped for the swing door and the stairs. The bald man crashed out at the same time, seized the pipes, and was hammering them to pieces on the railings when the police car drew up. (He was charged later with breach of the peace.)

Hugh says that when he burst into the flat Jean met him with – "I didn't tell you to run up here," and then smashed a casserole over his head. This was the story anyway that Hugh told at the wedding luncheon a month or two later, and he still had the sticking plaster on his scalp.

I believe they've been fairly happy since. They're both pretty thrawn, of course, and if there have been more clashes than tender moments, I suppose that's nobody's business but their's. I was interested in one part of the story the newsreel man told about the action at El Berba. The regiment was standing there on the brink of zero hour, and the colonel saw Hugh with his pipes, getting ready to play.

"All right, MacCallum," he said, "you can play us through. But for God's sake none of your lah-de-dah jig-times. Give us a tune with battle in it."

They went forward ten seconds later, and Hugh was playing, "The Girl With Red Hair."

Alastair M. Dunnett

Scottish Enigma

Experts have been puzzled by a new record of bagpipe music played by Pipe Major Iain McLeod. Now it turns out that the tapes were recorded backwards. More than 1000 records went out without anyone realising the mistake. And 400 were sold without complaint. After the sitar, could this be the next new sound?

Pendennis, [Observer] *1967*

Last Wish

I will nae priests for me shall sing,
Nor yet nae bells for me to ring,
But ae Bag-pype to play a spring.

Walter Kennedy

The Kilt

When I started with the Seaforth Highlanders, it was the kilt or nothing. Or rather it was the kilt *and* nothing. You had a mirror set in the concrete at the guardroom. You had to pass over it before you could get out of the barracks. The briefest flash of a pair of knickers and you were peeling tatties for a week. When the good Lord made the Jocks he did not design them to go upstairs in tramcars. There's no mystery nowadays about what the Jock wears under his kilt. He either does or he doesn't.

The kilt is a corruption of the original Highland feilidh-Mor, the big blanket or plaid. The blanket was made of wool and roughly dyed. The colours and patterns or setts didn't emerge for a long time. The blanket should be two yards wide and six yards long.

There's only one way to get into it – and the secret baffled the Sassenach for centuries. First of all you've got to lay out its entire length on top of a belt near one end and pleating the blanket to the width of the belt. You then lie down, adjusting the belt to your waist level, and buckle the belt. Sit up, kneeling, and allow the surplus blanket to drape over one shoulder. Arrange the pleats round your body and adjust the height of the kilt from the floor. In this kneeling position the cloth should *almost* touch the floor. Almost but not quite, otherwise you will earn (and deserve) the soubriquet "dreepy drawers".

If it's a cold day you can distribute the top end of the garment round your upper person. You can keep your sword arm and dirk arm free by coiling it over both shoulders. But if you get into a fight or want to charge in battle it's a hell of a handicap to be lumbered with twelve square yards of heavy wool, so, with one quick flick of the belt buckle you can be down to . . . well, the sight of *that*, with hairy bare hurdies gleaming in the sunlight, was enough to move the bowels of a sphinx.

Jock

Case Against Trews

The Highlander has an exclusive advantage, when halted, of drenching his kilt in the next brook, as well as washing his limbs, and drying both, as it were by constant fanning, without injury to either, but on the contrary feeling clean and comfortable; while the buffoon in tartan pantaloon, with all its hinged frippery (as some mongrel Highlanders would have it), sticking wet and dirty to their skin, is not easily pulled off and less so to get on again in cases of alarm or any other hurry, and all this time absorbing both wet and dirt, followed up by rheumatism and fevers which ultimately make great havoc in hot and cold climates . . . The proposed alteration must have proceeded from a whimsical idea more than the real comfort of the Highland soldier, and a wish to lay aside the national garb, the very sight of which has upon occasions struck the enemy with terror and confusion . . . I sincerely hope that his Royal Highness will never acquiesce in so painful and degrading an idea as to strip us of our native garb and stuff us into a harlequin tartan pantaloon.

Colonel Cameron (Cameron Highlanders)
[*1804*]

A Curse of Breeches

The chief of a Scotch clan, with his poniard and pistols, like a buccaneer, his *cacique* cap, his cloak resembling Grecian drapery, his party-coloured hose, which like all the stuffs of the country, recall to mind the tattooing of the ancient inhabitants, which they have thrown into oblivion, his club of laburnam bent back as the sign of his command, his savage demi-nudity, and, with all that, his noble and gentle mein, is a living tradition, perhaps the only one in Europe, of our ages of strength and liberty. Though proud, and very proud of the dazzling beauty of their dress, they do not walk – they fly without looking at anything; and traverse towns like lions that have lost their way. In fact they must feel there some painful sentiments. Their inhabitants were once free like themselves, but have precipitated themselves under the yoke of associations and laws, in order to gratify their idleness and cupidity. I can easily understand that the Highlanders must despise the breeches of the civilised man. Chains come after them.

Charles Nodier [*1810*]

"Join a Highland regiment, me boy. The kilt is an unrivalled garment for fornication and diarrhoea."

John Masters in Bugles and a Tiger.

Villainous Plaid

Various reasons are given both for and against the Highland dress. It is urged against it, that it distinguishes the nation as a body of people distinct and separate from the rest of the subjects of Great Britain, and therefore is one cause of their narrow adherence among themselves, to the exclusion of all the rest of the kingdom; but the part of the habit chiefly objected to is the plaid (or mantle), which, they say, is calculated for the encouragement of an idle life, in lying about upon the heath, in the day-time, instead of following some lawful employment; that it serves to cover them in the night when they lie in wait among the mountains, to commit their robberies and depredations; and is composed of such colours as altogether, in the mass, so nearly represent the heath on which they lie, that it is hardly to be distinguished from it until one is so near them as to be within their power if they have any evil intention; that it renders them ready, at a moment's warning, to join in any rebellion, as they carry continually their tents about with them: and, lastly, it was thought necessary, in Ireland, to suppress that habit by act of parliament, for the above reasons, and no complaint for the want of it now remains among the mountaineers of that country.

On the other hand, it is alleged, the dress is most convenient to those who, with no ill design, are obliged to travel from one part to another upon their lawful occasions, viz – That they would not be so free to skip over the rocks and bogs with breeches as they are in the short petticoat; that it would be greatly incommodious to those who are frequently to wade through waters, to wear breeches, which must be taken off on every such occurrence, or would not only gall the wearer, but render it very unhealthful and dangerous to their limbs, to be constantly wet in that part of the body, especially in winter-time, when they might be frozen; and with respect to the plaid in particular, the distance between one place of shelter and another, is often too great to be reached before night comes on; and, being intercepted by sudden floods, or hindered by other impediments, they are frequently obliged to lie all night in the hills, in which case they must perish, were it not for the covering they carry with them. That even if they should be so fortunate as to reach some hospitable hut, they must lie upon the ground uncovered, there being nothing to be spared from the family for that purpose.

And to conclude, a few shillings will buy this dress for an ordinary Highlander, who, very probably, might hardly ever be in condition to purchase a Lowland suit, though of that coarsest cloth or stuff, fit to keep him warm in that cold climate.

Edward Burt [1754]

England's Revenge

From and after the 1st day of August 1747 no man or boy within that part of Great Britain called Scotland, other than such as shall be employed as Officers and soldiers in His Majesty's Forces, shall wear or put on clothes commonly called Highland Clothes, that is to say, the Plaid, Philabeg or Little Kilt, Trowse, Shoulder Belts, or any part whatsoever of what peculiarly belongs to the Highlands.

Act for the Abolition and
Proscription of the Highland Dress

Nothing, indeed, seemed to hurt their spirits more, or to give them a meaner appearance, than this regulation, the wisdom of which might be questioned. At any rate, there ought to have been an exception in favour of the loyal clans, who were exceedingly attached to that ancient garb. Clad in it, they had oftener than once signalised themselves in behalf of the family on the throne; and, indeed, there was no more treason in tartan and the belted plaid than in Sir Thomas More's beard.

John Ramsay

Short Report

The relationship between the War Office and the kilt has always been somewhat strained. And nothing was improved in 1939 when, fearing the use of phosgene gas in the new war, the brass hats in London sent a sample set of pink knickers to the 1st Argylls. The knickers, of slightly feminine design, were supposed to protect the Highlander's unfeminine parts from the burning effects of the gases. The samples were sent "for trial and report".

There is no regimental evidence of any trial, and the report is believed to be the shortest in the whole history of the British Army.

Jock

"The Ladies from hell."

German definition of Scottish infantry, 1914–1918

The Naked Space

... some I have seen shod with a kind of pumps made out of a raw cowhide with the hair turned outward, which being ill made, the wearer's feet looked something like those of a rough-footed hen or pigeon: these are *quarrants*, and are not only offensive to the sight, but intolerable to the smell of those who are near them. The stocking rises no higher than the thick of the calf, and from the middle of the thigh to the middle of the leg is a naked space, which being exposed to all weathers, becomes tanned and freckled; and the joint being mostly infected with the country distemper, the whole is very dis-agreeable to the eye ... A Highland gentleman told me one day merrily, as we were speaking of a dangerous precipice we had passed over together, that a lady of a noble family had complained to him very seriously, That as she was going over the same place with a *gilly*, who was upon an upper path leading her horse with a long string, she was so terrified with the sight of the abyss, that, to avoid it, she was forced to look up towards the bare Highlander all the way long.

Edward Burt

Pour l'amour, oui, mais pour la guerre, non.

General Joffre

A Highland Fling

Now, in an eightsome reel, it doesn't matter how well the individuals dance the steps if the whole eightsome fails to stay in its allotted position. The unknown girls were expert dancers and it was the dawning look of horror on their faces that alerted me to a very nasty situation ... Somehow our entire eightsome, performing perhaps with too much verve and abandon, had started to creep slowly down the ballroom floor towards the Gordons. A crash was imminent. The "Gay" Gordons turned rather nasty, and hissed oaths came our way. We recoiled and began travelling inexorably in the direction of the Camerons who tried to avoid us and got into a really horrible mix-up with the Seaforths. Having started the rot and cleared a large portion of the floor for our own use, our eightsome settled down beautifully and never moved again. The other eightsomes were left cannoning into each other and generally behaving like goods trains at Clapham Junction often ricochetting off the Duke of Atholls's sixteensome in the centre. Trubshawe observed the Argylls trying to ignore a couple from the Black Watch who were now dancing dazedly in their midst and summed up things – "Bit of a fuck-up at the other end of the room, old man."

David Niven

Kilted King

A great mistake was made by the stage managers – one that offended all the southron Scots; the King [George IV] wore at the Lévee the Highland dress. I daresay he thought the country all Highland, expected no fertile plains, did not know the difference between the Saxon and the Celt. However, all else went off well, this little slur on the Saxon was overlooked, and it gave occasion for a laugh at one of Lady Saltoun's witty speeches. Some one objecting to this dress, particularly on so large a man, "Nay," said she, "we should take it very kind of him; since his stay will be so short, the more we see of him the better." Sir William Curtis was kilted too, and standing near the King, many persons mistook them, amongst others John Hamilton Dundas, who kneeled to kiss the fat Alderman's hand, when, finding out his mistake, he called, "Wrong, by Jove!" and rising, moved on undaunted to the larger presence.

Elizabeth Grant

The Tartan Alarm

Should you go search the globe throughout,
You will find none so pious & devout;
So modest, chaste, so handsome, and so fair,
As our dear Caledonian ladies are.

When awful beauty puts on all her charms,
Nought gives our sex such terrible alarms,
As when the hoop & tartan both combine
To make a virgin like a goddess shine.

James Thomson

The Gay and Grotesque

We dined at Hector Macdonald's with several Highlanders most of whom were in their garb, intending to go to a great fancy ball in the evening. There were young Cluny Macpherson, Campbell Airds, Campbell Saddell and others of the race of Diarmid. I went for an hour to the Ball where there were many gay and some grotesque figures. A dressed ball is for the first half hour a splendid spectacle; you see youth and beauty dressed in their gaiest attire, unlimited save by their own taste and enjoying the conscious power of charming which gives such life and alacrity to the features. But the charm ceases in this like every thing else. The want of masques takes away the audacity with which the disguized parties conduct themselves at a masquerade, and the sullen sheepishness which mingles makes them I suppose the worst maskers in Europe. At the only real masquerades which I have known in Edinburgh there were many, if not most of those who had determined to sustain characters who had more ill breeding than facetiousness. The jests were chiefly calculated to give pain and two or three quarrels were with difficulty prevented from ripening into duels.

Scott's Journal, March 5, 1828.

Plots and Personages

He either fears his fate too much,
  Or his deserts are small,
That dares not put it to the touch
  To gain or lose it all.

James Graham, Marquis of Montrose

Not Quite Couth

My Lawnmarket cousins spoke Scots while we were halfway towards English. The men in uniform out in the street were "sodgers". My Auntie Liz would "bile" the water for our tarry tea while I played with her cat on the "flair". And then we would put on our coats and go "hame".

The poet was born in Edinburgh. Scots . . . was not his mother tongue, but neither, for the matter of that, was English. What he spoke from earliest infancy was a bastard lingo, compounded of rudimentary Scots on the one hand, and mispronounced English on the other, and developing, with the aid of the Scottish educational system, into a nameless language, English in vocabulary and Doric in idiom, which he speaks (God help him) to this very day. But for the purposes of poetry he early realised he must find a language – so he proceeded to teach himself English, as Scott and his contemporaries had attempted to do, by purging his tongue of the national elements called in England "Scotticisms". But this process only left him with a greater regard for the separated national elements, which he now realised to form at least the rudimentary frame of another language, which came, if anything, easier to his tongue. The kind of English in which he had learned to write was not spoken by any but the rarest, most casual acquaintances, whereas he could find in the hinterland, and indeed in the streets of his own town, a whole world of people who spoke this Scots with remarkable purity. Two living tongues! One spoken in its entirety some three hundred miles from where he lives; the other a matter of no miles worth considering!

Albert D. Mackie
(about himself)

Since English became the literary language of Scotland there has been no Scots imaginative writer who has attained greatness in the first or even second rank through the medium of English.

Edwin Muir

Yet Scots is used for the full range of discourse by the great majority of Scots still (though, of course, they know English too and can screw themselves up to "speaking fine" when need be, albeit – in so far as thinking in any language is not a mere metaphor – they think in Scots and have to translate their thought into English utterance).

Hugh MacDiarmid [1940]

74

I don't think we were screwing ourselves up at Craigleith Hill. My mother and my Auntie Liz were sisters and had been brought up in a large family in Tron Square, an awful warren of pathetic little houses, all hugger-mugger in a quadrant that looks like the latrines of a Stalag Luft.

I have only one memory of my maternal grandfather. He came to Craigleith in the spring of my fourth or fifth year and was served something out of a bottle from the sideboard. He was a squat, fat, bald old man with a wooden leg. When I asked, much later, what was in the bottle I was told it was "Grandad's New Year". Like the question of the chosen and the damned, once again I was confused. How could the New Year be in a bottle? And why were there daffodils in January or, conversely, such unusual celebrations in March? Grandad was possessed by the demon drink.

Many years later (I was by this time a radio producer) one of our interviewers returned to the studios in triumph. A publican in the Lawnmarket had given him a splendid description of life in the Royal Mile at the turn of the century. It was, indeed, a warm and evocative memory, full of incident and character. "Listen to this bit," said the interviewer as the tape rolled towards the end . . .

Of course we had real drinkers in those days, really hard men who could put away a bottle a day and still do a day's work. They used whisky for water and water for nothing . . . I'll always remember the garrison shoemaker at the Castle, seeing him on a wet and frosty

night, stotting down Castle Hill, his peg-leg skitin' off the slippery cobbles but never losing his balance, fu' as a puggy, singin' his heid off, with a plum pudding under his arm for the weans, and wavin' the bottle in time to his tune.

I'm not sure that anyone believed me at the time when I told them we had been listening to a tale about my grandfather.

Drink, like cancer and tuberculosis, was not so much a forbidden subject as an unspoken subject in our household. A man down the road who always tottered home up the hill smelling like a bartender's apron was like that "because he works in a brewery". People died or "were taken" and I would catch my mother silently forming the letters "TB" when she was explaining the cause.

They fancied that the low tone in which they spoke and the curious language they employed effectually veiled the meaning of their gossip; instead, therefore, of sending us away when they had private communications to make, they merely bid us go to some other part of the room, while they tried to conceal the subject of their whisperings by the ingenious addition of "*vus*" to every word they spoke, as "Did*vus* you*vus* ever*vus* hear*vus* of*vus*," etc. At first we supposed this was another continental language different from French, which we were ourselves learning, but the proper names sometimes used instead of he*vus* she*vus* gave us a clue to the cypher, which soon enabled us to translate it.

Elizabeth Grant

No chest was more thoroughly "sounded", pounded, and X-rayed than mine. Other people got more palatable emulsions or small capsules, but I had to take my cod liver oil off a spoon, every day without fail, the only variety being additional doses of something red and sticky called Chemical Food – the sort of compound fertiliser that no self-respecting gardener would give his dahlias – and a white goo called Agorol which was supposed to keep my bowels in good working order. My mother's fear of tuberculosis was founded in the fact that my father's only brother and sister had both succumbed to it as young adults and it was therefore a scourge that "ran in the family". Today it is impossible to comprehend these fears of only 30 to 40 years ago because we have no comparable social disease – contagious, hereditary, and so often fatal – in western civilisation.

Speaking "fine" – that is, like the English – has been a curse of Scotland since the Act of Union in 1707. Whatever else the treaty was supposed to be, it was intended to bring about a union of the peoples as well as the parliaments of Scotland and England – not unlike the Common Market in many respects. Being "bought and sold for English gold", as the song says, angered many Scots then and now, but most of the culprits were Scots, and particularly those Scots gentry who imported English elocution teachers along with Italian singing masters in an attempt to smooth away the so-called vulgarities of Scottish society.

In the eighteenth century we were far from being "couth", it is true. Extreme drunkenness was not the prerogative of the street rabble but was known to extend even into the law-courts, some judges quaffing three and four bottles of claret in a single sitting.

Two vices especially were very prevalent, if not universal, among the upper ranks – swearing and drunkenness. Nothing was more common than for gentlemen who had dined with ladies, and meant to rejoin them, to get drunk. To get drunk in a tavern, seemed to be considered as a natural, if not intended consequence of going to one. Swearing was thought the right, and the mark, of a gentleman . . . The naval chaplain justified his cursing the sailors, because it made them listen to him; and Braxfield (Lord Justice Clerk) apologised to a lady whom he damned at whist for bad play, by declaring that he had mistaken her for his wife.

Henry Thomas Cockburn

People spat and belched and farted in public, still emptied their chamber-pots on to the populace from upper windows, and household refuse rotted in the streets where it had been dumped. Even the gentry spoke Scots, and these same drunken judges and advocates summed up or pleaded their cases in the same "rough" tongue.

Lord Cockburn was the last Scottish judge who habitually used the vernacular. His easy manners and intimate familiarity with provincial phrases rendered him expert in examining witnesses from the country. He was, as a counsel, associated with Francis Jeffrey in a cause in which their client sought to prove that the heir of a landed property was incapable of administering his affairs. A country farmer, who was understood to be favourable to the views of the pursuer, was examined by Mr Jeffrey, who failed to procure satis- factory answers to his questions. Cockburn came to the assistance of his learned colleague. "Ye ken David, I suppose?" said he to the witness. "Ou aye," responded the farmer, "I've kent him since he wasna muckle bigger than ma loof." "Ay, an' what d'ye think o' the cratur?" "Think of him?" said the farmer. "The cratur has naething in him ava." "Wad ye trust him in the market to sell a coo?" proceeded the counsel. "Deed no," answered the witness; "I maist think he disna ken a coo frae a calf." "That will do, John," said Mr Cockburn, who resumed his seat.

John Clerk, afterwards Lord Eldin, was sent to London to plead before Lord Chancellor Eldon in an important property cause. He was inveterate in his use of the Scottish accent. In the course of his speech he pronounced the word *enow* for enough. The Chancellor drily remarked, "Mr Clerk, in England we sound the ough as *uff* – enuff, not enow." "Verra weel, ma Lord," said Clerk, "of this we have said *enuff*; and I come, ma Lord, to the sub-division of the land in dispute. It was apportioned, ma Lord, into what in England would be called *pluff* land, a pluff land being as much land as a *pluffman* can pluff in one day." The Chancellor was convulsed by the happy repartee, and said "Proceed, Mr Clerk, I know *enow* of Scotch to understand your argument."

Rev. Charles Rogers [1867]

By the beginning of the Second World War I was ten. I had been out of Edinburgh only to carry spade and pail to the sand dunes of Gullane, and once to Glasgow, on a day-trip to the great Empire Exhibition, with its free soup and chocolate and the most terrifying helter-skelter in the world.

I suppose the sheer Protestant monotony of the present and the constant proximity of an alluring past drove me to an early fascination with Scotland's history, particularly since so much of it had been played out so bloodily on my Auntie Liz's doorstep. The fall of the Bastille, the Indian Mutiny, Balaclava and Waterloo, the American and Russian revolutions all happened on the moon so far as I knew or cared. Whereas this *was* the Heart of Midlothian, outside the auld kirk of St Giles where the Tolbooth had stood, where Knox had thundered at Mary down the hill in Holyrood with her French fiddlers and dancers. Burke and Hare had scuttered up and down these closes and vennels with their awful burdens, and in my reconstruction of Burke's execution in the Lawnmarket I had a front seat at my favourite auntie's parlour window.

By an unconscious process of absorption, by walking the streets and wynds of the Old Town, I sucked in more than the dusty record of the past – I lived it, fantasised about it, acted it out in my head, and played all the parts. This, my town, was Walter Scott's "own romantic town". And the dark duality of the place fired me as it had fired that other son of the city, Robert Louis Stevenson.

The Icy Blast

John Knox and the Reformers did their work earnestly and well . . . but they went about it with such terrible vengeance that we're still staggering under it now, four hundred years later.

The Holy Roman Empire conjured up colour and richness and ornament. There were great feast days, and merry music and dancing, and spiritual beauties even in the act of worship. But by kneeling to Rome you accepted the authority of the Pope. And you had to thole the corrupt administration of the Church, the punitive taxes and unfair favours, and close your eyes to the sexual shinnanigans of the Roman clergy.

The Reformers donned the bible black, outlawed music, banned colour from the land, and dressed the nation in hodden grey. Anything that smacked of merriment smacked of Rome. The General Assembly was God's government on earth and more powerful than any parliament or king . . . No bishops, no fat fornicating friars, no more kneeling. But no more singing or dancing. Fast days instead of feast days. No ornament. No joy. And work, Amen, and more work. And instead of a balmy wind from Italy, wafting all the warmth and humanity of the Renaissance, an icy blast of Calvinism from the frozen shores of Lake Geneva.

Jock

Poor Mary

Poor Mary Queen of Scots was born
With all the graces which adorn
Her birthday is so very late
That I do now forget the date
Her education was in France
There she did learn to sing and dance
There she was married to the dauphin
But soon he was laid in a coffin
Then she at once from France retired
Where she had been so much admired
Fare well dear France she cried at last
While a despairing look she cast.

Marjory Fleming

79

Knox and Mary

KNOX

What I have been to my country this unthankful age will not know.
Yet the ages to come will be compelled to bear witness to the truth. I
require all men who have to charge me with anything that they will do
it so plainly as that I make myself and all my doings manifest to the
world; for to me it seems a thing most unreasonable that, in this my
decrepit age, I shall be compelled to fight against shadows and houlets
that dare not abide the light . . .

The very face of heaven, the time of her coming, did manifestly
speak what comfort was brought into this country with her; to wit,
sorrow, dolour, darkness, and all impiety; for in the memory of man
was never seen a more dolorous face of the heaven; for beside the surface
wet, and corruption of the air, the sun was not seen to shine two days
before, nor two days after. That forewarning gave God unto us; but,
alas, the most part were blind. Aye, and within three days she is hearing
her idolatrous mass at Holyrood. One mass, I say, is more fearful to me
than if ten thousand armed enemies were landed in any port in the
realm . . . Madam!

MARY

I have knowledge of you, Maister Knox, and I am told that you have
raised my subjects against me, and that you have written a book set
against the authority of queens; furthermore, that in England you did
cause bloodshed and sedition, and that all you do is by black arts and
necromancy . . .

KNOX

May it please your majesty patiently to hear my simple answers. First,
if to teach the truth of God in sincerity, to rebuke idolatry, and to will
a people to worship God according to his word, be to raise subjects
against their princes, then I cannot be excused.

MARY

You think, then, that I have no just authority?

KNOX

Please, you majesty, learned men in all ages have had their judgements
free. I would be as well content to live under your grace as was Paul to
live under Nero. In very deed, madam, that book which is the cause of
offence was written most especially against that wicked Jezebel of
England.

MARY

But you speak of women in general.

KNOX

Now, madam, if I had intended to trouble your estate, because ye are a woman, I would have chosen a time more convenient for that purpose than I can do now, when your presence is within this realm. I preached no sedition in England, and as for necromancy . . .

MARY

Yet you have taught the people to receive another religion than their princes can allow.

KNOX

Madam, if all the seed of Abraham should have been of the religion of Pharaoh, what religion would have been on the face of the earth? Or if all men in the days of the apostles should have been of the religion of the Roman emperors?

MARY

But none of these men raised the sword against their princes.

KNOX

Yet you cannot deny, madam, but that they resisted. These that obey not, in some sense resist.

MARY

But they resisted not by the sword.

KNOX

God had not given unto them the power or the means.

MARY

Think you, then Maister Knox, that subjects having power may resist their princes?

KNOX

If their princes exceed their bounds, madam, no doubt they may be resisted, even by power. For no greater power or greater obedience is to be given to kings and princes than God has commanded to be given to father and mother. But the father may be struck with a frenzy, in which he would slay his children. Now, madam, if the children arise, join together, apprehend the father, take the sword from him, bind his hands, and keep him in prison till the frenzy be over, think ye, madam, that the children do any wrong? Even so, madam, is it with princes that would murder the children of God that are subjects unto them.

MARY

Well, then, I perceive that my subjects shall obey you and not me, and will do what they please and not what I command; so must I be subject to them, and not they to me.

KNOX

God forbid, madam, that ever I take upon me to command any to obey me. But my travail is, that both princes and subjects may obey God.

It is he who craves of kings that they may be as foster-fathers to his Kirk, and commands queens to be nurses to his people.

MARY

But you are not the kirk that I will nourish. I will defend the kirk of Rome, for, I think, it is the true kirk of God.

KNOX

Your will, madam, is no reason. Neither doth your thought make that Roman harlot to be the true and immaculate spouse of Jesus Christ. And wonder not, madam, that I call Rome a harlot; for that church is altogether polluted with all kind of spiritual fornication.

MARY

My conscience is not so.

KNOX

Conscience, madam, requires knowledge; and I fear that right knowledge ye have none.

MARY

But I have both heard and read.

KNOX

So, madam, did the Jews who crucified Jesus Christ read the law and the prophets.

MARY

Who shall I believe? Who shall be judge? You interpret the Scriptures in one way, Rome in another. If they were here they would answer you.

KNOX

Would God that the learnedest Papist in Europe were here to sustain the argument.

MARY

Well, you may get that wish sooner than you believe.

KNOX

Assuredly, if ever I get that in my life, I get it sooner than I believe. They cannot sustain debate, except fire and sword and their own laws be judges.

MARY

So say you.

KNOX

It has been so to this day. I pray God, madam, that ye may be as blessed within the commonwealth of Scotland, *if it be the pleasure of God*, as ever Deborah was within the commonwealth of Israel.

Knox [1974]

The Death of Mary

One of my great-grandfathers was with the Queen from the day she landed at Leith. He heard Knox rant at her that Rome was a harlot polluted with spiritual fornication.

He saw her fall hopelessly in love with a fool, but heard her say that Henry, Lord Darnley, was "the lustiest and best proportionit lang man" she had ever seen.

He served wine at her wedding and wiped up the blood when one of her courtiers, David Riccio, was dragged from her side at Holyrood and murdered by fifty dagger-blows.

He heard Knox cast caution aside and call upon God to "destroy that whore in her whoredom."

He was there in that tiny room at Edinburgh Castle where she gave birth to the first king of Scotland and England. And later, he saw the gleam in her eyes and recognised her hunger for the body of that brave rogue, the Earl of Bothwell. He understood her growing loathing of Darnley, who was so scarred by syphilis, scabies, or smallpox – or all three – that he had to cover his face with a silk mask.

That ancestor of mine, a servant of the Queen's Chamber, heard the terrible explosion at Kirk o'Field, and knew that Darnley had been strangled and did not die in the blast, but to the end of his days he remained loyal to somebody and shed no light on Scotland's greatest mystery.

He was with his Queen when, in a Protestant ceremony, she brought the nation's scorn on her head by marrying Bothwell. And he saw her kiss him goodbye at Dunbar. He rode south with her to ask asylum from her cousin, Elizabeth, and served her as well as he could during the nineteen years of her imprisonment.

He was by her side that February day at Fotheringhay when Elizabeth of England finally made up her mind and they came in the night to tell Mary that she would die in the morning.

She spent most of her last hours writing her will, dispensing small gifts to her loyal servants and praying in her private oratory. Then she was led out to the great hall at Fotheringhay, where three hundred people were gathered to see this greatest menace to Protestant England put to death.

She was calm, but pale, and dressed in black. She held a crucifix and prayer book. Two rosaries hung from her waist. A great fire burned against one wall of the hall. In the centre, a small stage, draped in black, bearing the block and a basket and a headsman's axe.

She was led to the stage and mounted it, and immediately the Protestant Dean began to preach at her.

"Mr Dean," she said, "I am settled in the ancient Catholic Roman religion, and mind to spend my blood in defence of it."

But the Dean prayed, and the Queen prayed, and the great hall rang to their contesting claims.

Her executioner asked her forgiveness in advance – as was the custom – and the Queen said: "I forgive you with all my heart, for now I hope you shall make an end of all my troubles."

They removed the Queen's black robe. She now stood dressed entirely in red, not a bright red or scarlet, but the colour of dark blood. Her auburn hair gleamed in the firelight, a mantle of red framing her pale but smiling face. A lady of the court came forward and began to bind Mary's eyes with the gold-edged white band that the Queen had selected for the purpose during the night.

Then the Queen knelt at the block. She felt it all over with her hands then laid her head in position, carefully placing her chin over the edge. Stretching out her arms and legs to their fullest extent she shouts, several times . . . "In manus tuas Domine, commendo spiritum meum . . . " "Into your hands, O Lord, I commend my spirit."

The first blow bit deeply into the back of her head. Many who were there swore that they heard the Queen whisper, "Sweet Jesus."

The second blow all but severed the neck. The executioner, using his axe like a saw, cut through the last strand of gristle, and the Queen's head fell. He plucked it up by the hair and shouted, "God Save the Queen".

The crowd was stunned into silence. The lips in the bloody head still moved and continued to move for another fifteen minutes.

The Queen's real hair was grey and cropped short. She was an old woman at forty-four.

The final horror of that black Wednesday was still to come. After all the provocative shouting over the bleeding corpse, the sugary salutes to Elizabeth and the condemnation of all Papists to the same gory end, there was a moment of silence while attendants prepared to carry the body to the embalmers. Across the great hall carried the distressed whimpering of a dog.

Out from under Mary Stuart's red petticoat crept a tiny Skye terrier, the Queen's pet, smuggled by his mistress into the place of her execution, to be with her when the axe fell, and now lost and afraid and unable to understand why the person who had doted over him and loved him . . . ended at the shoulders.

Jock

To Fire and Hell

Elisabeth was a cross old maid
Now when her youth began to fade
Her temper was worse than before
And people did not her adore
But Mary was much loved by all
Both by the great and by the small
But hark her soul to heaven did rise
And I do think she gained a prise
For I do think she would not go
Into that awfull place below
There is a thing that I must tell
Elisabeth went to fire and hell
Him who will teach her to be cevel
It must be her great friend the divil.

Marjory Fleming

Claret Beam

It is curious, and perhaps edifying, to note that John Knox, strongly as he denounced the luxurious and sensuous habits of the Catholic clergy of his time, retained till his dying day that relish for French wine which he had no doubt acquired when a priest. Much as he railed against the French mote in Queen Mary's eye, he was all unconscious of the beam of French claret in his own.

T. F. Henderson [1893]

Scotia's Darling

And Charlie is my darling,
My darling, my darling,
And Charlie is my darling,
  The Young Chevalier.

As he cam walking up the street,
  The pipes played loud and clear;
And young and auld cam out to greet
  The Young Chevalier.

You're Welcome

Had I the power as I've the will,
I'd make thee famous by my quill,
Thy foes I'd scatter, take, and kill,
  Frae Billingsgate to Duart.

You're welcome, Charlie Stuart,
You're welcome, Charlie Stuart,
You're welcome, Charlie Stuart,
  There's none so right as thou art!

A Pledge

I swear by moon and stars sae bright,
  And the sun that glances early,
If I had twenty thousand lives,
  I'd risk them a' for Charlie!

Traditional Songs

The Prince Incognito

A tall youth of most agreeable aspect, in a plain black coat, with a plain shirt, not very clean, and a cambrick stock fixed with a plain silver buckle, a fair round wig out of the buckle, a plain hatt with a canvas string haveing one end fixed to one of his coat buttons; he had black stockins and brass buckles in his shoes. I chanced to be one of those who were standing when he came in, and he took his seat near me, but immediately started up again and caused me to sitt down by him upon a chest. I, at this time taking him to be only a passenger or some clergyman, presumed to speak to him with too much familiarity, yet still retained some suspicion he might be one of more note than he was said to be. He asked me if I was not cold in that habite (viz. the highland garb). I answered, I was so habituated to it that I should rather be so if I was to change my dress for any other. At this he laugh'd heartily, and next enquired how I lay with it at night, which I explained to him; he said that by wraping myself so closs in my plaid I would be un-prepared for any sudden defence in the case of a surprise. I answered, that in such times of danger, or during war, we had a different method of useing the plaid, that with one spring I could start to my feet with drawn sword and cock'd pistol in my hand without being in the least incomber'd with my bed-cloaths. Several such questions he put to me; then rising quickly from his seat he calls for a dram . . .

Unknown Jacobite Officer

The End of the Road

The right of our army, commanded by Lord George Murray, had made a furious attack, cut their way through Barrel's and Munro's regiments, and had taken possession of two pieces of cannon; but a reinforcement of Wolfe's regiment, etc. coming up from the Duke's second line, our right wing was obliged to give way, being at the same time flanked with some pieces of artillery, which did great execution. Towards the left the attack had been less vigorous than on the right, and of course had made but little impression on the Duke's army; nor was it indeed general, for the centre, which had been much galled by the enemy's artillery, almost instantly quitted the field. The scene of confusion was now great; nor can the imagination figure it. The men in general were betaking themselves precipitately to flight; nor was there any possibility of their being rallied. Horror and dismay were painted in every counte-nance. It now became time to provide for the Prince's safety: his person had been abundantly exposed. He was got off the field and very

87

narrowly escaped falling in with a body of horse which, having been detached from the Duke's left, were advancing with incredible rapidity, picking up the stragglers, and, as they gave no quarter, were levelling them with the ground. The greater numbers of the army were already out of danger, the flight having been so precipitate. We got upon a rising ground, where we turned round and made a general halt. The scene was, indeed, tremendous. Never was so total a rout – a more thorough discomfiture of an army. The adjacent country was in a manner covered with its ruins. The whole was over in about twenty-five minutes. The Duke's artillery kept still playing, though not a soul upon the field. His army was kept together, all but the horse. The great pursuit was upon the road towards Inverness. Of towards six thousand men, which the Prince's army at this period consisted of, about one thousand were asleep in Culloden parks, who knew nothing of the action till awaked by the noise of the cannon. These in general endeavoured to save themselves by taking the road towards Inverness; and most of them fell a sacrifice to the victors, for this road was in general strewed with dead bodies. The Prince at this moment had his cheeks bedewed with tears; what must not his feelings have suffered!

Sir Robert Strange

The wounded were bayoneted where they lay. Prisoners were shot and their women raped. The countryside was burned and pillaged. Atrocities. An act of genocide matched only by what the white man did to the Red Indian. The clan system destroyed. The tartan and the bagpipes proscribed. The axe and the rope took their terrible revenge, and hundreds of families were sold to American plantations.

But Royal Charlie was weel awa', safely o'er the Border gaen, to live another forty years in Rome, the city of his birth and death, a drunken old roué who knocked hell out of his wife, whose vain and futile escapade ruined the very people who had shown him such unswerving loyalty and love.

Jock

Request Time

Upon the anniversary of the Battle of Culloden in 1749, some military officers attending the theatre in the Canongate, Edinburgh, called to the musicians for the tune of 'Culloden'; whereupon the audience, in resentment, demanded 'You're Welcome, Charlie Stuart', and had their request complied with. A riot, ending in the complete humiliation of the officers, was the consequence.

Robert Chambers

The Resurrectionists

No' last nicht, but the nicht before,
Twa dummy doctors cam' to oor door;
They askit ma mither tae let them in,
But she knocked them doon wi' th' rolling-pin!

Burke's the butcher,
Hare's the thief,
And Knox the boy
Who buys the beef.

Traditional Street Rhymes

When some Lasswade worthies one night, during the Resurrectionist scare, were watching in Lasswade churchyard they saw an object moving stealthily among the tombstones. They challenged it three times but receiving no reply, they fired a shot, and when they went to investigate they discovered that they had shot a sheep.

A natural, or "gangrel body", named Jock, used to wander about from place to place in the parish. In good weather he slept out of doors. One night, tired and weary, he slipped into Lasswade churchyard and lay down to sleep behind a tombstone. He was just falling asleep when he heard the sound of a horse and trap being driven up to the gate. Two resurrection men jumped down and began to dispute as to who was to hold the horse.

"I'll haud the horse", shouted Jock behind the tombstone.

The two men fled in terror, leaving horse and trap behind them.

Jock gave up his prize to the police, who sold it on Jock's behalf to the highest bidder a few days afterwards.

J. B. Cairns

89

Burke and Hare

The anatomy museum of Edinburgh University contains the skeleton of William Burke; the museum of the Royal College of Surgeons of Edinburgh exhibits a pocket-book or wallet fashioned out of Burke's tanned skin and a plaster cast of a bust of Burke showing the rope-marks round his neck. Neither of these museums is open in the normal course of events to the casual visitor, but access is usually granted to serious inquirers. When, in the course of my researches, I was offered access to both establishments I was happy to be able to decline without appearing to be immoderately squeamish.

James Bridie's first London production was of *The Anatomist*. Dylan Thomas' film script *The Doctor and the Devils* has yet to be realised for the cinema, but the text was dramatised and staged at an Edinburgh Festival. Dr Robert Knox, the anatomy lecturer, and his suppliers of corpses, William Burke and William Hare, are as world-famous as most Scottish personages, although both body-snatchers were born in Ireland.

The snatching was a lucrative trade at a time when the dissection of most corpses was illegal. Of course Burke and Hare were only two of a substantial band of resurrectionists throughout the land. Newly-buried bodies fetched up to £10 a time from the anatomists, and a surprising number found their way to the dissecting slab within twenty-four hours, despite the posting of armed guards in kirkyard watch-towers all over the country.

Burke and Hare took to murdering their victims, a system which ensured their prime condition and probably a higher price. We will never know how many drunks and social derelicts they waylaid, invited home for a dram, then suffocated, but fifteen is generally accepted as a conservative estimate.

Dr Knox, former dux of the city's famous High School, was not even called to give evidence at the trial of the body-snatchers. He suffered, however, by ostracism of society and his profession. His effigy was burned in the streets.

Hare turned King's evidence and escaped the gallows. His wife was also released. Helen M'Dougal, charged "art and part" as Burke's accomplice, was defended by Henry Cockburn, later Lord Cockburn, in such an able manner that the jury returned the peculiarly Scottish verdict "not proven" ("that bastard verdict", according to Sir Walter Scott) and she went free.

Cockburn's address to the jury contained some masterly pleading, including as it did his examination of the moral implications of that other peculiar Scottish state, marriage "by habit and repute":

M'Dougal's Defence

Now, what is the history of this woman's connection with this crime? The general features of it are not disputed. Both of the prisoners state, in their declarations, that "they were never married", – by which they plainly mean, that no regular marriage ceremony was ever performed between them. But the relation of husband and wife may be contracted by the law of Scotland, without this, – by merely living together as married persons; and, it is clearly proved, that these two have been living in this manner for nearly ten years; nor has there been any attempt to prove the existence of any legal impediment to their being thus married, by conjugal cohabitation. In all probability, therefore, they are married, – though neither of them may know it. But, at any rate, in a moral sense, she was as completely under his influence as any wife could be to any husband. Great allowance, therefore, must be made in judging of her conduct, from the control which he may have exercised over her; and for the interest which she may naturally and most properly, have had in concealing her husband's crimes. For it is impossible to shut one's eyes to the fact, that this husband was a professional resurrectionist. His trade consisted in supplying anatomical teachers with subjects; a trade which, when conducted properly, is not only lawful, but absolutely necessary. The remains of mortality form the materials of that science, by which the sufferings of mortality are to be alleviated, or its date prolonged. But however necessary this employment may be, there can be no doubt that it is one which necessarily corrupts those who are engaged in it. It is shocking in itself; – it is generally conducted in violation of law; – and it must always be conducted by a disregard of the most sacred and reverential feelings of our nature. So that, in judging of her delinquency, she is fairly entitled to have her proceedings weighed in reference to the situation in which she acted. She was the wife of a person who had a professional connection with dead bodies, and with whom no woman could live, without seeing many things, which are better imagined than told. A thousand circumstances may concur in the life of such a woman, even where she is perfectly innocent, any one of which would be fatal to the idea of innocence in an ordinary case.

From Cockburn's Address to the Jury

Scene in Court

By order from the Court a large window was thrown open as far as it could be done, and a current of cold damp air beat for twenty-four hours upon the heads of the whole audience . . . The greater part of the audience being Advocates and Writers to the Signet in their gowns, these were wrapped round their heads, and, intermingled with various coloured handkerchiefs in every shade and form of drapery, which gave to the visages that were enshrouded under them such a grim and grisly aspect as assimilated them to a college of monks or inquisitors, or characters imagined in tales of romance, grouped and contrasted fantastically with the costume of the bench and the crowded bar engaged in the trial.

Contemporary account

Memento Mori

The Lord Justice-Clerk, in addressing Burke prior to sentence, said:

In regard to your case, the only doubt that has come across my mind, is, whether, in order to mark the sense that the Court entertains of your offence, and which the violated laws of the country entertain respecting it, your body should not be exhibited in chains, in order to deter others from the like crimes in time coming. But, taking into consideration that the public eye would be offended with so dismal an exhibition, I am disposed to agree that your sentence shall be put in execution in the usual way, but accompanied with the statutory attendant of the punishment of the crime of murder, viz. – that your body be publicly dissected and anatomized. And I trust, that if it is ever customary to preserve skeletons, yours will be preserved, in order that posterity may keep in remembrance your atrocious crimes.

Delightful Horrors

Letter from Anne Scott, Sir Walter's daughter, to Charles Kirkpatrick Sharpe:

My dear Sir . . . I hope you will not think me very troublesome should I ask you to tell me something of these delightful horrors in Edinburgh. Papa tells me you were to be at the trial, and he is much inclined to share a window with you on the day Mr Burke is hanged . . . We have no news here, except that our next neighbour shot a man the other night, thinking him a robber or a doctor . . .

House Full

Letter to Charles Kirkpatrick Sharpe from Robert Seton, bookbinder, No 423 Lawnmarket, Edinburgh:

Mr Stevenson, bookseller, wished one window for Sir Walter Scott and yourself but on account of the number that had applied, that will be out of my power. But I shall be happy to accomodate [*sic*] Sir Walter and yourself with a share of one.

The Execution of William Burke

Shortly after mid-day of Tuesday, the 27th January [1829], preparations commenced at the place of execution. Strong poles were fixed in the street, to support the chain by which the crowd was kept at due distance, and on this occasion the space enclosed was considerably larger than usual. By half-past ten o'clock at night, the frame of the gibbet was brought to the spot; and, as the night was very wet. there was no time lost by the workmen, and by 12 o'clock, the whole preparations in this department were completed. So exceedingly anxious were all ranks, that in utter disregard of the "pelting of the pitiless storm", the operatives were constantly surrounded by a great assemblage. When their labours were finished, *the crowd evinced their abhorence of the monster Burke, and all concerned in the West Port murders, by three tremendous cheers.*

At a very early hour on Wednesday morning, although the rain fell in torrents, the people began to assemble; and by eight o'clock, one of the densest crowds had collected ever witnessed on the streets of Edinburgh – certainly there were not fewer than from 20,000 to 25,000 spectators. Every window and housetop from which a glimpse of the criminal could be obtained was occupied. For some days previous, great interest had been used to obtain windows commanding a full view of the scaffold, – the cost varying according to the local position, from five to twenty shillings. Crowds of people continued to arrive, not only from all parts of the city, but from all the neighbouring towns. The scene at this time was deeply impressive. No person could without emotion survey such a vast assemblage, so closely wedged together, gazing on the fatal apparatus, and waiting in anxious and solemn silence the arrival of the worst of murderers.

Burke slept soundly a great part of Tuesday night, and when he awoke, expressed some anxiety to have his irons struck off, which was done about half-past five o'clock ... About half-past six o'clock, the two Catholic clergymen (the Rev. Messrs Reid and Stewart) entered the Lock-up-house, and the former immediately waited upon the criminal in his cell. At seven o'clock, he walked into the keeper's room, with a firm step, followed by Mr Reid, and took his seat in an arm-chair

94

by the side of the fire. It was remarked, however, that twice or thrice he sighed heavily. At this time two of the magistrates were present, and were shortly after joined by the Rev. Messrs Marshall and Porteous. The criminal and his spiritual assistants of the Catholic persuasion had, in the meantime, commenced their devotions, Burke apparently taking a fervent interest in these solemn preparations for his end . . .

In retiring to another apartment, he was accidentally met by the executioner, who stops him rather unceremoniously, upon which he said, "I am not just ready for you yet." He was, however, followed by Williams, and returned shortly afterwards with his arms pinioned, but without any change in his demeanour. While the executioner was discharging this part of his duty, Burke made no remark, except to tell him that his handkerchief was tied behind. He was then offered a glass of wine, which he accepted, and drank "Farewell to all my *friends!*" and then entered into conversation for a few minutes with Mr Marshall and Mr Porteous. The magistrates, Bailies Crichton and Small, now appeared in their robes, with their rods of office.

At eight o'clock, the procession left the Lock-up-house, and Burke walked to the scaffold with a firm step, but leaning on the arm of Mr Reid. As soon as the officers by whom the culprit was preceded made their appearance at the head of Libberton's Wynd, *one loud and simultaneous shout was given by the crowd.* When he mounted the stair, it was with a step as if he were anxious to bring the tragedy to a conclusion; and having heard the shouts of the multitude, his presence of mind seemed to be disturbed a good deal, and he appeared to require more support than when he was walking from the Lock-up-house. When he was fairly upon the scaffold, loud and universal shouts and yells of *execration* burst from the spectators, and he cast a look of fierce and even desperate defiance at the multitude. He knelt immediately, and was engaged for a few minutes in his devotions, assisted by one of the Catholic priests. Mr Marshall concluded the religious exercises by a short prayer. At the time when the culprit was observed to kneel, which he did with his back to the crowd, the shouts were repeated, with cries, to the persons on the scaffold, of "Stand out of the way!" "Turn him round!" &c. Signals were made to the crowd by the magistrates to intimate that Burke was engaged in his devotions; but these were totally disregarded, and the clamours continued. Besides the cries above noticed, shouts were heard of "Hare! Hare! bring out Hare!" "Hang Knox!" "He's a *noxious* morsel!" When Burke rose from his knees he lifted a silk handkerchief upon which he had knelt, and put it with much care in his pocket; he then gave one single glance up to the gallows.

At ten minutes past eight, Burke took his place on the drop. While the executioner was adjusting the rope, one of the priests said to him, "Now say your creed; and when you come to the words 'Lord Jesus Christ', give the signal, and die with his blessed name in your mouth." During all this time shouts were heard of, "Burke him". "Give him no rope!" "Do the same for Hare!" "Weigh them together!" "*Wash blood from the land!*" &c. When the executioner was about to unloose his handkerchief, in order to adjust the rope, Burke said to him, "The knot's behind"; which were the only words he uttered on the scaffold. Precisely at a quarter past eight, Burke gave the signal, and amidst the most tremendous shouts, died almost without a struggle.

On the body being cut down, about five minutes before nine o'clock, another shout was sent forth by the multitude. There was evidently a great desire to get hold of the dead body, and the people were only restrained by the numerous body of police, aided by the strong barriers. A scramble took place among the assistants under the scaffold for portions of the rope, and knives and scissors were actively at work. Even a handful of shavings from the coffin was pocketed as a relic. Not the slightest accident of any kind occurred.

The body of Burke was removed, during the night, to Dr Monro's classroom, and on Thursday it was in part dissected. The brain was the portion of the subject which was lectured upon; it was described as unusually soft; but peculiar softness is by no means uncommon in criminals who suffer the last punishment of the law. The anxiety to see the body was great. A prodigious crowd collected at an early hour in the forenoon, and besieged the classroom door, eager to gain admission. The regular students were provided with tickets. It was with great difficulty, however, that these could be made available, even with the assistance of the police. Those having been accommodated who were entitled to admission, others were then admitted till the room was filled.

The lecture began at one o'clock, and is usually over by two, but from the nature of the subject it was necessarily protracted, and did not terminate till after three. About half-past two o'clock, however, a body of young men, consisting chiefly of students, assembling in the area, and becoming clamorous for admission, which of course was quite impracticable, it was found necessary to send for a body of police to preserve order.

But this proceeding had quite an opposite effect from that intended. Indignant at the opposition they met with, conceiving themselves to have a preferable title to admission, and exasperated at the display of force, the young men made several attempts, in which they had nearly succeeded, to overpower the police, and broke a good deal of glass in the windows on either side of the entrance to the anatomical theatre. The police were in fact compelled to use their batons; and several hard blows were exchanged on both sides . . . Several of the policemen, we regret to learn, were severely hurt, as also were some of the students.

On Friday an order was given to admit the public generally to view the body of Burke, and of course many thousands availed themselves of the opportunity thus afforded them. Indeed, so long as daylight lasted, a stream of persons continued to flow through the College Square, who, as they arrived, were admitted by one stair to the anatomical theatre, passed the table on which lay the body of the murderer,

and made their exit by another stair. By these means no inconvenience
was felt, except what was occasioned by the impatience of the crowd to
get forward to the theatre.

As if to preserve a uniformity in the disgusting details connected
with this monster, it remains to be recorded that seven females pressed
in among the rest of the crowd to view the corpse. They were roughly
handled, and had their clothes torn by the male spectators.

From a contemporary account

Greedy for More

Burke the Murderer hangd this morning. The mob which was
immense demanded Knox and Hare but though greedy for more
victims received with shouts the solitary wretch who found his way
to the gallows out of five or six who seem not less guilty than He.

But the story begins to be stale insomuch that I believe a doggrel
ballad upon it would be popular how brutal soever the wit. This is
the progress of human passion. We ejaculate, exclaim, hold up to
heaven our hand, like the rustic Phidele – next morning the mood
changes and we dance a jig to the tune which moved us to tears.

Scott's Journal, January 28, 1829

Come all you resurrection men, I pray you now beware,
You see what has happened William Burke, and likewise
William Hare.

Contemporary Ballad

Deacon Brodie

If the gruesome deeds of Burke and Hare stoked the fires of Stevenson's imagination so successfully that 'The Body Snatcher', and perhaps, 'The Wrong Box' emerged from the flames, it is generally accepted that his best-known work, *The Strange Case of Dr Jekyll and Mr Hyde*, also came from an Edinburgh source. The moral ambiguity of the individual being one of Stevenson's favourite themes, he could have searched the folk-lore of Europe without finding a better illustration of his thesis than the one in his own backyard – the strange case of Deacon Brodie.

Fatal Facility

This was a man of respectable connections, and who had moved in good society all his life, unsuspected of any criminal pursuits. It is said that a habit of frequenting cockpits was the first symptom he exhibited of a decline from rectitude. His ingenuity as a mechanic gave him a fatal facility in the burglarious pursuits to which he afterwards addicted himself. It was then customary for the shopkeepers of Edinburgh to hang their keys upon a nail at the back of their doors, or at least to take no pains in concealing them during the day. Brodie used to take impressions of them in putty or clay, a piece of which he would carry in the palm of his hand. He kept a blacksmith in his pay, who forged exact copies of the keys he wanted, and with these it was his custom to open the shops of his fellow-tradesmen during the night. He thus found opportunities of securely stealing whatever he wished to possess. He carried on his malpractices for many years, and never was suspected till, having committed a daring robbery upon the Excise Office in Chessel's Court, Canongate, some circumstances transpired which induced him to disappear from Edinburgh.

Suspicion then becoming strong, he was pursued to Holland, and taken at Amsterdam, standing upright in a press or cupboard. At his trial, Henry Erskine, his counsel, spoke very eloquently in his behalf, representing, in particular, to the jury how strange and improbable a circumstance it was that a man whom they had themselves known from infancy as a person of good repute should have been guilty of such practices as those with which he was charged.

He was, however, found guilty, and sentenced to death, along with his accomplice Smith.

At the trial he had appeared in a full-dress suit of black clothes, the greater part of which was of silk, and his deportment throughout the affair was composed and gentlemanlike. He continued during the period which intervened between his sentence and execution to dress well and keep up his spirits. A gentleman of his acquaintance, calling upon him in the condemned room, was surprised to find him singing . . . Having contrived to cut out the figure of a draughtboard on the stone floor of his dungeon, he amused himself by playing with any one who would join him, and, in default of such, with his right hand against his left. This diagram remained in the room where it was so strangely out of place till the destruction of the jail.

His dress and deportment at the gallows (October 1, 1788) displayed a mind at ease, and gave some countenance to the popular notion that he had made certain mechanical arrangements for saving his life. Brodie was the first who proved the excellence of an improvement he had formerly made on the apparatus of the gibbet. This was the substitution of what is called the *drop* for the ancient practice of the double ladder. He inspected the thing with a professional air, and seemed to view the result of his ingenuity with a smile of satisfaction.

When placed on that insecure pedestal, and while the rope was adjusted round his neck by the executioner, his courage did not forsake him. On the contrary, even there he exhibited a sort of levity; he shuffled about, looked gaily around, and finally went out of the world with his hand stuck carelessly into the open front of his vest.

Robert Chambers

Creak in the Night

A great man in his day was the Deacon; well seen in good society, crafty with his hands as a cabinetmaker, and one who could sing a song with taste. Many a citizen was proud to welcome the Deacon to supper, and dismissed him with regret at a timeous hour, who would have been vastly disconcerted had he known how soon, and in what guise, his visitor returned. Many stories are told of this redoubtable Edinburgh burglar, but the one I have in my mind most vividly gives the key of all the rest. A friend of Brodie's, nested some way towards heaven in one of these great *lands*, had told him of a projected visit to the country, and afterwards detained by some affairs, put it off and stayed the night in town. The good man had lain some time awake; it was far on in the small hours by the Tron bell; when suddenly there came a creak, a jar, a faint light. Softly he clambered out of bed and up to a false window which looked upon another room, and there, by the glimmer of a thieves' lantern, was his good friend the Deacon in a mask. *It is characteristic of the town and the town's manners that this little episode should have been quietly tided over*, and quite a good time elapsed before a great robbery, an escape, a Bow Street runner, a cock-fight, an apprehension in a cupboard in Amsterdam, and a last step into the air off his own greatly-improved gallows drop, brought the career of Deacon William Brodie to an end. But still, by the mind's eye, he may be seen a man harassed below a mountain of duplicity, slinking from a magistrate's supper-room to a thieves' ken [*sic*], and pickeering among the closes by the flicker of a dark lamp.

Robert Louis Stevenson

Sir Walter Scott

This morning [March 15, 1826] I leave No. 39 Castle Street for the last time . . . In all my former changes of residence it was from good to better; this is retrograding. I leave this house for sale, and I cease to be an Edinburgh citizen, in the sense of being a proprietor, which my father and I have been for sixty years at least.

Scott's Journal

Of all the Edinburgh houses in which Scott had lived and worked as lawyer and writer only the first and last could no longer be seen. Above the fanlight of "dear old 39" I used to see the small bust put up in his memory. George Kemp's incredible Gothic steeple dominates Princes Street. And "Ma" Castles had carried the fiery torch for him all her teaching life.

If I were ever asked the desert island question about a book other than the Bible or Shakespeare, I think it would be a book of Walter Scott's. Not a Waverley novel, or a collection of his poetry and song, not even *Tales of a Grandfather* which set me off on so many roads in my own life. It would have to be Scott's *Journal*, the honest, always fascinating, and incredibly detailed record of his last stormy years.

The Old Wizard Dies

At a very early hour on the morning of Wednesday the 11th [July, 1832], we again placed him in his carriage, and he lay in the same torpid state during the first two stages on the road to Tweedside. But as we descended the vale of the Gala he began to gaze about him, and by degrees it was obvious that he was recognising the features of that familiar landscape. Presently he murmured a name or two – "Gala Water surely – Buckholm – Torwoodlee!" As we rounded the hill at Ladhope, and the outline of the Eildons burst on him, he became greatly excited and when turning himself on the couch his eye caught at length his own towers, at the distance of a mile, he sprang up with a cry of delight. The river being in flood, we had to go round a few miles by Melrose bridge; and during the time this occupied, his woods and house being within prospect, it required occasionally both Dr Watson's strength and mine, in addition to Nicolson's to keep him in the carriage. After passing the bridge, the road for a couple of miles loses sight of Abbotsford, and he relapsed into his stupor; but on gaining the bank immediately above it, his excitement became again ungovernable.

Mr Laidlaw was waiting at the porch, and assisted us in lifting him into the dining-room, where his bed had been prepared. He sat bewildered for a few moments, and then resting his eye on Laidlaw, said – "Ha! Willie Laidlaw! O man, how often have I thought of you!" By this time his dogs had assembled about his chair – they began to fawn upon him and lick his hands, and he alternately sobbed and smiled over them, until sleep oppressed him.

On Monday he remained in bed, and seemed extremely feeble; but after breakfast on Tuesday the 17th he appeared revived somewhat, and was again wheeled about on the turf. Presently he fell asleep in his chair, and after dozing for perhaps half an hour, started awake, and shaking the plaids we had put about him from off his shoulders, said – "This is sad idleness. I shall forget what I have been thinking of, if I don't set it down now. Take me into my own room, and fetch the keys of my desk." He repeated this so earnestly, that we could not refuse; his daughters went into his study, opened his writing-desk, and laid paper and pens in the usual order, and I then moved him through the hall and into the spot where he had always been accustomed to work. When the chair was placed at the desk, and he found himself in the old position, he smiled and thanked us, and said – "Now give me my pen, and leave me for a little to myself." Sophia put the pen into his hand, and he endeavoured to close his fingers upon it, but they refused their office – it dropped on the paper. He sank back among his pillows, silent tears rolling down his cheeks; but composing himself by and by, motioned to me to wheel him out of doors again. Laidlaw met us at the porch, and took his turn of the chair. Sir Walter, after a little while, again dropt into slumber. When he was awaking, Laidlaw said to me – "Sir Walter has had a little repose." – "No, Willie," said he – "no repose for Sir Walter but in the grave." The tears again rushed from his eyes. "Friends," said he, "don't let me expose myself – get me to bed – that's the only place."

As I was dressing on the morning of Monday the 17th of September, Nicolson came into my room, and told me that his master had awoke in a state of composure and consciousness, and wished to see me immediately. I found him entirely himself though in the last extreme of feebleness. His eye was clear and calm – every trace of the wild fire of delirium extinguished. "Lockhart," he said, "I may have but a minute to speak to you. My dear, be a good man – be virtuous – be religious – be a good man. Nothing else will give you any comfort when you come to lie here." – He paused, and I said – "Shall I send for Sophia and Anne?" – "No," said he, "don't disturb them. Poor souls! I know they were up all night – God bless you all!" – With this he sunk into a very tranquil sleep, and, indeed, he scarcely afterwards gave any sign of consciousness, except for an instant on the arrival of his sons. – They, on learning that the scene was about to close, obtained a new leave of absence from their posts, and both reached Abbotsford on the 19th. About half-past one P.M., on the 21st of September, Sir Walter breathed his last, in the presence of all his children. It was a beautiful day – so warm, that every window was wide open – and so perfectly still, that the sound of all others most delicious to his ear, the gentle ripple of the Tweed over its pebbles, was distinctly audible as we knelt around the bed, and his eldest son kissed and closed his eyes.

John Gibson Lockhart [1837–8]

Dear Mortimer Street:

I'm concerned to represent those whom you would call the eccentrics – and, as a race, we have more than our share. In my own lifetime I've supped warm banana and grated nutmeg with the old ladies who were the first performers of Ibsen in English. I've been shown how to bend steel bars by a man who ran in the Powderhall Sprint and once challenged Harry Lauder to three rounds of boxing, a quarter-mile race, four verses of "When Irish Eyes Are Smiling", and a ten-minute clog-dance. Lauder refused. A lady who walks past my window every day in coloured tights and doublet sincerely believes she is the re-incarnation of a Scottish king yet in all other respects is unremarkable. And the older I get the more normal they all seem to become.

Dear Gordon Smith:

You're in your mid-forties, you wear your hair down your back, you've refused all offers to move out of Scotland, you still believe in the living theatre, you take snuff, you support Hibernian, and you have a belief, bordering on the mystical, in the ultimate superiority of Scottish football . . . and you find it difficult to define eccentricity!

A Man's A Man

The film Western isn't something that needs immaculate research or anything like that. Essentially it needs an affection for the genre and I think I qualify for that. And I always put Scotsmen into them. You know, the first Westerns with Greenockian-type people in them. A new art form.

Alan Sharp

For A' That

My Auntie Liz's man, my Uncle Alex, spent his afternoons and evenings in a uniform that looked like one of Hermann Goering's cast-offs. Bright blue it was with enormous gold epaulettes and scrambled egg all round the brim of his hat. He earned his basic wages as a doorman, probably *the* doorman, at the picture palace down the High Street.

His mornings and Sundays, however, were spent on his real work as a kind of folk-doctor to the teeming tenement community. He was a masseur when that trade had more to do with embrocation than masturbation. He was also an apothecary of sorts, prescribing and mixing herbal remedies for everything from athlete's foot to quinsy throats. He was comprehensively unqualified, of course, a quack by any other name, and my father, who made his many certificates from the St Andrew's Ambulance Association sound like an honorary degree in medicine, scorned him too, particularly when my mother seemed to take Uncle Alex's solemn advice about her chronic rheumatism.

The folk-doctor of the Lawnmarket, who also happened to be my Uncle Alex, who looked like Mr Punch when he took his teeth out and "saucered" his tea, who despised organised religion almost as much as organised medicine, whose patients died in two wars and colonised the world, who lived up a stair so narrow and curved that undertakers had to bring corpses down before *rigor mortis* set in, my Uncle Alex was what is known as a character, a worthy, fit to rank alongside a legion of worthies, rich and poor, famous and infamous, who have graced and disgraced their native land. The one thing that distinguished them all, good and bad, was their independent mind, a characteristic so marked in the Scots that they have been known to go to hell and back to establish some trivial point.

What the Butler Saw

At the failure of Sir Walter I did not hear of it until the afternoon, but I see that all was not right with them, for they were sitting with millincoly countinances. Dinner was taken up the same as usual. I, taking off the cover of the tureen, Sir Walter says: "Dalgleish, just leave us and I will ring the bell when we want you."

In about ten minutes the bell rings, "Take away dinner," nothing touched.

As soon as dinner was down, I went out, and passing down South Castle Street, I meets a friend of Sir Walter's, he stopping me ast how the family was. I said I could scarcely answer his question with satisfaction.

"How is Sir Walter in spirits?"

"I cannot say that any of them is in good spirits."

"No wonder," says the gentleman.

"Pray Sir, do you know anything that has taken place?"

"Have you not heard of it? Sir Walter has lost seventy thousand pound."

I turned back and went into the house.

Tea being taken up at the usual hour. In a quarter of an hour the bell rings.

"Take away tea." No soiled cups.

Taking up supper at ten o'clock it was ordered away.

"No porter to-night, Dalgleish." This Sir Walter always had instead of supper.

Off to bed they goes. Nothing said.

I called Sir Walter at seven. "Verrey well, I hear you."

No word of Sir Walter until nine o'clock. Thinks I, this is not your ordinary way, however it is excusable.

They assembled in the dining-room to breakfast. In the course of an hour the bell rings. "Take away the things." The same way, nothing touched.

About twelve o'clock hir Ladyship called me upstairs. We went into the diningroom. "Dalgleish, I suppose you have heard what has happened with Sir Walter?"

"Yes, my Lady."

"Well, you will have to look out for a situation as we will be obliged to part with all our servants and the carrage and horses."

"I am very sorry to hear it, but I shall not leave you."

"Oh, you know we will have nothing, so we cannot pay your wages."

"I don't care, I will not go."

So in six weeks after this hir Ladyship told me to let the servants know, to keep their minds easy, they would be the same as ever.

But I return back to where they had tasted nothing. I was determined if possible to get them to taste something, so about one o'clock I took in a few mutton chops and placing them upon the table Lady Scott ast what this was.

"What a fine chop, do have one papa, since Dalgleish has been so kind," (said Miss Scott).

Sir Walter, giving me a look, went forward and partook, Miss following the example. After they had satisfied themselves so far they thanked me kindly. So after things was brought to an understanding they came wonderful round, but still something always preyed upon their minds, although they did not show anything before strangers, yet I knew how they were feeling; they were not the same people.

William Dalgleish, butler to Sir Walter Scott

My Lady of the Rats

When Johnson and Boswell returned from their tour to the Hebrides' they visited Lady Eglintoune at Auchans [in Ayrshire]. She was so well pleased with the doctor, his politics, and his conversation that she embraced and kissed him at parting, an honour of which the gifted tourist was ever afterwards extremely proud. Boswell's account of the interview is interesting. "Lady Eglintoune," says he, "though she was now in her eighty-fifth year, and had lived in the country almost half a century, was still a very agreeable woman. Her figure was majestic, her manners high-bred, her reading extensive, and her conversation elegant. She had been the admiration of the gay circles, and the patroness of poets. Dr Johnson was delighted with his reception here. Her principles in church and state were congenial with his. In the course of conversation, it came out that Lady Eglintoune was married the year before Dr Johnson was born; upon which she graciously said to him that she might have been his mother, and she now adopted him."

This venerable woman amused herself latterly in taming and patronising rats. She kept a vast number of these animals in her pay at Auchans, and they succeeded in her affections to the poets and artists whom she had loved in early life. It does not reflect much credit upon the latter that her ladyship used to complain of never having met with true gratitude except from four-footed animals. She had a panel in the oak wainscot of her dining-room, which she tapped upon and opened at meal-times, when ten or twelve jolly rats came tripping forth and joined her at table. At the word of command, or a signal from her ladyship, they retired again obediently to their native obscurity – a trait of good sense in the character and habits of the animals which, it is hardly necessary to remark, patrons do not always find in two-legged protégés.

Her ladyship died in 1780, at the age of ninety-one, having preserved her stately mien and beautiful complexion to the last. The latter was a mystery of fineness to many ladies not the third of her age. As her secret may be of service to modern beauties, I shall, in kindness to the sex, divulge it. *She never used paint, but washed her face periodically with* SOW'S MILK!

Robert Chambers

The Dalkeith Dominie

He seldom whipped, but when in a passion, substituting different degrees of shame according to the offence, viz., setting them on the floor with their breeches down; making them crawl round the school, which he called licking the dust; or putting them naked to bed in a play afternoon, and carrying off their clothes. This method soon rendered him exceedingly popular, both with parents and children, and contributed not a little to the flourishing of his school. He was indeed showy, and carried on the boys fast by means of translations, which were then in high request. His manners were very kind and pleasing, but he chiefly excelled in a sort of intuition into the character and genius of boys, in which he was seldom mistaken. His mode of punishing trespassers proved, however, more beneficial to himself than to his pupils. Ere long shame, which had at first wrought wonders, lost its terrors and became matter of ridicule to the wilder lads, some of whom took a comfortable nap on a play afternoon.

John Ramsay [1736–1814]

Proposal by Proxy

When Professor Aytoun was making proposals of marriage to his first wife, a daughter of the celebrated Professor Wilson (Christopher North, author of *Noctes Ambrosiani*), the lady reminded him that it would be necessary to ask the approval of her sire. "Certainly," said Aytoun, "but as I am a little diffident in speaking to him on this subject, you must just go and tell him my proposals yourself." The lady proceeded to the library, and taking her father affectionately by the hand, mentioned that Professor Aytoun had asked her to become his wife. She added, "shall I accept his offer, papa? He says he is too diffident to name the subject to you himself." "Then," said old Christopher, "I had better write my reply and pin it to your back." He did so, and the lady returned to the drawing-room. There the anxious suitor read the answer to his message, which was in these words, – "With the author's compliments."

Rev. Charles Rogers

Legal Luminaries

Lord Monboddo, an eminent judge of the Supreme Court, laboured under the singular hallucination that the human race were originally possessed of tails. He had persuaded himself that these were removed by accoucheurs so soon as children were born. When a birth took place in his house, he kept watch at the door of the apartment, and demanded that the young stranger might immediately be presented to him. He was much disappointed that he could never discover any evidence of a caudal appendage having been wrenched off.

Lord Kames was a very eccentric judge. He had acquired the ridiculous habit of familiarly styling his friends by the term which designates a female dog. At an advanced age he retired from the bench. After taking farewell of his colleagues in a solemn address, and shaking hands with them all round, he was about to retire from the court-room, when the deep feelings of the moment re-awakened his peculiarity, and he cried, with a broken utterance "Fareweel – fare ye a' weel, ye bitches!" Dr David Doig, Rector of the grammar school of Stirling, a person of remarkable learning, published anonymously two letters to Lord Kames respecting certain extravagant opinions advanced in his *Sketches of the History of Man.* Having ascertained the authorship of the criticisms, his lordship called upon Dr Doig, and finding him in his schoolroom, saluted him with, "Are you the bitch that wrote those letters?" "I am the Dog who did so, my lord," responded the rector.

Lord Braco was excessively fond of money. Walking in the avenue which conducted through his demesne, he saw a farthing at his feet, which he took up, cleaned, and deposited in his pocket. A mendicant who happened to come up, begged that his lordship would bestow upon him the small coin which he had picked up. "Fin' a farthing for yoursel', my man," said his lordship, as he slowly pursued his walk.

Lord Auchinlech was possessed of considerable powers of sarcasm. His son, James Boswell, was not exempted from its frequent application. Referring to his son's accompanying Johnson in his Scottish tour, and otherwise courting his society, the old judge remarked that he had often heard of bears being led about by men, but that Jamie was the first man he had ever heard of who was led about by a bear.

James Boswell was one day expatiating to his father on the learning and other good qualities of Dr Johnson, in the hope of removing his prejudices against the lexicographer. "He is," concluded James, "the grand luminary of our hemisphere – quite a constellation, sir." "Ursa Major, I suppose?" drily responded his lordship.

Lord Hailes was celebrated for his minute accuracy in business affairs. He had an only daughter, whose succession to his estates depended on his having destined them to her by testamentary deed. But after his lordship's death no document of the nature of a will could be found. His daughter, Miss Dalrymple, was preparing, in consequence, to vacate the paternal home to make room for the heir male, when one of the domestics, in closing the window-shutters, discovered a document resting behind one of the panels, which she handed to her mistress. It proved to be his lordship's will, which was found to secure her in possession of his estates.

Lord President Dundas had six clerks. He characterized them thus: "Two cannot read, two cannot write, and the other two can neither read nor write." One of those who could not read was the eccentric Sir James Colquhoun. His lordship's remarks were of course hypercritical; but it is related of Lord Gardenstoun, as an historical fact, that he was unable to spell the most common words. His lordship was author of several respectable publications. James Boswell persisted in misspelling certain words. The word friend he uniformly wrote freind.

Lord Braxfield possessed eminent forensic talents, but was excessively coarse in his judicial procedure. During the trial of Muir, one of the political prisoners of 1793–4, he said to one of the jury, as he passed behind the bench to get into the jury–box, "Come awa', Maister Horner; come awa', and help us to hang ane o' thae daamned scoondrels."

The clerk of the Criminal Court, Mr Joseph Norris, was an authority in forms and precedents. When any doubts were started regarding the validity of a criminal indictment, Braxfield used to say, "Hoot! just gie me Josie Norrie and a gude jury, an' I'll do for the fellow."

Rev. Charles Rogers [1867]

It is impossible to condemn his [Braxfield's] conduct as a criminal judge too gravely, or too severely. It was a disgrace to the age . . .

It may be doubted if he was ever so much in his element as when tauntingly repelling the last despairing claim of a wretched culprit, and sending him to Botany Bay or the gallows with an insulting jest; over which he would chuckle the more from observing that correct people were shocked. Yet this was not from cruelty, for which he was too strong and jovial, but from cherished coarseness ... "Let them bring me prisoners, and I'll find them law" used to be openly stated as his suggestion when an intended political prosecution was marred by anticipated difficulties.

I heard him, Lord Eskgrove, in condemning a tailor to death for murdering a soldier by stabbing him, aggravate the offence thus, "and not only did you murder him, whereby he was berea-ved of his life, but you did thrust, or push, or pierce, or propell the le-thall weapon through the belly-band of his regimen-tal breeches, which were his Majes-ty's."

Henry Thomas Cockburn

Oh, My Dear!

The fat, vulgar Mrs Jobson, whose low husband had made his large fortune at Dundee by pickling herrings, on being congratulated at the approaching marriage of her daughter to Sir Walter Scott's son, said the young people were attached, otherwise her Jane might have looked higher; "it was only a baronetcy, and quite a late creation."

Elizabeth Grant

Poets' Pleas

2 SULYARDE TERRACE, TORQUAY,
Respected Paternal Relative,   THURSDAY (APRIL, 1866)

I write to make a request of a most moderate nature. Every year I have cost you an enormous – nay, elephantine – sum of money for drugs and physician's fees, and the most expensive time of the twelve months was March.

But this year the biting Oriental blasts, the howling tempests, and the general ailments of the human race have been successfully braved by yours truly.

Does this not deserve remuneration?

I appeal to your charity, I appeal to your generosity, I appeal to your justice, I appeal to your accounts, I appeal, in fine, to your purse.

My sense of generosity forbids the receipt of more – my sense of justice forbids the receipt of less – than half-a-crown – Greeting from, Sir, your most affectionate and needy son,

R. Stevenson

Honoured Sir, – I have purposely delayed writing, in the hope that I should have the pleasure of seeing you on New-Year's Day; but work comes so hard upon us, that I do not choose to be absent on that account, as well as for some other little reasons, which I shall tell you at meeting. My health is nearly the same as when you were here, only my sleep is a little sounder; and, on the whole, I am rather better than otherwise, though I mend by very slow degrees ...

As for this world, I despair of ever making a figure in it. I am not formed for the bustle of the busy, nor the flutter of the gay. I shall never again be capable of entering into such scenes. Indeed, I am altogether unconcerned at the thoughts of this life. I foresee that poverty and obscurity probably await me. I am in some measure prepared, and daily preparing to meet them. I have but just time and paper to return you my grateful thanks for the lessons of virtue and piety you have given me, which were too much neglected at the time of giving them; but which, I hope, have been remembered ere it was too late. Present my dutiful respects to my mother ... and with wishing you a merry New-Year's Day, I shall conclude.

I am, honoured sir, your dutiful son,

Robert Burns

P.S. My meal is nearly out, but I am going to borrow till I get more.

IRVINE, DECEMBER 27, 1781

Mr Spurgeon

Oh! mighty city of London, you are wonderful to see,
And thy beauties no doubt fills the tourist's heart with glee,
But during my short stay and while wandering there,
Mr Spurgeon was the only man heard speaking proper English
    I do declare.

William McGonagall

William McGonagall, the pathetic butt of intellectuals in his own lifetime and increasingly over the past decade, was born in Edinburgh in
1825. But it is the city of Dundee, where McGonagall spent most of
his life, which is most closely identified with the world's worst poet.
The following is an extract from "A Summary History of Poet McGonagall", in McGonagall's own handwriting, which is now the property of
Dundee Public Library.

And his father bought the Living as a Pedlar, and supported the
family by selling hardware, among the peasantry In the Orkney
Isles, and returning home every night to his family, when circumstances would permit him. Charles the eldest son was herding
Cows to a Farmer in the Island of Southronaldsay, and his eldest
Sister Nancy, was in the service of a Farmer in the same locality,
and William, the Poet, and Thomas, the second eldest brother, was
sent to School to be teached by Mr James Forbes, the parish School-
master, Who was a very Strict Dominie indeed, of which our readers
shall hear of as a proof of his strictness, a rather curious incident.
William, the Poet, chanced to be one day in his garden behind the
school, and Chanc'd to espy a live Tortoise, that the Dominie kept
in the garden and never having seen such a curious kind of a reptile
before, his Curiousity was therefore excited no doubt to see it, and
he stooped down and lifted the Tortoise with both hands, thereon
admiring the varied beautiful Colours of its shell. when behold it
dunged upon both hands of William the poet, which was rather
aggravating to William, no doubt, and he dash'd the Tortoise on
the ground which almost killed it. And the Dominie Chanc'd to see

him, at the time through the back window of the Schoolroom, and he rattled on the window with his Cane to William, which startled him, and as soon as William came in to the School, he layd hold of him and began to beat him unmercifully about the body and face, untill his face was blackened in many places, with his hard Taws. and persisted in it until some of the elder Scholars cried out to him to Stop! beating William. and when William went home to his dinner, and told his kind father all about it as it had happened his father flew into a rage and said he would be revenged upon him for beating William so unmerciful, and accordingly he went to a Magistrate, with William, and related the Case to him as it had happened. and when the Magistrate examined Williams face, and seen the marks, the Dominie had left thereon he ask'd Williams father if he was willing to put him from ever being a Schoolmaster in the parish again, but Williams Father would not consent to hear of that owing to the Kindness he had shown towards his Son, Thomas, and he simply ask'd the Magistrate, to give him a line, to certify, to Mr Forbes, that he could put him from ever being a Schoolmaster in that parish again if he would just say the word. so Williams Father went with him to the Dominie, and showed him the line he had got from the Magistrate, to certify that he could put him from being a School-master again in the parish if he would say the word. and when the Dominie read he was very much surprised and began to make an Apology to Williams Father for what he had done, and promised he would never do the like again. so William and his Father were well satisfied for getting such a sweet revenge, upon that Dominie, and ever after that William was a great favourite of the Dominies and just acted as he pleased and was always very unwilling to go to School. Williams Father had to beat him very often before he would go to School, so that he never got a very great share of education.

The Tay Bridge Disaster

Beautiful Railway Bridge of the Silv'ry Tay!
Alas! I am very sorry to say
That ninety lives have been taken away
On the last Sabbath day of 1879,
Which will be remember'd for a very long time.

'Twas about seven o'clock at night,
And the wind it blew with all its might,

And the rain came pouring down,
And the dark clouds seem'd to frown,
And the Demon of the air seem'd to say –
"I'll blow down the Bridge of Tay."

When the train left Edinburgh
The passengers' hearts were light and felt no sorrow,
But Boreas blew a terrific gale,
Which made their hearts for to quail,
And many of the passengers with fear did say –
"I hope God will send us safe across the Bridge of Tay."

But when the train came near to Wormit Bay,
Boreas he did loud and angry bray,
And shook the central girders of the Bridge of Tay
On the last Sabbath day of 1879,
Which will be remember'd for a very long time.

So the train sped on with all its might,
And Bonnie Dundee soon hove in sight,
And the passengers' hearts felt light,
Thinking they would enjoy themselves on the New Year,
With their friends at home they lov'd most dear,
And wish them all a happy New Year.

So the train mov'd slowly along the Bridge of Tay,
Until it was about midway,
Then the central girders with a crash gave way,
And down went the train and passengers into the Tay!
The Storm Fiend did loudly bray,
Because ninety lives had been taken away,
On the last Sabbath day of 1879,
Which will be remember'd for a very long time.

As soon as the catastrophe came to be known
The alarm from mouth to mouth was blown,
And the cry rang out all o'er the town,
Good Heavens! the Tay Bridge is blown down,
And a passenger train from Edinburgh,
Which fill'd all the people's hearts with sorrow,
And made them for to turn pale,
Because none of the passengers were sav'd to tell the tale
How the disaster happen'd on the last Sabbath day of 1879
Which will be remember'd for a very long time.

It must have been an awful sight,
To witness in the dusky moonlight,
While the Storm Fiend did laugh, and angry did bray,
Along the Railway Bridge of the Silv'ry Tay.

Oh! ill-fated Bridge of the Silv'ry Tay.
I must now conclude my lay
By telling the world fearlessly without the least dismay,
That your central girders would not have given way,
At least many sensible men do say,
Had they been supported on each side with buttresses,
At least many sensible men confesses,
For the stronger we our houses do build,
The less chance we have of being killed.

William McGonagall

Toad in a Stone

I have my doubts whether it was in the beginning of this year, or in the end of the last, that a very extraordinary thing came to light in the parish; but, howsoever that may be, there is nothing more certain than the fact, which it is my duty to record. I have mentioned already how it was that the toll, or trust-road, was set a-going, on account of the Lord Eaglesham's tumbling on the midden in the Vennel. Well, it happened to one of the labouring men, in breaking the stones to make metal for the new road, that he broke a stone that was both large and remarkable, and in the heart of it, which was boss, there was found a living creature, that jumped out the moment it saw the light of heaven, to the great terrification of the man, who could think it was nothing but an evil spirit that had been imprisoned therein for a time. The man came to me like a demented creature, and the whole clachan gathered out, young and old, and I went at their head to see what the miracle could be, for the man said it was a fiery dragon, spewing smoke and flames. But when we came to the spot, it was just a yird toad, and the laddie weans nevelled it to death with stones, before I could persuade them to give over. Since then I have read of such things coming to light in the *Scots Magazine*, a very valuable book.

John Galt [1769]

The Early Detective – The Cock and Trumpet

There are certain duties we perform of which we are scarcely aware, and which consist in a species of strolling supervision among houses, which, though not devoted to resetting, are often yet receptacles of stolen goods. Among these there was a well-known house, known as the Cock and Trumpet, for the reason that a bantam was represented on the sign as blowing a huge French horn. It was a favourite of mine – the more by token that I had several times brought off rather wonderful things. On one occasion I issued triumphantly with a Dunlop cheese weighing thirty pounds, on another with a dozen of Italian sausages, and on another with two live geese.

It was a feature of the portly landlady that she never knew (not she) that such things were in the house. "And got ye that in *my* house, Mr McLevy? Whaur in a' the earth did it come frae? And wha brought it to the Cock and Trumpet? I wish I kent."

But the sound of *her* trumpet was changed one morning after she had taken to herself a certain Mr Alexander Dewar to be lord of her, her establishment, and the crowing bantam. Sandy was himself a great thief.

One morning I happened to be earlier on my rounds than usual, and though houses like the Cock and Trumpet do their business during night, and are therefore late openers, I found the door open.

Something more than ordinary, I said to myself. The bantam must have been roused by some cock that has seen the morning's light sooner than it reaches the deep recesses of that wynd.

And going straight in, I came to the bed-room of the new master himself. The mistress was enjoying in bed the repose due to her labours, snoring as deep as a woman of her size and suction could do, and beside her, in a chair, sat Sandy himself plucking lustily at fowls. He had finished nine hens, and was busy with the last of nine ducks. No wonder that the bantam had crown so early.

"What a fine show of poultry, Sandy, man," said I. "Where got you so many hens and ducks?"

"A man has surely a right to what comes into his ain trap," replied the rogue, as unmoved as one of the dead hens. "They flew in at the window."

And he proceeded with the operation of plucking.

My voice had in the meantime awakened his helpmate.

"Whaur can the hens hae come frae?" snorted the jolly woman.

Said I: "They flew in at the window."

"Weel, maybe they did."

"Just in the way the Bologna sausages did," said I.

"I'm an innocent woman. Was I no sleeping when ye cam in? Does

119

a sleeping woman catch hens in her sleep as she does flees in her mooth?"

"Well," said I, turning to Sandy, "you're the man."

"The Lord's will be dune," said the wife, "If Sandy has disgraced the house I made him master o', ay, and a gentleman to boot, he maun just dree the dregs (take the consequences)."

Nor was I much surprised at this turn, for I had heard that she was losing conceit of Sandy, and had been repenting that she had raised him to the rank of a gentleman as well as lord of the Cock and Trumpet. Here was a good opportunity of getting rid of him, and the shrewd Jezebel saw her advantage.

"Now, Sandy," said I again to the cool rogue, still occupied with his work, and who had now arrived at the head feathers of the last duck, which head feathers (though generally left by poultry pluckers) I observed he had carefully taken from every victim; "lay down the duck and get a pillow-slip."

"Here's ane," cried his wife on the instant, as she began to undo the strings of her head cushion, ay, even that which had frequently been pressed by the head of her lord. "There," she added, as she threw the article out of the bed.

"Put these feathers into that bag," said I; "every feather, and I'll wait till I see the last put in."

"Ye'll find that a kittle job, Mr McLevy. A fleeing feather's no easily catched."

"Weel," said Sandy, as he threw a wrathful glance at the mistress of his affection, now about to be lost to him, a loss of fifteen stones of solid beef – "I'll do your bidding," and then relaxing into a chuckle – "but will you tell me hoo the devil ony judge or jury can tell, after a' these feathers are mixed, which belongs to ae duke, and no to anither, and which to ae hen, and no to its neeghbour; and then after a' that, to whom the hens or the dukes belang? Ye see there's no a head feather left."

I saw in a moment that the cunning rogue had caught me. But I had gone too far to recede. "Put in the feathers quick," said I. "Here," cried Mrs Dewar, "there's some on my bed." And commencing to pick them up, "Nae man shall say that a stown (stolen) feather was left in my house."

"And now, Sandy," said I, when there was scarcely a feather to be seen, "you'll bind all the legs of the corpses together." A command which was obeyed slowly and reluctantly.

"Throw them over your back," continued I, "and the bag will go over all."

Having got my man laden with his dead spoil, "And now we'll march to the Office," said I.

"And fareweel, Sandy," cried a voice from the bed; "we'll maybe never see ane anither again. May the Lord prosper ye and mend ye!"

I bent my head over the lump of innocence –

"Now, Mrs Dewar," whispered I, "just tell me how Sandy came by the ducks and hens."

"Aweel," said she in return, disappointing my hopes of an admission, "I'll say naething against my lawfu' husband. If the dukes and hens didna flee in at the window, it's now dead certain they'll no flee oot at the door."

These were the last words of the sonsy landlady, and I marched Sandy, with his burden, through an admiring crowd to the Office, where, having locked him up, I began to examine the dead bodies. The heads, as I have said, had been all taken care of, not a feather left upon one of them. Every corpse was so provokingly like another, that I could see no way of proving that they belonged to any one; and if, as was likely, Sandy had not been observed by any person about the place, I had no evidence to rest on. I was in difficulty.

A short time afterwards there came in a charge from Mr Beaton, Hope Park, Meadows, to the effect that nine ducks had been stolen from his premises on the previous night; and after the lapse of another hour, a second charge, involving the nine hens, came from Mr Renton of Hope Park End. To these places I repaired, and saw the servants, who could, of course, have had no difficulty about the identity of their favourites, fed and tended by them every morning, but they all laughed at the idea of knowing their lamented favourites with bare bodies. As to the thief, no one could say that he was seen, or even heard. Sandy had done his work well. I then got the lasses to accompany me to the Office, where we soon arrived.

So the girls turned over and over the bodies, examining them with all the minuteness in their power. Jenny declared it impossible, and Helen was in despair; Peggy thought she observed something, and Barbara declared it to be nothing. At the long run, a happy thought struck Jenny.

"But where's the 'pensioner'?" cried she.

"Ay, the 'pensioner'?" responded her neighbour Nelly.

"Had he a spliced leg?" inquired I.

"Yes," replied the first, "a dog broke it, and Nelly and I bound it up with two thin pieces of wood and a string."

"Ay, and he got aye the best handful of barley," rejoined Nelly; "but the leg of the 'pensioner' was cured a month ago, and the bandage removed."

"Is that the 'pensioner'?" said I, as I shewed the leg of one which I had observed in the forenoon as having on it the appearance of a healed-up sore.

"Ay, just the creature," they both exclaimed. "It was the right leg, and you'll see yet the marks of the string."

"So much for the ducks," said I; "and now for the hens and cocks; was there no pensioner among them?"

"No," cried Barbara, "but there was the 'corporal'."

"Any mark beyond the coat?" inquired I.

"Ay," cried Peggy, "he was stone-blind in the right eye; he lost his sight in a battle and never recovered his eyesight again."

"Is that the blind 'corporal'?" said I.

"The very creature," cried Barbara, as she examined the white orb of the animal which I had detected in the morning; "but oh," she added, "I am vexed to see him in that condition!"

The scene was renewed before the Sheriff. Sandy got sixty days' imprisonment for the ducks, and six months for the hens, as a kind of second offence; and Luckie Dewar could afford a few tears (common to certain amphibious animals on the banks of the Nile) over the misfortunes of Sandy Dewar, who had thus fallen from being master of the Cock and Trumpet to being the occupant of a prison.

James McLevy

Burying his Mistakes

It happened at a small country town [in England] that Scott suddenly required medical advice for one of his servants, and, on enquiring if there was any doctor at the place, was told that there was two – one long established, and the other a new comer. The latter gentleman, being luckily found at home, soon made his appearance; – a grave, sagacious-looking personage, attired in black, with a shovel hat, in whom, to his utter astonishment, Sir Walter recognised a Scotch blacksmith, who had formerly practised, with tolerable success, as a veterinary operator in the neighbourhood of Ashestiel. – "How, in all the world!" exclaimed he, "can it be possible that this is John Lundie?" – "In troth is it, your honour – just *a' that's for him.*" – "Well, but let us hear; you were a *horse*-doctor before; now, it seems, you are a *man*-doctor; how do you get on?" – "Ou, just extraordinar weel; for your honour maun ken my practice is vera sure and orthodox. I depend entirely upon twa *simples*." "And what may their names be? Perhaps it is a secret?" – "I'll tell your honour," in a low tone; "my twa simples are just *laudamy* and *calamy*!" – "Simples with a vengeance!" replied Scott. "But John, do you never happen to *kill* any of your patients?" – "Kill? Ou ay, may be sae! Whiles they die, and whiles no; but it's the will o' Providence. *Ony how, your honour, it wad be lang before it makes up for Flodden!*"

John Gibson Lockhart

Omicron *Lick-Devil, Esq

Printer in London.

> * It may not be improper to observe, for the information
> of those who have never yet committed any of their
> thoughts to the press, that the Printers Errand-boys
> are dignified with the names of Devils.

Sir, as I live at such a distance from the press, I must take the liberty
to offer you a few directions, with regard to the manner of printing the
work which will be put into your hands, by my worthy friend Dribble-
verse Pufftrash, Esq. the bookseller. In the first place, I desire the
type may not be invisibly small, nor even such a one, as is only to be
perused by the microscope. It is true your small character looks neat
and pretty; but then its troublesome to those, who do not consider
books as mere furniture, but are of opinion that one use of them is to
be read. By Gad, Sir, this minute way of printing is enough to reduce
the clearest and most transparent writers to a level with those that are
the most dark, muddy, profound, mysterious and obscure: and if
Brindley, and a parcel of them, carry their improvements in micography
a very little further; that most perspicuous poet the divine Virgil, even
divested of his thick cloud of commentators, will, in a little time,
become as unintelligible as the most puzzled prose or rhime meta-
physician, that ever labour'd of abortive meanings, or sat upon the
wind eggs of philosophy. This is all for the sake of meer neatness. –
Good God! into what will this little age dwindle? . . .
    I had something else to say – Oh! it was about the choice of Mottos.
In this article at least, I have it still in my power to out-do (without
vanity be it said) even the most learned of my contemporaries. And by
Gad I will. There is nothing like good, apt and pertinent mottos in
various languages to shew an author's reading; and sometimes let me
tell you the motto is the only well said thing in a whole book. But to
let you into a piece of secret history, you must know, Sir, that I am no
great linguist myself; for as to the ancient languages, I cannot honestly
pretend to be perfect in any of them, escept the Latin, Greek, Hebrew,
Syriac, Chaldaic, Troglodite, and Carthaginian; in which last, particularly, I may say without vaunting, I am as well versed, thank heaven!
as most men of my inches in Europe; be the other who he will. In the
modern, or if you will, the living languages, (for some of these may,
perhaps, be reckoned among the number of the ancient) I find myself
equally imperfect. For though I speak as familiarly as my own mother
tongue, the French, English, Chinese, Italian, German, Allemagne,
High-Dutch, Portuguese, Spanish, Irish, the Russ like any bear,
Persian or Persic, which you will, the Laplandic, Turchestan, most of
the African languages; and have a little smattering of Low-Dutch, just

enough to make myself understood by a Porpus: yet I must own myself most deplorably ignorant, as to many of the American languages; particularly those that are spoke in some of the more inland parts of that vast continent, and towards the sources of the river of the Amazons, and the Oroonoko; and especially that beautiful, pybald, black and white Lingo, pallaber'd in its greatest purity by the Creolians of Jamaica. Being thus deficient in languages, I have wrote to my good friend Mr All-Tongue Tasteless, principal of Waxen-Nose College, in the university of Coxcomb-Den; who will, for the sake of our old friendship, supply you with plentiful forage of mottos in all languages dead and alive. But I abhor prolixity; and therefore without more words at present assure yourself, that I am at all hours, days, minutes, and seconds (till such time as you give me some cause, either real or imaginary, to become your bitter enemy)

Sir, your most unalterable friend,
and humble servant,

Datchet-Bridge,
Nov. 1748   NOUREDDIN ALI

[*John Armstrong 1709–1779*]

The Comic Singers

Where the pools are bright and deep
Where the grey trout lies asleep
Up the river and o'er the lea,
That's the way for Billy and me.

Where the blackbird sings the latest,
Where the hawthorn blooms the sweetest,
Where the nestlings chirp and flee,
That's the way for Billy and me.

Where the mowers mow the cleanest,
Where the hay lies thick and greenest,
There to trace the homeward bee,
That's the way for Billy and me.

Where the hazel bank is steepest,
Where the shadow falls the deepest,
Where the clustering nuts fall free,
That's the way for Billy and me.

Why the boys should drive away
Little sweet maidens from the play,
Or love to banter and fight so well,
That's the thing I never could tell.

But this I know, I love to play,
Through the meadows, among the hay,
Up the water and o'er the lea,
That's the way for Billy and me.

James Hogg

The Frugal Muse

I met my first poet, real or otherwise, when I was about twelve. So unreasoning were the demands of total war that even my father had been sucked into full-time ARP duty in a shed in Inverleith Park. I think they were supposed to rescue us from blazing rooftops or burrow for us in blitzed basements, but with one or two nasty exceptions the Luftwaffe left Edinburgh off their flight plans, so my father's duty hours were spent in arduous training for tasks which were never necessary. He spent several nights a week on duty at the park; we all grinned and bore that hardship.

Another unlikely civil defender at Inverleith came home sometimes for tea. He was the poet Alexander Reid. That sounds unbearably grand . . . like "the poet Sacheverell Sitwell", or Robert Burns himself. It would be truer to say that Alex "wrote poetry" in those days, and I was twenty before I read a word he had written, but my father very properly sensed his worth and celebrated it with us.

He looked poetic, I suppose, with long hair (for those days), dreamy eyes, always blinking, and incredibly long (and usually filthy) fingernails which my mother shuddered about to her dying day. He had a French wife whose name, Genevieve, I enjoyed saying aloud because it sounded so beautiful. Thinking back on it, it is extremely unlikely that Alexander Reid had anything to do with the International Brigade and the Spanish Civil War, I don't think he met Trotsky, saw action at the wide Ebro river, almost went to jail for his pacifist/humanist/socialist beliefs, or any of the wildly romantic things I imagined that all poets did.

Meanwhile the Church Hymnary, authorised by Presbyterians from Cork to Christchurch, provided almost the only formal poetry of my young life.

> By cool Siloam's shady rill
>   How sweet the lily grows!
> How sweet the breath, beneath the hill,
>   Of Sharon's dewy rose!
>
> *Reginald Heber*

> In the bleak mid-winter
>   Frosty wind made moan,
> Earth stood hard as iron,
>   Water like a stone;
> Snow had fallen, snow on snow,
>   Snow on snow,
> In the bleak mid-winter,
>   Long ago.
>
> *Christina Georgina Rossetti*

No clumsy choir, no quavering exhibitionist soprano, could spoil these two or three good lyrics for me, then or now.

Alexander Reid, despite all my mother's dire predictions, achieved fame and a period of considerable success as a dramatist. His comedy, *The Lass Wi' the Muckle Mou'*, deserves its permanent place in the dramatic literature of Scotland and, more importantly, is remembered with great affection by the many thousands who saw it in that daft post-war decade when the emergence of a Scottish National Theatre seemed inevitable. The old Border legend of Muckle Mou'd Meg is intertwined with the great ballad, "Thomas the Rhymer", in a most satisfying dramatic style and shape.

> He has gotten a coat of the even cloth,
>   And a pair of shoes of velvet green;
> And till seven years were gane and past,
>   True Thomas on earth was never seen.

In another play, a modern morality based upon medieval witchcraft, *The World's Wonder*, Reid uses that celebrated enchanter, Sir Michael Scott, as his hero.

Sir Michael Scott of Balwearie flourished during the thirteenth century. He was a man of much learning, chiefly acquired in foreign countries. He wrote a commentary upon Aristotle, printed at Venice in 1496; and several treatises upon natural philosophy, from which he appears to have been addicted to the abstruse studies of judicial astrology, alchymy, physiognomy, and chiromancy. Hence he passed among his contemporaries for a skilful magician . . . The magic books of Michael Scott . . . could not be opened without danger, on account of the malignant fiends who were thereby invoked. Michael Scott, was, once upon a time, much embarrassed by a spirit, for whom he was under the necessity of finding constant employment. He commanded him to build a cauld, or Dam-head, across the Tweed at Kelso; it was accomplished in one night, and still does honour to the infernal architect. Michael next ordered that Eildon Hill, which was then a uniform cone, should be divided into three. Another night was sufficient to part its summit into the three picturesque peaks which it now bears. At length the enchanter conquered this indefatigable demon, by employing him in the hopeless and endless task of making ropes out of sea-sand.

> Note [1890] to *Sir Walter Scott's*
> "The Lay of the Last Minstrel."

Anyone who has seen the sea-haar come off the Firth of Forth and gobbling up Edinburgh will enjoy this youthful poem by Alexander Reid.

The Monster

Humpbacked and wet and grey as grief
I saw him crawlin' up frae Leith
Dumfoundered watched him while he licked
The High Street tenements frae sicht
Swallowed the Tron and then St Giles,
Then rested in the Gardens, whiles
He eyed wi' bleary weary een
What lay ayont that haugh o' green.
It garred him grue. He changed his mind,
Spat oot the lave and wi' the wind
Trauchled tae Portobello Bay
And doon the Firth and sae away.

The poetry of the streets constantly rang in our ears. My sister and her friends inherited at least a century of skipping-game songs, ball-game songs, rhymes to run, hop, and jump to, sad songs to sing to dolls or smaller sisters, funny jingles, naughty poems, often gibberish, sometimes innocent and pretty.

I'm going in the train
And you're no' coming wi' me,
I've got a laddie o' my ain
His name is Bonnie Jamie

Jamie wears a kilt
He wears it in the fashion,
And every time I look at him
I canna help frae laughin'.

La donna mobilé
My legs are wobble-y
Nae bloomin' wonder,
Look what they're under!

The Salvation Army, full of sin,
Went to heaven in a corned-beef tin,
The corned-beef tin began to smell
So the Salvation Army went to . . .
Helensburgh Castle stands on a rock;
If you want to pass you've got to show your . . .
Cocktails and soda, tuppence a glass,
If you won't want them, stick them up your . . .
Ask no questions, you'll be told no lies,
Shut your mouth and you'll catch no flies.

Skinny malinky lang legs,
Umbrella feet,
Went tae the pictures
An' couldna' find a seat
He got the bus hame
An' he wouldna' pey his fare,
So the wee bald conductor
Kicked him doon the stair.

Auntie Mary
Had a canary
Up the leg o' her drawers:
It whistled for 'oors
And frightened the Boers
And won the Victoria Cross.

My brother Bill is a fireman bold;
He pits oot fires.
He's only twenty-five years old;
He pits oot fires.
He went to fight a fire one night,
When somebody shouted dynamite,
Wherever he is he'll be all right;
He pits oot fires.

And the most memorable singing-game of all, probably because of its catchy tune, is undoubtedly the "Golden City", common to Dublin, Liverpool, and other cities.

The wind, the wind, the wind blows high
The snow comes falling from the sky;
Jeannie Macpherson says she'll die
For the want of the Golden City

She is handsome, she is pretty,
She is the girl of the Golden City;
She is handsome, one-two-three,
Come and tell me who shall be!

O Jenny Cock-a-lee
Come to bed and cuddle me
And I'll gie you a cup o' tea
Tae keep your belly warm!

One, two, three, a-leerie
I saw Wallace Beery
Sittin' on his bumbaleerie
Kissing Shirley Temple.

The big ship sails through the Eely-Alley-o,
The Eely-Alley-o, the Eely-Alley-o;
The big ship sails through the Eely-Alley-o
On the fourteenth of December.

How many miles to Babylon?
Three score and ten.
Will I get there by candlelight?
Yes, and back again!

There she goes, there she goes,
Like an elephant on her toes;
Look at her feet, she thinks she's neat,
Black stockings and smelly feet.

I had a sausage,
A bonny, co-operative sausage,
I put it in the oven for my tea;
I went down the lobby
To meet my Uncle Bobby
And the sausage came after me.

My teenage daughters confirm that their version of Plainie-Clappie is modified to include some minor amendments from Kincardineshire where they spent most of their summers:

"Plainie"	– bounce the ball against a wall.
"Clappie"	– both hands clapped before the bouncing ball returns.
"Roll-up-in"	– hands rolled over each other.
"To backie"	– clap hands behind back.
"Right hand"	– catch with right hand.
"Left hand"	– catch with left hand.
"High si-toosh"	– catch ball with upturned clasped hands.
"Low si-toosh"	– catch ball with downturned clasped hands.
"Touch my heel"	– hand touches heel.
"Touch my toe"	– hand touches toe.
"Through ye go"	– ball goes through legs and is caught.
"And birly-O!"	– a final turn around and catch.

Is "first love" fact or fancy?

It's unimportant, and who in middle-age will truthfully separate wish from fulfilment, ambition from conquest? Her name was Rita Schnabel and, like my sister, she was a Brownie. The fact that she was a Brownie of German extraction at or about 1939 was irrelevant then and even more so now.

Escorting my sister home from the Brownies became, therefore, excuse and reason for furtive fumbles in wet bushes and wetter kisses that were closer to collisions than anything else. But the tom-toms talked, the smoke signals soared above the playgrounds, and it seemed that our initials were going to be carved on trees or passed in classroom notes for ever more.

> Water water wallflower
> Growing up so high
> We are all maidens
> And we must all die;
> Except for Rita Schnabel (or whoever)
> For she's the fondest lover
> She can dance and she can sing
> And she can lick the sugar:
> Fie, fie, fie for shame
> Turn your face to the wall again!

The wallflower song, always so sweetly sung by girls in such a wobbly piped treble, refers to whoever is "het" or "he" (as they now have it) in whatever game is afoot. I love the counting-out rhyme, "Maister Mundie", used to decide who is "het" in a game of Tig, or any other game that requires a nominated victim, as most games do:

Maister Mundie, hoo's yer wife?
   Verra sick an' like to die.
Can she eat onie meat?
   Aye, as muckle's I can buy.
A platefu' o' parritch verra thin,
A pund o' butter meltit in;
Black fish, white troot,
Eetle, ottle, you're oot!

Since childhood, in retrospect, seems to have been compounded of one ritual after another, perhaps the most powerful were the invocations used to vouchsafe one's willingness to tell the truth, the whole truth, and nothing but . . .

I ring, I ring, a pinky
If I tell a lee;
I'll go to the bad place
Whenever I dee.
White pan, black pan,
Burn me to death,
Tak a muckle gully
An' cut my breath,
Ten miles below the earth!

At its best, indigenous folk song and rhyme is splendid frugal poetry. "If You Will Marry Me" and "Queen Mary" were common to many districts of Scotland before they were taken up by the folk-song revivalists.

Oh, I'll gie you a dress o' red,
A' stitched roon' wi' a silver thread,
If you will marry, arry, arry, arry,
If you will marry me.

Oh, I'll no' tak your dress o' red,
A' stitched roon' wi' a silver thread,
An' I'll no' marry, arry, arry, arry,
An' I'll no marry you.

Well, I'll gie you a silver spoon,
Tae feed the bairn in the afternoon,
If you will marry, arry, arry, arry,
If you will marry me.

Oh, I'll no tak your silver spoon, etc.,

Well, I'll gie you the keys o' my chest,
An' all the money I possess,
If you will marry, etc.,

Oh, yes, I'll tak the keys o' your chest,
An' all the money that you possess,
An' I will marry, arry, arry, arry,
An' I will marry you.

Oh, my God, you're helluva funny,
Ye dinna love me but ye love my money,
An' I'll no' marry, arry, arry, arry,
An' I'll no' marry you!

Queen Mary, Queen Mary,
My age is sixteen,
My father's a farmer
On yonder green;
He's plenty of money
To dress me fu' braw,
But there's nae bonnie laddie
Will tak me awa'.

One morning I rose
And I looked in the glass,
Said I to myself,
"With a shove ye might pass,"
Put my hands by my side,
And I gave a "Ha! Ha!"
But there's nae bonnie laddie
Will tak me awa'.

For those who were lucky enough to share the experience, it's worth while adding that the first time I heard "Queen Mary" was when Roddy McMillan sang it along with a clutch of other childhood songs so hauntingly remembered.

Some unfortunate children were forced, for reasons best known only to their parents, to attend elocution lessons. Some perfectly good poetry got itself a bad name through its association with this activity.

The Whistle

He cut a sappy sucker from the muckle rodden-tree,
He trimmed it, an' he wet it, an' he thumped it on his knee;
He never heard the teuchat when the harrow broke her eggs,
He missed the craggit heron nabbin' puddocks in the seggs,
He forgot to hound the collie at the cattle when they strayed,
But you should hae seen the whistle that the wee herd made!

He wheepled on't at mornin' an' he tweetled on't at nicht,
He puffed his freckled cheeks until his nose sank oot o' sicht,
The kye were late for milkin' when he piped them up the closs,
The kitlins got his supper syne, an' he was beddit boss;
But he cared na doit nor docken what they did or thocht or said,
There was comfort in the whistle that the wee herd made.

For lyin' lang o' mornin's he had clawed the caup for weeks,
But noo he had his bonnet on afore the lave had breeks;
He was whistlin' to the porridge that were hott'rin' on the fire,
He was whistlin' ower the travise to the bailie in the byre;
Nae a blackbird nor a mavis, that hae pipin' for their trade,
Was a marrow for the whistle that the wee herd made.

He played a march to battle, it cam' dirlin' through the mist,
Till the halflin' squared his shou'ders an' made up his mind
          to 'list;
He tried a spring for wooers, though he wistna what it meant,
But the kitchen-lass was lauchin' an' he thocht she maybe kent;
He got ream an' buttered bannocks for the lovin' lilt he played –
Wasna that a cheery whistle that the wee herd made?

He blew them rants sae lively, schottisches, reels an' jigs,
The foalie flang his muckle legs an' capered owre the rigs,
The grey-tailed futt'rat bobbit oot to hear his ain strathspey,
The bawd cam' loupin' through the corn to "Clean Pease
          Strae";
The feet o' ilka man an' beast gat youkit when he played –
Hae ye ever heard o' whistle like the wee herd made?

But the snaw it stopped the herdin' an' the winter brocht
         him dool,
When in spite o' hacks an' chilblains he was shod again for
         school;
He couldna sough the catechis nor pipe the rule o' three,
He was keepit in an' lickit when the ither loons got free,
But he aften played the truant – 'twas the only thing he played,
For the maister brunt the whistle that the wee herd made.

Charles Murray

The Puddock

A puddock sat by the lochan's brim,
An' he thocht there was never a puddock like him,
He sat on his hurdies, he waggled his legs,
An' cockit his heid as he glower'd throu' the seggs,
The bigsy wee cratur' was feelin' that prood,
He gapit his mou' an' he croakit oot lood:
"Gin ye'd a' like tae see a richt puddock," quo' he,
"Ye'll never, I'll sweer, get a better nor me.
I've fem'lies an' wives an' a weel-plenished hame,
Wi' drink for my thrapple an' meat for my wame.
The lasses aye thocht me a fine strappin' chiel,
An' I ken I'm a rale bonny singer as weel,
I'm nae gyaun tae blaw, but the truth I maun tell –
I believe I'm the varra MacPuddock himsel'."

A heron was hungry an' needin' tae sup,
Sae he nabbit th' puddock and gollup't him up;
Syne runkled his feathers: "A peer thing," quo' he,
"But – puddocks is nae fat's they eesed tae be."

J. M. Caie

For entertainment value and mordant wit the poetry of the graveyard rivals the ditties of the streets and pubs. The circular tomb of David Hume on Edinburgh's Calton Hill bears the inscription:

Within this circular idea,
    Call'd vulgarly a tomb,
The ideas and impressions lie
    That constituted Hume.

Glasgow's Necropolis is one of Britain's most impressive burial grounds – a vast vulgar monument to the city's material wealth when she was the second city of the British Empire. Somewhere, in the middle of all these toppling effigies and crumbling masonry, is a simple stone, saying:

Here lyes Bessy Bell,
But whereabouts I cannot tell.

A stone, dated 1757, in Montrose intimates:

Here lies the bodeys of George Young
and Isobel Guthrie, and all their
posterity for fifty years backwards.

Sir Walter Scott loved no man more than his servant Tom Purdie, a
former poacher who had come before Sir Walter in his capacity as
sheriff. Purdie referred to the Waverley Novels as "*our* books". It was
he who had the markings of the Abbotsford sheep changed from "W.S."
to "S.W.S." after Scott received his knighthood, and of him that his
master is believed to have said:

Here lies one who might have been
trusted with untold gold, but not
with unmeasured whisky.

A Scots wool worker had a similar problem:

Here lies the bones of Tammy Messer,
Of tarry woo' he was a dresser;
He had some faults and mony merits,
And died of drinking ardent spirits.

Robert Burns was, of course, maestro of the epitaph as well as so much
else.

On a Schoolmaster

Here lie Willie Michie's bones;
   O Satan, when ye tak him,
Gie him the schoolin' of your weans,
   For clever deils he'll mak them!

On William Nicol

Ye maggots, feed on Nicol's brain,
   For few sic feasts ye've gotten,
And fix your claws in Nicol's heart,
   For deil a bit o't's rotten.

On a Suicide

Earthed up, here lies an imp of hell
   Planted by Satan's dibble:
Poor silly wretch, he's damned himsel
   To save the Lord the trouble.

On a Wag in Mauchline

Lament him, Mauchline husbands a',
   He aften did assist ye;
For had ye staid whole weeks awa,
Your wives they ne'er had miss'd ye.

Ye Mauchline bairns, as on ye pass
    To school in bands thegither,
O tread ye lightly on his grass;
    Perhaps he was your father.

Dear Gordon Smith:

So far, not bad at all, but we'll need more serious attention to your dear old Robbie Burns. I thought he was your national hero. I can understand them translating him in Moscow – all that incipient socialism even in his love lyrics – but I was reading only the other day that a tribe of hitherto unknown Patagonian Indians came out of the jungle and greeted their discoverers with a spirited rendering of something called "Willie Brew'd a Peck o' Maut" in faultless Scotch. Surely this is going too damnably far!

Dear Mortimer Street:

You should know that we have peopled the earth. Over the centuries we have been hounded, transported, battened down in holds, shackled and manacled, bought and sold, and frustrated into voluntary exile. Our mercenaries have fought the world's wars for whoever paid the highest price – regardless of cause, colour, creed or religion. Have Burns, will travel. And we take no prisoners.

For the umpteenth time, it's Scots, not Scotch. And "Auld Lang Zyne" to you too!

There was a Lad

Burns possessed the power of a crushing sarcasm, which he was not loth, on fitting occasion, to administer. He was standing on the quay at Greenock, when a prosperous merchant of the place happened to fall into the water. Being unable to swim, he had certainly perished had not a sailor at once plunged after him, and, at the risk of his own life, rescued him from his perilous situation. The merchant drew his purse, and gave the sailor a shilling. The bystanders protested as to the contemptible nature of the reward, when Burns, coming forward, entreated them to refrain. "Surely," said he, with a smile of scorn, "the gentleman is the best judge of the value of his own life."

Rev. Charles Rogers

The Haggis Club

We didn't celebrate Robert Burns in our house. His birthday came and went without any haggis-bashing, and I don't remember the street outside running with whisky or the night air reverberating to shrill cries of pagan joy. Come to think of it, we didn't celebrate all that much in our house – a good example of Presbyterian rectitude carried to reckless excess.

My mother loved Burns's songs and sang them about the house, simply and sweetly as they should be sung, not screeched by kilted tenors and sashed sopranos. They are some of the greatest love lyrics in the world, rivalling Catullus:

> Ae fond kiss, and then we sever!
> Ae fareweel, alas, for ever!
> Deep in heart-wrung tears I'll pledge thee,
> Warring sighs and groans I'll wage thee.
>
> Had we never lov'd sae kindly,
> Had we never lov'd sae blindly,
> Never met – or never parted,
> We had ne'er been broken-hearted.

My Love is Like a Red Red Rose

> My love is like a red red rose
>   That's newly sprung in June:
> My love is like the melodie
>   That's sweetly play'd in tune.
>
> So fair art thou, my bonnie lass,
>   So deep in love am I:
> And I will love thee still, my dear,
>   Till a' the seas gang dry.
>
> Till a' the seas gang dry, my dear,
>   And the rocks melt wi' the sun:
> And I will love thee still, my dear,
>   While the sands o' life shall run.

143

And fare thee weel, my only love,
    And fare thee weel, awhile!
And I will come again, my love,
    Tho' it were ten thousand mile.

Ye Banks and Braes

Ye banks and braes o' bonnie Doon,
    How can ye bloom sae fresh and fair?
How can ye chant, ye little birds,
    And I sae weary fu' o' care?
Thou'lt break my heart, thou warbling bird,
That wantons thro' the flowering thorn:
Thou minds me o' departed joys,
    Departed never to return.

Aft hae I rov'd by bonnie Doon,
    To see the rose and woodbine twine;
And ilka bird sang o' its love,
    And fondly sae did I o' mine,
Wi' lightsome heart I pu'd a rose,
    Fu' sweet upon its thorny tree;
And my fause lover stole my rose,
    But ah! he left the thorn wi' me.

Mary Morison

O Mary, at thy window be,
    It is the wish'd, the trysted hour!
Those smiles and glances let me see,
    That make the miser's treasure poor:
How blythely wad I bid the stoure,
    A weary slave frae sun to sun,
Could I the rich reward secure,
    The lovely Mary Morison.

Yestreen, when to the trembling string
   The dance gaed thro' the lighted ha',
To thee my fancy took its wing,
   I sat, but neither heard nor saw:
Tho' this was fair, and that was braw,
   And you the toast of a' the town,
I sigh'd, and said amang them a',
   'Ye are na Mary Morison.'

O Mary, canst thou wreck his peace,
   Wha for thy sake wad gladly die?
Or canst thou break that heart of his,
   Whose only faut is loving thee?
If love for love thou wilt na gie,
   At least be pity to me shown!
A thought ungentle canna be
   The thought o' Mary Morison.

Within a week of going to my first Burns supper I had been to six. By this time I was a junior reporter with the *Dalkeith Advertiser*, and that predominantly socialist Midlothian mining and farming community loves its Burns. As a matter of fact, at that time I was junior reporter, senior reporter, sub-editor and editor rolled into one, and it stayed that way, fourteen hours a day, for nearly three years. Invaluable experience, said everybody, and so it was, although my mother kept wondering when I was going to get a "steady job" and settle down.

The reporting of events at a Burns Supper is no more hazardous than reporting, say, grand prix motor racing. In both cases the level of performance depends to some extent on very superior high-octane fuel. The ritual seldom varies: a hired piper of variable dexterity leads in the trencher which bears the sacrificial haggis. The noise in even a large dining room is unbearable, the chords ululating on in one's head long after the piper has quaffed the large ceremonial dram which he is offered, never refuses, then goes in search of more. A man with dagger then recites Robert Burns's "Address to the Haggis", stabbing it savagely at the appropriate moment in his script. I have seen the "warm-reeking gushing entrails" splattered across a room under such a vehement attack. That great authority on Scottish food and custom, F. Marian McNeill, sensibly prescribed the cutting of a small St Andrew's cross ($\times$) in the haggis to reduce the risks of second-degree burns to impatient diners.

There are always graces and toasts and songs and recitations, sometimes some good fiddling, even some exhibition dancing. But the principal toast, "to the Immortal Memory of Robert Burns", is supposed to be the cornerstone of the evening. Many of these "memories" are works of scholarship and wit, often delivered by ministers of religion, lawyers, headmasters, trade unionists, and politicians. Six in a week is a bit much, but six successive helpings of haggis and turnip and champit tatties, no matter how much neat whisky smoothed the passages, was an act of professional loyalty and daring which ought to be recognised.

It was, of course, a foolproof way to discover what Burns meant to different people. And as one listened to the toasts and eulogies it was impossible not to wonder if they were all honouring the same person.

Like many a folk-hero before him Burns is adapted to fit any image, quoted to substantiate any cause. The sketch of the ploughman poet, the rough country lad, the noble savage tamed by Edinburgh society is the most familiar distortion, employed for romantic or sentimental reasons in one dining-room, for political persuasion in another. Agnostic or atheistic followers chant his satires against the church as condemnation of all religion and religious attitudes; dog-collared apologists will find true spirituality wherever they seek it. By admitting that Robin "was a bit of a lad" his extraordinary sexual free-wheeling has been played down.

Jean [Armour] I found banished like a martyr – forlorn, destitute and friendless: all for the good old cause: I have reconciled her to her fate: I have reconciled her to her mother: I have taken her a room: I have taken her to my arms: I have given her a mahogany bed: I have given her a guinea: and I have fucked her till she rejoiced with joy unspeakable and full of glory. But – as I always am on every occasion – I have been prudent and cautious to an astounding degree; I swore her, privately and solemnly, never to attempt any claim on me as a husband, even though anybody should persuade her she had such a claim, which she has not, neither during my life nor after my death. She did all this like a good girl, and I took the opportunity of some dry horse-litter, and gave her such a thundering scalade that electrified the very marrow of her bones.

Letter from Burns to Robert
Ainslie, March, 1788.

Sir Walter retained a vivid recollection of his interview with the Ayrshire poet. He was particularly struck with his large dark eye. He writes, "It literally glowed. I never saw such another eye in a human head, though I have seen the most distinguished men in my time." The writer was informed by Mrs Begg, the poet's sister, that the expression of her brother's eye, once seen, was never to be forgotten. She added, "His entire countenance beamed with genius. So striking was his look, that a stranger passing him on the highway would, though ignorant who he was, have turned round to look at him a second time."

Rev. Charles Rogers

... the affair [began] merely in a "gaieté de coeur", and, to tell the truth, a vanity of showing my parts in courtship, particularly my abilities at a "billet-doux", which I always piqued myself upon, made me lay siege to her; and when I had battered myself into a very warm affection for her, she told me one day, in a flag of truce, that her fortress had been for some time before the rightful property of another, but with the greatest friendship and politeness she offered me every alliance, except actual possession."

Burns on Montgomerie's Peggy

On the other hand, Burns's drinking has been shamefully exaggerated, a fact not unrelated to his misfortune in having a moralising teetotaller as his first biographer.

When, at every Burns supper, his great narrative poem "Tam o' Shanter" is delivered – usually with ebullient style and brio – the moral of the tale is not lost on those members of the audience who, by that time, are themselves well on the way to "getting fou and unco happy".

When chapman billies leave the street,
And drouthy neibors neibors meet,
As market-days are wearing late,
An' folk begin to tak the gate;
While we sit bousing at the nappy,
An' getting fou and unco happy,
We think na on the lang Scots miles,
The mosses, waters, slaps, and styles,
That lie between us and our hame,
Where sits our sulky sullen dame,
Gathering her brows like gathering storm,
Nursing her wrath to keep it warm.
   This truth fand honest Tam o' Shanter,
As he frae Ayr ae night did canter –
(Auld Ayr, wham ne'er a town surpasses
For honest men and bonnie lasses.)
   O Tam! hadst thou but been sae wise
As ta'en thy ain wife Kate's advice!
She tauld thee weel thou was a skellum,
A bletherin', blusterin', drunken blellum;
That frae November till October,
Ae market-day thou was na sober;
That ilka melder wi' the miller
Thou sat as lang as thou had siller;
That every naig was ca'd a shoe on,
The smith and thee gat roarin' fou on;

That at the Lord's house, even on Sunday,
Thou drank wi' Kirkton Jean till Monday.
She prophesied that, late or soon,
Thou would be found deep drown'd in Doon;
Or catch'd wi warlocks in the mirk
By Alloway's auld haunted kirk.

   Ah, gentle dames! it gars me greet
To think how mony counsels sweet,
How mony lengthen'd sage advices,
The husband frae the wife despises!

   But to our tale: Ae market night,
Tam had got planted unco right,
Fast by an ingle, bleezing finely,
Wi' reaming swats, that drank divinely;
And at his elbow, Souter Johnny,
His ancient, trusty, drouthy crony;
Tam lo'ed him like a very brither;
They had been fou for weeks thegither.
The night drave on wi' sangs and clatter.
And aye the ale was growing better:
The landlady and Tam grew gracious,
Wi' favours secret, sweet, and precious;
The souter tauld his queerest stories;
The landlord's laugh was ready chorus:
The storm without might rair and rustle,
Tam did na mind the storm a whistle.

   Care, mad to see a man sae happy,
E'en drown'd himsel amang the nappy.
As bees flee hame wi' lades o' treasure,
The minutes wing'd their way wi' pleasure;
Kings may be blest, but Tam was glorious,
O'er a' the ills o' life victorious!

   But pleasures are like poppies spread –
You seize the flow'r, its bloom is shed;
Or like the snow falls in the river –
A moment white, then melts for ever;
Or like the borealis race,
That flit ere you can point their place;
Or like the rainbow's lovely form
Evanishing amid the storm.
Nae man can tether time nor tide;
The hour approaches Tam maun ride;
That hour, o' night's black arch the key-stane,
That dreary hour, he mounts his beast in;
And sic a night he taks the road in,
As ne'er poor sinner was abroad in.

   The wind blew as 'twad blawn its last;

The rattling show'rs rose on the blast;
The speedy gleams the darkness swallow'd;
Loud, deep, and lang, the thunder bellow'd:
That night, a child might understand,
The Deil had business on his hand.
   Weel mounted on his gray mare, Meg,
A better never lifted leg,
Tam skelpit on thro' dub and mire,
Despising wind, and rain, and fire;
Whiles holding fast his gude blue bonnet;
Whiles crooning o'er some auld Scots sonnet;
Whiles glow'ring round wi' prudent cares,
Lest bogles catch him unawares.
Kirk-Alloway was drawing nigh,
Whare ghaists and houlets nightly cry.
   By this time he was cross the ford,
Where in the snaw the chapman smoor'd;
And past the birks and meikle stane,
Where drunken Charlie brak's neck-bane;
And thro' the whins, and by the cairn,
Where hunters fand the murder'd bairn;
And near the thorn, aboon the well,
Where Mungo's mither hang'd hersel.
Before him Doon pours all his floods;
The doubling storm roars thro' the woods;
The lightnings flash from pole to pole;
Near and more near the thunders roll:
When, glimmering thro' the groaning trees,
Kirk-Alloway seem'd in a bleeze;
Thro' ilka bore the beams were glancing,
And loud resounded mirth and dancing.
   Inspiring bold John Barleycorn!
What dangers thou canst make us scorn!
Wi' tippenny, we fear nae evil;
Wi' usquebae, we'll face the devil!
The swats sae ream'd in Tammie's noddle,
Fair play, he car'd na deils a boddle!
But Maggie stood right sair astonish'd,
Till, by the heel and hand admonish'd,
She ventur'd forward on the light;
And, vow! Tam saw an unco sight!
Warlocks and witches in a dance!
Nae cotillon brent new frae France,
But hornpipes, jigs, strathspeys and reels,
Put life and mettle in their heels.
A winnock-bunker in the east,
There sat auld Nick, in shape o' beast –

A touzie tyke, black, grim, and large!
To gie them music was his charge:
He screw'd the pipes and gart them skirl.
Till roof and rafters a' did dirl.
Coffins stood round like open presses,
That shaw'd the dead in their last dresses:
And by some devilish cantraip sleight
Each in its cauld hand held a light,
By which heroic Tam was able
To note upon the haly table
A murderer's banes in gibbet-airns;
Twa span-lang, wee, unchristen'd bairns;
A thief new-cutted frae the rape –
Wi' his last gasp his gab did gape;
Five tomahawks, wi' blude red rusted;
Five scymitars, wi' murder crusted;
A garter, which a babe had strangled;
A knife, a father's throat had mangled,
Whom his ain son o' life bereft –
The gray hairs yet stack to the heft;
Wi' mair of horrible and awfu',
Which even to name wad be unlawfu',
   As Tammie glowr'd, amaz'd and curious,
The mirth and fun grew fast and furious:
The piper loud and louder blew;
The dancers quick and quicker flew;
They reel'd, they set, they cross'd, they cleekit,
Till ilka carlin swat and reekit,
And coost her duddies to the wark,
And linkit at it in her sark!
   Now Tam, O Tam! had thae been queans,
A' plump and strapping in their teens;
Their sarks, instead o' creeshie flannen,
Been snaw-white seventeen hunder linen!
Thir breeks o' mine, my only pair,
That ance were plush, o' gude blue hair,
I wad hae gi'en them off my hurdies,
For ae blink o' the bonnie burdies!
   But wither'd beldams, auld and droll,
Rig woodie hags wad spean a foal,
Louping and flinging on a crummock,
I wonder didna turn thy stomach.
   But Tam kent what was what fu' brawlie
There was ae winsome wench and walie
That night enlisted in the core,
Lang after kent on Carrick shore!
(For mony a beast to dead she shot,

And perish'd mony a bonnie boat,
And shook baith meikle corn and bear,
And kept the country-side in fear.)
Her cutty sark, o' Paisley harn,
That while a lassie she had worn,
In longitude tho' sorely scanty,
It was her best, and she was vauntie.
Ah! little kent thy reverend grannie
That sark she coft for her wee Nannie
Wi' twa pund Scots ('twas a' her riches)
Wad ever grac'd a dance of witches!
    But here my muse her wing maun cour;
Sic flights are far beyond her pow'r –
To sing how Nannie lap and flang,
(A souple jade she was, and strang);
And how Tam stood, like ane bewitch'd,
And thought his very een enrich'd;
Even Satan glowr'd, and fidg'd fu' fain,
And hotch'd and blew wi' might and main:
Till first ae caper, syne anither,
Tam tint his reason a' thegither,
And roars out "Weel done, Cutty-sark!"
And in an instant all was dark!
And scarcely had he Maggie rallied,
When out the hellish legion sallied.
    As bees bizz out wi' angry fyke
When plundering herds assail their byke,
As open pussie's mortal foes
When pop! she starts before their nose,
As eager runs the market-crowd,
When "Catch the thief!" resounds aloud.
So Maggie runs; the witches follow,
Wi' mony an eldritch skriech and hollow.
    Ah, Tam! ah, Tam! thou'll get thy fairin'!
In hell they'll roast thee like a herrin'!
In vain thy Kate awaits thy comin'!
Kate soon will be a woefu' woman!
Now do thy speedy utmost, Meg,
And win the key-stane o' the brig:
There at them thou thy tail may toss,
A running stream they darena cross,
But ere the key-stane she could make,
The fient a tail she had to shake!
For Nannie, far before the rest,
Hard upon noble Maggie prest,
And flew at Tam wi' furious mettle!
Ae spring brought off her master hale,

But left behind her ain gray tail:
The carlin claught her by the rump,
And left poor Maggie scarce a stump.
   Now, wha this tale o' truth shall read,
Each man and mother's son, take heed;
Whene'er to drink you are inclin'd,
Or cutty-sarks rin in your mind,
Think! ye may buy the joys o'er dear;
Remember Tam o' Shanter's mare.

The Merry Muses

It is not the fault of Burns that generations of Scots – the worst of them exiled abroad – have turned him into a symbolic mouthpiece for the worst excesses of nationalism and maudlin sentimentality. He would have flailed their hypocrisy and mocked their mimsy English ways.

It is only ten years since the general publication of *The Merry Muses of Caledonia,* a collection of bawdy poems and folk-song much of which is attributed to Burns. It is usually assumed that this great poet was one of the world's best songsmiths, and probably the greatest song-cobbler of all time. But there are cases where even his good judgment failed him and the "cleaning-up" process undoubtedly bowdlerised some songs. Throughout *The Merry Muses,* however, sex is there in all its animal heat; sex is the great leveller; and it is a reasonable assumption that the hand of Burns set down the best and most bawdy of these songs. We know for a fact that he enjoyed delivering his own compositions to his drinking cronies of the Crochallan Fencibles in his most riotous Edinburgh days.

Wha'll Mow Me Now?

O wha'll mow me now, my jo,
    And wha'll mow me now?
A sodger with his bandeleers,
    Has bang'd my belly fu'.

O I hae tint my rosy cheek,
    Likewise my waist sae sma',
O wae gae wi' the sodger loon,
    The sodger did it a'!

O wha'll mow me now, my jo, etc.

For I maun thole the scornfu' sneer,
    O mony a saucy queen,
When, curse upon her godly face,
    Her cunt's as merry as mine.

O wha'll mow me now, my jo, etc.

Our dame holds up her wanton tail,
    As oft as down she lies,
And yet misca's a young thing,
    The trade if she but tries.

O wha'll mow me now, my jo, etc.

Our dame has aye her ain gudeman,
    And mows for glutton greed,
And yet misca's a poor thing,
    That mows but for its bread.

O wha'll mow me now, my jo, etc.

Alack! sae sweet a tree as love,
    Sae bitter fruit should bear,
Alas that e'er a merry cunt
    Should draw so many a tear.

O wha'll mow me now, my jo, etc.

But devil tak' the lousy loon,
    Denies the bairn he got;
Or leaves the merry lass he lo'ed
    To wear a ragged coat.

O wha'll mow me now, my jo, etc.

Gie the Lass her Fairin

O gie the lass her fairin lad,
    O gie the lass her fairin,
An' something else she'll gie to you
    That's waly worth the wearin;
Syne coup her o'er amang the creels
    When ye hae taen your brandy,
The mair she bangs the less she squeals,
    An' hey for houghmagandie.

Then gie the lass a fairin, lad,
    O gie the lass her fairin,
And she'll gie you a hairy thing,
    An' of it be na sparin.

But coup her o'er amang the creels
    An' bar the door wi baith your heels;
The mair she bangs the less she squeals,
    An' hey for houghmagandie.

Green Grow the Rashes

O wat ye ought o fisher Meg,
    And how she trow'd the webster, O;
She loot me see her carrot cunt,
    And sell'd it for a labster, O.
    Green grow the rashes, O;
        Green grow the rashes, O;
    The lassies they hae wimble-bores,
        The widows they hae gashes, O.

Mistress Mary cow'd her thing
    Because she wad be gentle, O
And span the fleece upon a rock
    To waft a highland mantle, O.
    Green grow, etc.

An' heard ye o the coat o arms
    The Lyon brought our lady, O?
The crest was couchant sable cunt,
    The motto "*ready, ready,* O."
    Green grow, etc.

An' ken ye Leezie Lundie, O,
    The godly Leezie Lundie, O?
She mows like reek thro a' the week,
    But finger-fucks on Sunday, O.
    Green grow, etc.

John Anderson, My Jo

John Anderson, my jo, John,
  I wonder what ye mean,
To lie sae lang i' the mornin',
  And sit sae late at e'en?
Ye'll bleer a' your een, John,
  And why do ye so?
Come sooner to your bed at e'en,
  John Anderson, my jo.

John Anderson, my jo, John,
  When first that ye began,
Ye had as good a tail-tree,
  As ony ither man;
But now its waxen wan, John,
  And wrinkles to and fro;
I've twa gae-ups for ae gae-down,
  John Anderson, my jo.

I'm backit like a salmon,
  I'm breastit like a swan;
My wame it is a down-cod,
  My middle ye may span:
Frae my tap-knot to my tae, John,
  I'm like the new-fa'n snow;
And it's a' for your convenience,
  John Anderson, my jo.

O it is a fine thing
  To keep out o'er the dyke;
But it's a meikle finer thing,
  To see your hurdies fyke;
To see your hurdies fyke, John,
  And hit the rising blow;
It's then I like your chanter-pipe,
  John Anderson, my jo.

When ye come on before, John,
  See that ye do your best;
When ye begin to haud me,
  See that ye grip me fast;
See that ye grip me fast, John,
  Until that I cry "Oh!"
Your back shall crack or I do that,
  John Anderson, my jo.

John Anderson, my jo, John,
  Ye're welcome when ye please;
It's either in the warm bed
  Or else aboon the claes:
Or ye shall hae the horns, John,
  Upon your head to grow;
An' that's the cuckold's mallison,
  John Anderson, my jo.

The Scottish Poets

At an argument, [Thomas] Campbell was apt to betray an embarrassing keenness of speech. Dr John Leyden, the eminent poet and Orientalist, was afflicted with similar impatience. The bards had quarrelled, but they remained, amidst their disputes, warm admirers of each other's genius. Sir Walter Scott relates how he repeated "Hohenlinden" to Leyden, who immediately said, in his own peculiar style, "Dash it, man, tell the fellow that I hate him; but dash him, he has written the finest verses that have been published these fifty years." Scott communicated this singular message, and received from [Campbell] the reply, "Tell Leyden that I detest him, but I know the value of his critical approbation."

Rev. Charles Rogers

A Wheen Sangs

When the mountaineer was asked why he climbed mountains he replied, "because they are there". When Louis MacNeice was asked why he wrote poetry he said, "because it *ought* to be there."

Carol

For us that blissit bairne was borne
For us he was baith rent and torne
For us he was crounit with thorne
Christ has my hart ay
    For us he sched his precious blude
    For us he was naillit on the rude
    For us he in mony battell stude
    Christ has my hart ay
Nixt him to lufe his Mother fair
With steid fast hart for ever mair
Scho bure the byrth, fred us from cair
Christ has my hart ay.

Scottish Psalter

Three Things

If you would lufe and luvit be,
In mynd kept weill these thingis three,
And sadly in thy breast imprent;
Be secret, true and patient.

Anonymous

159

Love's Lament

Wae's me, wae's me!
The acorn's no' yet
Fa'en frae the tree
That's to grow the wood,
That's to mak the creddle,
That's to rock the bairn
That's to grow a man
That's to lay me.

Anonymous

Sir Patrick Spens

The king sits in Dunfermline town
  Drinking the blude-red wine;
"O whare will I get a skeely skipper
  To sail this new ship o' mine?"

O up and spak an eldern knight,
  Sat at the king's right knee:
"Sir Patrick Spens is the best sailor
  That ever sail'd the sea."

Our king has written a braid letter,
  And seal'd it with his hand,
And sent it to Sir Patrick Spens,
  Was walking on the strand.

"To Noroway, to Noroway,
  To Noroway o'er the faem;
The king's daughter o' Noroway,
  'Tis thou must bring her hame."

The first word that Sir Patrick read
  So loud, loud laugh'd he;
The neist word that Sir Patrick read
  The tear blinded his e'e.

"O wha is this has done this deed
  And tauld the king o' me,
To send us out, at this time o' year,
  To sail upon the sea?

"Mak ready, mak ready, my merry men a'!
  Our gude ship sails the morn" –
"O say no' that, my master dear,
  I fear a deadly storm.

"I saw the new moon late yestreen
  Wi' the auld moon in her arm;
And if we gang to sea, master,
  I fear we'll come to harm."

They hadna sailed a league, a league,
  A league but barely three,
When the lift grew dark, and the wind blew loud,
  And gurly grew the sea.

O laith, laith were our gude Scots lords
  To wet their cork-heel'd shoon;
But lang or a' the play was play'd
  They wat their hats aboon.

F

O lang, lang may the ladies sit,
   Wi' their fans into their hand,
Before they see Sir Patrick Spens
   Come sailing to the strand!

And lang, lang may the maidens sit
   Wi' their gowd kames in their hair,
A-waiting for their ain dear loves!
   For them they'll see nae mair.

Half-owre, half-owre to Aberdour,
   'Tis fifty fathoms deep
And there lies gude Sir Patrick Spens,
   Wi' the Scots lords at his feet.

Anonymous

Roderick

Roderick, Roderick,
Roderick of yonder dun,
Thou art my mirth
   and my merry music,
Thou art my rosary
   and the comb of my hair,
Thou art my fruit-garden
   wherein are apples.

Anonymous [from the Gaelic]

The Siller Croun

And ye sall walk in silk attire,
   And siller ha'e to spare,
Gin ye'll consent to be his bride,
   Nor think o' Donald mair.

Oh, wha wad buy a silken goun,
    Wi' a puir broken heart?
Or what's to me a siller croun,
    Gin frae my love I part?

The mind whase every wish is pure,
    Far dearer is to me;
And ere I'm forced to break my faith,
    I'll lay me doun and dee;
For I ha'e pledged my virgin troth,
    Brave Donald's fate to share,
And he has gi'en to me his heart,
    Wi' a' its virtues rare.

His gentle manners wan my heart,
    He gratefu' took the gift;
Could I but think to seek it back,
    It wad be waur than theft.
For langest life can ne'er repay
    The love he bears to me;
And ere I'm forced to break my troth,
    I'll lay me doun and dee.

Anonymous

A lesser-known Scottish poet than that great master, Anon, is Francis
Sempill of Beltrees who lived a long life in the seventeenth century and
left us one of the best songs in the language.

Maggie Lauder

Wha wadna be in love
    Wi' bonnie Maggie Lauder?
A piper met her gaun to Fife,
    And spier'd what was't they ca'd her:
Richt scornfully she answered him,
    Begone, you hallenshaker!
Jog on your gate, you bladderskate!
    My name is Maggie Lauder.

Maggie! quoth he; and, by my bags,
    I'm fidgin' fain to see thee!
Sit down by me, my bonnie bird;
    In troth I winna steer thee;
For I'm a piper to my trade;
    My name is Rob the Ranter:
The lasses loup as they were daft,
    When I blaw up my chanter.

Piper, quo Meg, hae ye yer bags,
    Or is your drone in order?
If ye be Rob, I've heard o' you;
    Live up upo' the Border?
The lasses a', baith far and near,
    Have heard o' Rab the Ranter;
I'll shake my foot wi' richt gude will,
    Gif ye'll blaw up your chanter.

Then to his bags he flew wi' speed;
    About the drone he twisted:
Meg up and wallop'd ower the green;
    For brawly could she frisk it!
Weel done! quo he. Play up! quo she,
    Weel bobb'd! quo Rab the Ranter;
It's worth my while to play, indeed,
    When I hae sic a dancer!

Weel hae ye play'd your part! quo Meg;
    Your cheeks are like the crimson!
There's nane in Scotland plays sae weel,
    Sin' we lost Habbie Simson.
I've lived in Fife, baith maid and wife,
    This ten years and a quarter.
Gin ye should come to Anster Fair,
    Spier ye for Maggie Lauder.

Also in the seventeenth century, during the great plague of 1645, two young women left their home in the town and sought the safety of a country bower. Unfortunately, one of the girls had a lover who could not resist coming to see her and brought the plague with him:

Bessie Bell and Mary Gray

O Bessie Bell and Mary Gray,
   They war twa bonnie lasses!
They biggit a bower on yon burn-brae,
   And theekit it oer wi' rashes.

They theekit it oer wi' rashes green,
   They theekit it oer wi' heather,
But the pest cam frae the burrows toun,
   And slew them baith thegither!

They thought to lye in Methven kirk-yard,
   Amang their noble kin,
But they maun lye in Stronach Haugh,
   To biek forenent the sin.

And Bessie Bell and Mary Gray,
   They war twa bonnie lasses!
They biggit a bower on yon burn-brae,
   And theekit it oer wi' rashes.

Anonymous

George MacDonald came from rural Aberdeenshire and never lost his sure ear for the Scottish tongue, even though he spent the greater part of his life in London. He was dismissed from his charge as a Congregational minister for preaching heresy; he wrote over twenty novels, including some extraordinary fantasies; and Lewis Carroll tried out *Alice's Adventures in Wonderland* on MacDonald's children before offering them to the world.

Ane by Ane

Ane by ane they gang awa',
The Gatherer gathers great an' sma',
Ane by ane mak's ane an' a'.

Aye when ane sets doun the cup,
Ane ahint maun tak it up,
Yet thegither they will sup.

Golden-heided, ripe an' strang,
Shorn will be the hairst ere lang,
Syne begins a better sang!

Payment in Kind

When Allan Ramsay commenced business in Edinburgh . . . he was
unable to meet his first half-year's rent. Some time after the rent had
become due he chanced to meet his landlord, a country farmer, who
was attending the Hallow Fair. The farmer hailed him to a neighbouring tavern. When they sat down, Allan referred to the subject of the
rent, and expressed his distress of mind that he was unable to
satisfy it. The farmer told him not to vex himself about the matter;
he saw he was a lad of some genius and would give him time.
"Indeed," proceeded the farmer, "if you'll give me a rhyming
answer to four questions in as many minutes, I'll quit you the rent
altogether." Allan said he would try. The questions put were these:
"What does God love? What does the devil love? What does the world
love? What do I love?" Within the specified time Ramsay produced
the following verse:

God loves man when he refrains from sin;
The devil loves man when he persists therein;
The world loves man when riches on him flow,
And you'd love me could I pay what I owe.

"The rent is paid," said the farmer, giving his young tenant a hearty
slap across the shoulders . . .

Rev. Charles Rogers

To You Let Snow and Roses . . .

To you let snow and roses
And golden locks belong.

These are the world's enslavers,
  Let these delight the throng.
For her of duskier lustre
  Whose favour still I wear,
The snow be in her kirtle,
  The rose be in her hair!

The hue of highland rivers
  Careering, full and cool,
From sable on to golden,
  From rapid on to pool –
The hue of heather-honey,
  The hue of honey-bees,
Shall tinge her golden shoulder,
  Shall gild her tawny knees.

Robert Louis Stevenson

Robert Louis Stevenson's "hills of home" were his beloved Pentlands, guarding Edinburgh to the south. Even in Samoa, his last port of call in a lifelong search for a healthy body, he was able to conjure the magic of the place he knew as home.

To S. R. Crockett (on receiving a Dedication)

Blows the wind today, and the sun and the rain are flying
  Blows the wind on the moors today and now,
  Where about the graves of the martyrs the whaups are crying,
    My heart remembers how!

Grey recumbent tombs of the dead in desert places,
  Standing-stones on the vacant wine-red moor,
Hills of sheep, and the howes of the silent vanished races,
  And winds, austere and pure.

Be it granted me to behold you again in dying,
  Hills of home! and to hear again the call;
Hear about the graves of the martyrs the peewees crying,
  And hear no more at all.

167

John Davidson is most closely associated with Greenock where he grew up. He led a troubled life, almost revelling in his capacity to withstand hardship, and he took his own life by walking off the cliffs at Penzance. Compare his end to the death of the stag in his most famous poem, written three years before they fished Davidson's body out of the English Channel.

A Runnable Stag

When the pods went pop on the broom, green broom,
　　And apples began to be golden-skinned,
We harboured a stag in the Priory coomb,
　　And we feathered his trail up-wind, up-wind,
　　We feathered his trail up-wind –
　　　　A stag of warrant, a stag, a stag,
　　　　A runnable stag, a kingly crop,
　　　　Brow, bay and tray and three on top,
　　　　A stag, a runnable stag.

Then the huntsman's horn rang yap, yap, yap,
　　And "Forwards" we heard the harbourer shout;
But 'twas only a brocket that broke a gap
　　In the beechen underwood, driven out,
　　From the underwood antlered out
　　　　By warrant and might of the stag, the stag,
　　　　The runnable stag, whose lordly mind
　　　　Was bent on sleep, though beamed and tined
　　　　He stood, a runnable stag.

So we tufted the covert till afternoon
　　With Tinkerman's Pup and Bell-of-the-North;
And hunters were sulky and hounds out of tune
　　Before we tufted the right stag forth,
　　Before we tufted him forth,
　　　　The stag of warrant, the wily stag,
　　　　The runnable stag with his kingly crop,
　　　　Brow, bay and tray and three on top,
　　　　The royal and runnable stag.

It was Bell-of-the-North and Tinkerman's Pup
  That stuck to the scent till the copse was drawn.
"Tally ho! tally ho!" and the hunt was up,
  The tufters whipped and the pack laid on,
  The resolute pack laid on,
    And the stag of warrant away at last,
    The runnable stag, the same, the same,
    His hoofs on fire, his horns like flame,
    A stag, a runnable stag.

"Let your gelding be: if you check or chide
  He stumbles at once and you're out of the hunt;
For three hundred gentlemen, able to ride,
  On hunters accustomed to bear the brunt,
  Accustomed to bear the brunt,
    Are after the runnable stag, the stag,
    The runnable stag with his kingly crop,
    Brow, bay and tray and three on top,
    The right, the runnable stag."

By perilous paths in coomb and dell,
  The heather, the rocks, and the river-bed,
The pace grew hot, for the scent lay well,
  And a runnable stag goes right ahead,
  The quarry went right ahead –
    Ahead, ahead, and fast and far;
    His antlered crest, his cloven hoof,
    Brow, bay and tray and three aloof,
    The stag, the runnable stag,

For a matter of twenty miles and more,
  By the densest hedge and the highest wall,
Through herds of bullocks he baffled the lore
  Of harbourer, huntsman, hounds and all,
  Of harbourer, hounds and all –
    The stag of warrant, the wily stag,
    For twenty miles, and five and five,
    He ran, and he never was caught alive,
    This stag, this runnable stag.

When he turned at bay in the leafy gloom,
  In the emerald gloom where the brook ran deep,
He heard in the distance the rollers boom,
  And he saw in a vision of peaceful sleep,
  In a wonderful vision of sleep,
    A stag of warrant, a stag, a stag,
    A runnable stag in a jewelled bed,
    Under the sheltering ocean dead,
    A stag, a runnable stag.

So a fateful hope lit up his eye,
   And he opened his nostrils wide again,
And he tossed his branching antlers high
   As he headed the hunt down the Charlock glen,
   As he raced down the echoing glen,
      For five miles more, the stag, the stag,
      For twenty miles, and five and five,
      Not to be caught now, dead or alive,
      The stag, the runnable stag.

Three hundred gentlemen, able to ride,
   Three hundred horses as gallant and free,
Behind him escape on the evening tide,
   Far out till he sank in the Severn Sea,
   Till he sank in the depths of the sea –
      The stag, the buoyant stag, the stag
      That slept at last in a jewelled bed
      Under the sheltering ocean spread,
      The stag, the runnable stag.

Christopher Murray Grieve, who, as Hugh MacDiarmid, is Scotland's most celebrated poet since Burns, hates the English. In fact he is the one man I know who makes even the word sound despicable. I have often suspected that he is not so unreservedly Marxist, or atheist, or Scottish nationalist as he professes to be; I have never doubted his – I was going to say hatred or loathing, but contempt is more accurate – his utter contempt for the race whose territory begins only a few yards from where he was born in Langholm.

Few dispute that he is our greatest poet since Burns. Many claim, with persuasive force, that MacDiarmid is an even greater poet, and I believe he would agree with them so long as he was in the mood to pursue such a pointless debate.

Burns was the logical extension of a tradition. The genius of Burns was his capacity to sing his songs for himself *and* for a whole race of people – now enlarged to include much of mankind – who could identify with the poet.

MacDiarmid's genius, hitched to a more informed and universal concern for the human predicament, has been to invent almost a new music using an old language. When he began to write in Scots, Mac-Diarmid, far from following the same tradition as Burns, had to cut a path to freedom through thickets of Kailyaird undergrowth – Burns-imitators, sentimental rhymers, the ditty-dabblers who genteelly followed the Scottish muse. MacDiarmid began the revolution which led to a renaissance of the Scots tongue.

When he was only a year or two short of the age at which Robert Burns died, MacDiarmid published what many people still regard as his greatest work, his long poem, "A Drunk Man Looks at the Thistle", of which this is a superb, free-standing fragment:

> O wha's the bride that cairries the bunch
> O' thistles blinterin' white?
> Her cuckold bridegroom little dreids
> What he sall ken this nicht.
>
> For closer than gudeman can come
> And closer to'r than hersel',
> Wha didna need her maidenhead
> Has wrocht his purpose fell.
>
> O wha's been here afore me, lass,
> And hoo did he get in?
>   *– A man that deed or I was born*
> *This evil thing has din.*
> And left, as it were on a corpse,
> Your maidenheid to me?
>   *– Nae lass, gudeman, sin' Time began*
> *'s had ony mair to gi'e.*
>
> *But I can gi'e ye kindness lad,*
> *And a pair o' willin hands,*
> *And you sall ha'e my breists like stars,*
> *My limbs like willow wands.*
>
> *And on my lips ye'll heed nae mair,*
> *And in my hair forget,*
> *The seed o' a' the men that in*
> *My virgin womb ha'e met . . .*

MacDiarmid's output has been prodigious. With characteristic good sense he once compared himself to a volcanic eruption – no matter how many flames and bright fires, a lot of smoke and dust as well. For those who heard in him the authentic socialist voice of Scotland, there was surprise, to say the least, when it came to:

Cattle Show

> I shall go among red faces and virile voices,
> See stylish sheep, with fine-heads and well-wooled,
> And great bulls mellow to the touch,

Brood mares of marvellous approach, and geldings
With sharp and flinty bones and silken hair.

And through th' enclosure draped in red and gold
I shall pass on to spheres more vivid yet
Where countesses' coque feathers gleam and glow
And, swathed in silks, the painted ladies are
Whose laughter plays like summer lightning there.

Christopher Grieve has lived a hard and sometimes harrowing life of material poverty. All of his so-called secure, mature years – honorary doctorate of literature and all, Civil List pension and all – have been spent in a farm-labourer's cottage near Biggar, and if the Grieves or MacDiarmids eventually got drains, and power, and running water they had some few friends to thank for it and not an ungrateful nation.

The Caledonian Antisyzygy

I write now in English and now in Scots
To the despair of friends who plead
For consistency; sometimes achieve the true lyric cry,
Next but chopped-up prose; and write whiles
In traditional forms, next in a mixture of styles.
So divided against myself, they ask:
How can I stand (or they understand) indeed?

Fatal division in my thought they think
Who forget that although the thrush
Is more cheerful and constant, the lark
More continuous and celestial, and, after all,
The irritating cuckoo unique
In singing a true musical interval,
Yet the nightingale remains supreme,
The nightingale whose thin high call
And that deep throb,
Which seems to come from different birds
In different places, find an emotion
And vibrate in the memory as the song
Of no other bird – not even
The love-note of the curlew –
                     can do!

So, by his own testament, we are left with the image of the nightingale, not the eagle or some other wild, proud spirit soaring in lofty spirals of convoluted disdain, but that most English of birds, with the high melody sung over a pedal that jars the heart. The image goes well, too, with the stories he has told me about his "drill", learned in the First World War, "in the dark".

After a happy night with his friends in the great democracy of Milne's Bar or some other howff in Edinburgh, the fittest of them would see him on to the bus for Biggar. All of the conductors, if not every traveller, knew him well and knew his road-end in the dark. He would be shaken awake if necessary and steered out into the night.

Then the fumbling would begin – first money, then spectacles, finally false teeth. He would keep his eyes shut all this time in the hope that even some fugitive starlight would see him home. But no matter, whatever the conditions, full moon and snow up to the dyke or darkness as black as Auld Nick's waistcoat, the valuables – money, specs and teeth – were carefully deposited under a stone or behind a tuft of grass at the side of the road.

Then Scotland's greatest living poet found his way up the hill and home. As all poets have discovered, Parnassus can be a wee brae when you're passing fu'.

The Tryst

O luely, luely, cam she in,
and luely she lay doun:
I kent her by her caller lips
and her breists sae smaa and round.

Aa throu the nicht we spak nae word
nor sindered bane frae bane:
aa through the nicht I heard her hert
gang soundin wi my ain.

It was about the waukrif hour
when cocks begin to craw
that she smooled safely throu the mirk
afore the day wad daw.

Sae luely, luely cam she in,
sae luely was she gane;
and wi her aa my simmer days
like they had never been.

William Soutar

Soutar died at the age of 45 having spent the last fourteen years of his life confined to bed with spinal paralysis. He had been an athlete, a sailor in the 1914–1918 war, and destined to become a teacher. He could move only his arms and legs in the bed that was an island in a sea of books. His was "the true lyric cry", and we all knew it.

So Many Summers

Beside one loch, a hind's neat skeleton,
Beside another, a boat pulled high and dry:
Two neat geometries drawn in the weather:
Two things already dead and still to die.

I passed them every summer, rod in hand,
Skirting the bright blue or the spitting gray,
And, every summer, saw how the bleached timbers
Gaped wider and the neat ribs fell away.

Time adds one malice to another one –
Now you'd look very close before you knew
If it's the boat that ran, the hind went sailing.
So many summers, and I have lived them too.

Norman MacCaig

Sleeping Compartment

I don't like this, being carried sideways
through the night. I feel wrong and helpless – like
a timber broadside in a fast stream.

Such a way of moving may suit
that odd snake the sidewinder
in Arizona: but not me in Perthshire.

I feel at rightangles to everything,
a crossgrain in existence. – It scrapes
the top of my head, and my footsoles.

To forget outside is no help either –
then I become a blockage
in the long gut of the train.

I try to think I'm a through-the-looking-glass
mountaineer bivouacked
on a ledge five feet high.

It's no good. I go sidelong.
I rock sideways . . . I draw in my feet
to let Aviemore pass.

Norman MacCaig

After MacDiarmid, MacCaig is probably more widely read than any
other contemporary Scottish poet. Much of his work is rooted in his
love of landscape, particularly the north-west Highlands and the people
of these parts, but he is a fascinating mixture of urban scholar and
frustrated gamekeeper. His eye is as keen and penetrating as any eagle's;
he sees more than most poets; and what he does with the information,
how he processes it, is individual, often ironic, and disturbing in its
lazy muscularity.

Power Dive

He spent a fortune on architects and builders.
He signed tickertapes of cheques for furniture,
carpets, paintings, filmstar beds. He surrounded the

house with plantations and parterres, hahas and gazebos.
And in the right place, the properest place
at last he saw completed a swimmingpool
that glittered like ancient Rome.

It was just before he hit the water
in his first dive that he glimpsed
the triangular fin cutting the surface.

Norman MacCaig

It has been my great good fortune to be on nodding terms with most
Scottish poets and intimate terms with some. The following selection
of contemporary verse has been chosen in all cases because it serves
the book's purpose and I like it; and in some cases as a passing salute
to my friends.

One Day at Shieldaig

Behind rolled Vauxhall windows
two women, sealed in homely Aran sweaters,
knitted their fingers into sweated Arans.

Two men, cast off for
"a breath of air" (discreetly to water themselves),
came sweating back, two strolling Arans homing.

Even the clouds and mountains
got knitted up in patterns of each other,
the sea's fingers glinted incredibly.

Maurice Lindsay

Aberdeen Train

Rubbing a glistening circle
on the steamed-up window I framed
a pheasant in a field of mist.

The sun was a great red thing somewhere low,
struggling with the milky scene. In the furrows
a piece of glass winked into life,
hypnotized the silly dandy; we
hooted past him with his head cocked,
contemplating a bottle-end.
And this was the last of October,
a Chinese moment in the Mearns.

Edwin Morgan

Love Letter

To Mistress Madeline Corston, widow
At Quoy, parish of Voes, in the time of hay:

> The old woman sat in her chair, mouth agape,
> At the end of April.
> There were buttercups in a jar at the window.
>
> The floor is not a blue mirror now
> And the table has flies and bits of crust on it.
>
> Also the lamp glass is broken.
>
> I have the shop at the end of the house
> With sugar, tea, tobacco, paraffin
> And, for whisperers, a cup of whisky.
>
> There is a cow, a lady of butter, in the long silent grass.
>
> And seven sheep on Moorfea.
>
> The croft girls are too young
> Nothing but giggles, lipstick, and gramophone records.
>
> Walk over the hill Friday evening.
> Enter without knocking
> If you see one red rose in the window.

George Mackay Brown

The Larch Tree

One of these mornings I shall leave
shall have the bank arrange long credits
at out of the way places
shall pack my cases and the hold-all

with the broken zipper and heave
them into the boot of the car:
changing gear at the intersection I'll feel
faintly constipated about my wife and children

and after a hindu honeymoon with myself
I'll rent a flat near the Botanic Gardens
with a girl, a bidet and a Toshie lantern

and if I should spot them any afternoon, "Hullo,
hello!" I'll shout across the street, "The sky
was too hard a blue, the larch tree was too green."

Tom Buchan

Freia

When the long swathe of her desire
is harvested, the skin is kind:
the warm arm under the neck can
more than thigh or vulva love
and without torpor satisfy

and more than her agility can tell
is said by her
remaining still to be alive
as still she gathers me
the last sheaf in.

Tom Buchan

Witches

Coveys of black witches gather
at corners, closes.
Their thin red pointed noses
are in among the mash of scandal.

Poking red fires with
intense breath, hot as the imagined
rape riding the hot mind.
The real one was more moral

and more admirable because animal.
In an empty air they convene
their red, sad envious beaks. The clean
winter rubs them raw

in a terrible void, hissing
with tongues of winter fire.
Pity them, pity them. Dare
to ring them with your love.

Iain Crichton Smith

Sea and Sky

Sea and sky. Earthbound as I am
I've never yet been able to decide
which one I like best. I'd live,
I think, for preference on the sea.
I'd farm there a more fruitful soil
than what surrounds me here.
I'd be a connoisseur of gulls
and every day I'd open a new horizon.

I'd choose the sky for burial,
though, if such were possible.
I'd have mountains at my head and feet.
When Gabriel blew his trumpet I'd arrive
before God's kindness became strained.
The clouds would ease my bones
more than the hard rocks of Ardnamurchan.
Not worms would feed on me but larks.

Alasdair Maclean

When Children Sing

The first time I felt famous
I was standing in a ring
The others knew my fortune
And they began to sing
Of always how the hero falls
Forever in the game
And rises to the chorus
Of his mortal name.

I saw the meadows fallen
To the bright soldiery
The boys of war were boasting
To girls in cramasie
There were infants at the kneeling
Of a mariner from Spain
Who came to bind a widow
With a royal chain.

O seal me in a circle
Where boyhoods come and go
And songs of drums and sailormen
Are all we need to know
I could face the chaplin water
And the sentry of the ring
If the parody could happen
When children sing.

Roddy McMillan

Inventory

You left me
> nothing but nail
> parings orange peel
> empty nutshells half filled
> ashtrays dirty
> cups with dregs of
> nightcaps an odd hair
> or two of yours on my
> comb gap toothed
> bookshelves and a
> you-shaped
> depression in my pillow.

Liz Lochhead

The Coming of the Wee Malkies

Whit'll ye dae when the wee Malkies come,
if they dreep doon affy the wash-hoose dyke,
an pit the hems oan the sterr-heid light,
an play wee heidies oan the clean close-wa,
an blooter yir windae in wi the baw,
missis, whit'll ye dae?

Whit'll ye dae when the wee Malkies come,
if they chap yir door an choke yir drains,
an caw the feet fae yir sapsy weans,
an tummle thur wulkies through yir sheets,
an tim thur ashes oot in the street,
missis, whit'll ye dae?

Whit'll ye dae when the wee Malkies come,
if they chuck thur screwtaps doon the pan,
an stick the heid oan the sanit'ry man;
when ye hear thum shauchlin doon yir loaby,
chantin, "Wee Malkies – the gemme's a bogey!"
Haw, missis, whit'll ye dae?

Stephen Mulrine

Villanelle de Noël

The Robin owre aa birds is blest
At this time of the year, Nowel:
The bluid o Christ is on his breist.

Frae Sicily til Hammerfest
The bairns relate the sely tale,
That the Robin owre aa birds is blest,

For on Calvarie he tried to wrest
Frae Yeshu's palm the cruel nail:
The bluid o Christ is on his breist.

Sensyne he's been Yuill's dearest guest,
Nae ither sae welcome as himsel:
The Robin owre aa birds is blest.

He wears the Yuilltide like a vest,
And his sang's the peal o a ferlie bell:
The bluid o Christ is on his breist.

Nae starred and medalled hero's chest
Can eer wi greater merit swell:
The Robin owre aa birds is blest
The bluid o Christ is on his breist.

Tom Scott

Iris, Messenger of the Gods

On a recent trip to Paris, from London by night,
I thought I'd do some "Reflections on Woman".
As the boat moved, girls' faces grew more white,
Lovely jaws sagged, and normally tight
Muscles slackened bizarrely, hardly human.

In the Tuileries, by the pond la Concorde,
I saw three female generations, the hips
Were the clues – straight, curved, and blurred –
And I was obsessed by the sounds that slurred
From the oldest, scooping with her gallic lips.

Then to the Rodin Museum, rue de Verenne,
I headed, for an hour or so of art,
Watching flesh more than bronze, when
I saw *Iris Messager des Dieux*, and women
Avoiding her – because she keeps her legs apart.

Alan Bold

Person

i have no thum
i am a little
deformed

i don't wear gloves
but i suffer very much
from the insolence
of those who are thumbed
and find in that
their distinction

Alan Jackson

The Good Thief

heh jimmy
yawright ih
still wayz urryi
ih

heh jimmy
ma right insane yirra pape
ma right insane yirwanny uz jimmy

see it nyir eyes
wanny uz

heh

heh jimmy
lookslik wirgonny miss thi gemm
gonny miss thi GEMM jimmy
nearly three a cloke thinoo

dark init
good jobe theyve gote thi lights

Tom Leonard

Dear Mortimer Street:

I resent the implication in your recent postcard (I get the impression that you'd go to hell itself to see that team playing away from home) that Scottish humour is nothing more than English humour decked out in tartan or Yiddish humour in the kilt. Where have you been since Harry Lauder?

(By telegraph)

BELGRADE

SMITH, EDINBURGH, UNDERSTAND AND ACKNOWLEDGE EXISTENCE GOOD INDIGENOUS JOKES STOP BUT DO SCOTCH EVER LAUGH AT THEM? – STREET

Scotch Humour

I muse how any man can say that the Scotch, as a people, are deficient in humour! Why, Sawney has a humour of his own so strong and irrepressible that it broke out all the stronger in spite of wordly thrift, kirk-session, cutty-stool and lectures.

Hartley Coleridge

This Happy Breed

As a race the adjective most commonly used to describe us is "dour". Maybe some commentators would say "mean", because of all those self-perpetuated Aberdonian jokes – fifteen persons killed in a crash between two taxis, moth-filled sporrans, and all that kidmaleerie. Maybe people think dour is less offensive when they really mean mean in the English and not the American sense of the word. But the Scots a dour people – grim, solemn, glum?

Scottish humour is sardonic, more reductive than English humour, and capable of sustaining surrealist non-sequiturs that most strangers to it are unable initially to comprehend.

Gaelic E.S.P.

The social anthropologist was investigating a convincing case of telepathy in Machrihanish: an aged mother merely "communicated" her special needs to her policeman son in Glasgow and they duly arrived by the next post. The scientist asked the old lady to demonstrate her method. She took him outside, walked to a tree, and with her mouth close against the bark spoke to it in earnest Gaelic. "Why do you speak to the tree?" he asked. "Because I am poor," she said. "Otherwise, I'd just use the telephone like everybody else."

The Bydand Myths

Deafness in Frogs

The Glaswegian lecturer shouted, "Attend, I am about to prove something of great importance." He cupped his hands round a frog on his desk. His students craned forward. "Jump!" said the lecturer, taking his hands away, and the frog dutifully sailed through the air. It was retrieved and encompassed once again in the lecturer's grasp. "Jump!" he said again, and the frog obeyed. The lecturer took out a penknife and cut off the frog's legs. "Jump!" he ordered. "Jump!" he said again. And finally, "Jump!" "You see," he told the class, "when you cut off the legs of a frog he has difficulty in hearing properly."

The Bydand Myths

Scottish Logic

One of the most essential attributes of the Scottish mind is its orderly, methodical, in a word, its logical character; this has often given to its preaching a bony appearance, or eminently doctrinal method. It was very important that the minister should fulfil these conditions, that he should be "*soun*", or sound. Some ministers had the reputation even of being "*awfu soun*", and hence a more sprightly or flowing manner came to be regarded with suspicion. Alexander Fletcher, before he went to London, was exceedingly popular at Stow. On the evening before he received "the call' to become the co-pastor there, with the Rev. M. Kidstone, there had been some doubt as to the perfect orthodoxy of his views; but on this occasion he preached a sermon to the delight, and even surprise, of a great gathering of people. Coming down from the pulpit, and going into the manse, Mr Kidstone met him and thanked him, saying with great suavity, "Weel Sandie, I must admit you're vara 'soun', but, oh, man! You're na deep!"

Paxton Hood

I think the Scots, as a people, have a deep comprehension of the possibility that the fountainhead of all laughter is incongruity.

Logic on the Wing

Say you and me are neighbours, leaning over the dyke and having a big barney about something. Well, not a barney, a discussion. It's about something highly intellectual and technically specialised like . . . like, whether Jimmy Johnstone's a better winger than George Best. I'm for Johnstone. You're for Best. We analyse them thoroughly. We compare their styles, we set Johnstone's shimmy against Best's swing of the hips, we compare their capacity to ride the tackle, read the game, accelerate, dribble, pass the ball, head it, deedle-dawdle with it – all that. And we get to the stage where we've marked up all the points, claimed the pros and admitted the cons – and we're no further forward.

I say, "Johnstone's got it".

And you say, "He has not."

And I say, "There's not another like him."

And you say, "Georgie's the greatest."

And I say, "There's nothing that you can say or do that will convince me that Jimmy Johnstone's not the best winger the world has ever seen."

And you say, "Jimmy Johnstone isn't fit to lace the boots of George Best."

And I say, "It's high time you gave that bloody greenhouse of yours a new coat of paint."

There was this Edinburgh merchant who happened to be a bailie and who also happened to be an elder of the kirk. Come to think of it, most of them are. Anyway, the bailie dies and arrives at the pearly gates, presents his credentials, and assumes instant admittance.

St Peter was in no mood to be rushed.

"You were a merchant," he says.

"Aye," says the Edinburgh man, "and I traded fair and square and looked after my workers like a father."

"So you did," said St Peter, consulting the big book. "And I see you were a bailie as well." "Aye, so I was," said the Edinburgh man, "and I dealt fearlessly and without favour to all wrongdoers, tempering my judgements, of course, with appropriate mercy."

"Aye, so you did, too" says St Peter.

"And as a kirk elder," says the Edinburgh man, "I served the Lord in all things and at all times."

St Peter looked in vain for any blemish on the record. "You've certainly led an honest and examplary life," he said. "Where was it you said you came from?"

"Edinburgh," says the Edinburgh man.

"Well, you can come in," says St Peter, throwing open the pearly gates. "But you'll not like it here."

In Dundee, not so very long ago, they used to buy in the police, in bulk, from the towns round about – big sonsy country lads with the strength of two bullocks. And before the Overgate was turned into a glorified supermarket it used to be the swinging heart of downtown Dundee on a Saturday night. They still have the big municipal barrow, shaped like a coffin, for hurling home the Saturday drunks. A very civilised place, Dundee.

Big Eck Thomson was a Dundee policeman from Forfar, where the bridies come from. Six-feet-six and seventeen stones in his summer semmit.

Constable Thomson went to the Overgate this night to investigate a disturbance. He arrived at the reported scene of the aforesaid disturbance, looked up at a first-floor window, and saw a broken pane. He went up the stair, chapped on the door, had a word with the wifie, then entered in his notebook the first piece of vital evidence.

"Window . . . broken . . . on . . . inside."

He clumps off back down the stairs, and when he gets to the street he looks up at the window again, then writes in his book:

"Window . . . also . . . broken . . . on . . . outside."

Now Big Eck Thomson hadn't chewed his pencil at the parish school for nothing. There was a conclusion to be drawn from all this. So, with great deliberation, and the flush of triumph that sometimes attends moments of divine inspiration, he wrote again in his book.

"Window . . . broken . . . on . . . both . . . sides."

Jock

Sometimes our laughter has a hollow ring to it, like the laughter of the lost, as if we too earnestly take the attitude that all life, even humour, must have a serious undertone, that we are all damned anyway. There is, of course, no original Scottish joke or anecdote, but if there were it would probably be some variation of the tale about the sinner on the stool of repentance who, in abject humility, moaned, "Lord, Lord, Ah didna ken . . ." And from the pulpit (if not from the heavens themselves) thunders the reply: "Weel, ye ken noo!"

The hunt for the archetype could also veer towards the "gallus" humour of the graveyard, where auld Tam (or Sandy or Wattie or Wullie) is coughing his way through the burial service, to be told by the minister at the end: "Well, Thomas, it's hardly worth your while going home, is it?" And the Glasgow classic (in which Edinburghers take perverse pleasure):

- Has your mother got a sewing-machine?
- Of course!
- Well, tell her to stitch that ... (the only sound that follows being the swish of an open-razor)
- Ha, ha! Missed me!
- Aye, but try shakin' yer heid!

The apogee of this *genre* was surely achieved by the black-hearted wit who asked:

- How do you get thirty-two Celtic supporters into a 1969 Mini traveller?
- Cremate them!

I suspect that the Scot's blackest humour is usually reserved for his adversaries, real or imaginary, in whom he does not recognise elements of courage and honesty, those moral qualities which are essential if one is going to make fun of oneself. So, recognising the deficiencies of his opponent, and secretly despising him, it would then be dishonest to allow discretion to blunt the bright shafts of truth. Which is the very moment when the Scots become insufferably pompous.

It's this wee joke, you must have heard it because everybody's claimed it now – the Russians, the Israelis, they've all pinched it. But it happened here in Scotland, and you'll not have heard the original, unexpurgated, unadulterated version.

This English king brought a great army as far as the Cheviots to crush the Scots. A sort of prehistoric Alf Ramsay. Just as they reached a mountain pass a solitary figure appeared on a hilltop and danced up and down and waved a sword at them. The King asked for volunteers, and a platoon of his best pikemen rushed the hilltop and swept the Scotsman over the top. The English listened to the clash of steel and waited. And waited. But their comrades did not return.

The King sent a troop of cavalry to investigate. They charged over the hill and loud and terrible was the sound of battle. Then silence, with only peeweeps calling in the clear air.

The King then set his entire army, thousands of men, against the hilltop, but being an English king he waited down below on his big white horse. Over the hills and along the valleys came the screams of dying men, and the king trembled in his saddle. The battle reached a climax, then the air became still again and the King was sore afraid.

He was turning his horse's head for England when he saw one of his men, an archer, stumbling and falling down the hill. The man clutched at his belly and the dark blood squirted through his fingers.

"Sire . . . Sire," he croaked as he approached his King. The King rode towards him. The archer buckled to his knees and with his last breath told the King: "Sire, it was a trap. There were two of them."

Jock

If it is true that having to explain a joke or anecdote will surely destroy it, then it is also true that the analysis of humour is an unrewarding and singularly unfunny activity. It is also very boring, particularly when otherwise lovable professional entertainers put on their Ph.D faces and identify humour as the "great human escape valve", or (I have even heard) "the ultimate proof of the existence of God."

Above all, humour should speak for itself.

A Day in the Country

A country dominie was walking over the hill with the wee fellow from a working man's club in Glasgow who was spending the first day of his life in the country. As they passed a hole in the ground the Glasgow man asked the teacher to explain the mound of small brown pellets outside the hole.

"Oh, they're rabbit droppings," said the Dominie, "and that's the wee chap's burrow."

They went on a bit farther and the Glasgow man stopped by a pile of larger pellets, black this time, on the green hillside.

"They're sheep's droppings," said the Dominie, and hurried on.

The Glasgow man caught up, but in his hurry he stepped on what the Girl Guides call a country pancake.

The dominie managed a wintry smile. "That's a cow-pat," he said. "Wipe your feet in that long grass."

The Glasgow man caught up again. "Back there," he said, "in the long grass there were large balls, about the size of oranges, reddish brown, with bits of straw in them . . ."

The dominie was already nodding. "Horse dung," he said.

They walked on in silence for a while, stopping now and again to admire the view.

Suddenly the Glaswegian grabbed hold of the dominie's lapel.

"What's the longest river in Nicaragua?" he shouted.

The dominie was startled out of his wits, but he thought for a moment, then shook his head and said: "I'm afraid I don't know."

"There y'are," said the Glasgow man. "What did I tell ye? Education? My God, are ye no' ashamed o' yoursel? Ye ken everything there is to ken aboot four different kinds o' shite, but nothin' at a' aboot geography."

Jock

In Scotland's most rural regions the sub-post office is often the only manifestation of the so-called civilisation of the cities. And because post offices handle cash and stamps and pensions and postal orders, no matter how small their turnover, they all have to be "audited" from time to time.

A friend of mine was at one time a cross between an accountant and a detective, employed by the Post Office to spring surprise audits on offices big and small, urban and rural. And preserving the element of surprise proved more difficult than any other aspect of his job. If big offices in towns and cities presented their own special security problems, out in the hinterland there seemed no way to sabotage the early warning system of the bush telegraph, a system of communication whose efficiency is in direct relationship to the number of miles one travels in a northerly direction.

There came the day when a spot-check on a tiny island's sub-post office could be delayed no longer. My friend and a colleague – we insist on corroborated evidence in Scotland – having had their cover blown before took the most elaborate precautions to disguise their intentions. They arrived at the mainland port of embarkation (almost certainly Mallaig) after dark, booked into a small private hotel, and in a quayside pub later that evening negotiated the hire of a boatman and his craft to ferry them to the island the next morning.

Without actually saying so they gave the impression that they were ornithologists and interested in the island's remarkable colony of sea birds.

They sailed, as arranged, soon after dawn and whiled away the two-hour crossing by trawling a mackerel line behind the boat.

All the inhabitants of the island live in a cluster of houses perched in the lee of the prevailing winds among rowan trees overlooking a bouldered bay.

The boat came in on the blind side, nosed round a headland, then

G

made all speed for the jetty. By the time it came alongside the island post-mistress was standing above them, arms akimbo, her head tilted playfully to one side, and saying: "come away up to the house, then, your breakfast's on the stove waiting for you."

Law of Averages

— Haw Jim, wud ye no' say, speakin' fur the proletariat the likes o' uz, that if we wuz tae drop a slice o' breid on the flair, especially if it wuz oor *only* slice o' bried, wad ye no' say that it wuz inevitable, in fac', beyond ony prospec' o' peradventure, that the bloody breid wud fa' butter-side doon?

— Oh aye, oh Christ aye, nae doot aboot yon.

— Ye wud say that wud ye?

— Never fails!

— Weel Jim, wud ye believe me, Ah dropped a slice o' toast this mornin', and it laundit flat on its erse, Y'unnerstaun'?

— Butter-side up?

— Aye.

— Christ yer kiddin' me. That's no' possible pal.

— Sure's Ah'm sittin' here.

— My God!

— Ah says to the wife Ah says, there'll be twa bloody moons in the sky the night . . . aye, flat on its erse it was, y'unnerstaun'?

— Ah never thought Ah'd hear tell o' . . . Haw here, pal, haud oan . . . Naw, Ah believe ye, leave me . . . naw, naw, Ah ken whit's happened. Listen tae me. Wheesht! Dinnae worry aboot it, son. Ah ken whit ye've done. Ye buttered yer toast oan the wrang side this mornin', that's a'.

The Bydand Myths

The Auld Maid in the Garret

Noo I've aft times heard it said by my faither and my mither,
That tae gang tae a waddin' is the makins o' anither;

If this be true, then I'll gang wi' oot a biddin' –
O kind Providence won't you send me tae a waddin'.
    For it's, Oh dear me, whit will I dae
    If I dee an auld maid in a garret?

Noo, there's my sister Jean, she's no' handsome or goodlookin',
Scarcely sixteen an' a fellow she was coortin';
Noo she's twenty-four, wi' a son an' a dochter,
An' I'm forty-twa an' I've never had an offer.

I can cook an' I can sew, I can keep the house right tidy
Rise up in the mornin' and get the breakfast ready;
But there's naethin' in this wide world would mak' me half so
                                cheery
As a wee fat man that would ca' me his ain dearie.

Oh, come tinker, come tailor, come soldier or come sailor
Come ony man at a' that would tak me frae my faither,
Come rich man, come poor man, come wise man or come witty
Come ony man at a' that would mairry me for pity.

Oh, I'll awa hame for there's naebody heedin',
Naebody heedin' tae puir Annie's pleadin';
I'll awa hame tae my ain wee bit garret –
If I canna get a man then I'll surely get a parrot.

                                 Traditional Song

Turn and Turn About

Two farmers from Stonehaven, eating fish and chips, walked up to
the Rolls-Royce stand at last year's Motor Show. They're a real pair

o' heather-loupers in cockit buits. Black pudden benders – to trade!

They schauchle round a big shiny Silver Ghost, munching away at their chips, and discussing the size of the boot and how many chickens and bags of tatties it could hold. The wee dapper man from Roll-Royce hops about after them, polishing the paintwork where they've dulled it with their greasy breath.

Big Davey opens a back door of the car. "C'm'awa' in, Andra'," he says, "an handsel this room an' kitchen at the back."

The assistant sees his whole career falling in ruins as Big Davey and Andra' settle down in the leather upholstery. They stretch their legs and carry on with their meal. Andra' presses a button and the electrically-operated window whispers down. Big Davey turns a handle and a well-stocked cocktail cabinet glides open. Andra' drops chips on the carpeted floor. He ignores them. Big Davey wipes his fingers on the leather seat.

"Gentlemen," squeaks the assistant, "I'll have to ask you to be more careful." He picks up the fallen chips with great distaste and hides them in his pocket. "And I'll have to ask, with great respect, if you've any serious interest in this limousine."

Big Davey squashes up his chip bag. He presses the window button on his side and throws it out. He wipes his fingers – on the carpet this time – and climbs out of the car. Andra' follows him. In silence thay walk round the car again, as if it were a heifer at the Highland Show. The assistant squawks and flutters like a broody hen. Big Davey stops in front of the famous radiator.

"How much did you say it was?"

The assistant draws himself up to his full five-feet-two. "Twelve thousand pounds," he says, "on the road." And he sniffs as he says it, like the wee snob that he is.

Big Davey and Andra' look hard at each other. Then Andra' nods and Big Davey announces: "We'll have twa."

The assistant is sure he's misunderstood. "You'll have . . . ?"

"Aye, two o' them," says Big Davey. "One each."

The assistant rushes to his desk, mentally spending his commission on the way. Big Davey starts to fumble for his hip pocket.

"Na, na," says Andra'. "It's my turn, Davey, you got the fish suppers."

Jock

Kohebrahama did my Teeth

It seems a far cry from the Market Place in Wick to the White House in Washington. And an even further one from President Truman to a roguish old coon called Kohebrahama who ruined my teeth when I was a lad of twelve. But they came together yesterday when I received a message from one of Truman's "trusties" in the American capital. Before I come to that, however, I must tell you who this old rogue was. Though he has long been dead and gathered to his jungle gods he stands out in my mind as one of the major, and certainly one of the most colourful influences in my life.

Kohebrahama looked for all the world as if he had been created by the joint genius of Mark Twain, O. Henry and Al Jolson. He looked like a cross between Uncle Tom, Monolulu and a boot polish advertisement. His skull, which was smooth and shiny as a black billiard ball, was fringed with lambswool curls, and when he laughed his teeth glimmered like snowdrops in a crimson cave. He wore a shepherd tartan suit and a yellow waistcoat with mother-of-pearl buttons, patent leather shoes which answered the shine of his skull, green spats and a vermilion topper on which appeared the words "Whiter than snow" in silver letters.

At night he lit a lamp inside his hat – the first illuminated sign ever seen in Wick. To gather a crowd he played Negro melodies like "Swanee", "Camptown Races", and "Poor Old Joe", and when we crowded round his cart recited poems about Dixie and Tennessee which he said were written by Burns, Shakespeare, Milton and John Bunyan. Then when we were all in a jolly mood Kohebrahama put his hat and banjo aside, produced a mysterious wicker basket and asked for a lad to join him on his cart. That is where I came in and my teeth began to come out. For, I regret to report retrospectively, I became Kohebrahama's assistant for one whole summer. Need I tell you he was a quack dentist? Or that his basket was packed with magical new radio-active tooth powders which not only kept the teeth white and the breath pure, but aided digestion, staved off night starvation, cured heartburn and generally improved the system.

My job was to have my teeth covered with soot and then polished with the magic powder. Kohebrahama was kind, efficient and excitingly entertaining and every night he gave me 6d. and a tin of the powder, which was just chalk and fishbone. It did for my teeth in record time and for every 6d. I earned as Boy Friday I must have spent £6 putting them right.

This all came back to me when I read the report from Washington about the Quacks Chamber of Horrors run by the Food and Drug Administration. In the letter which accompanied it Truman's friend – a famous labour leader who also suffered under Kohebrahama – tells me that in spite of the Government's vigilance America is

197

getting more quack-ridden every day. Only the other day a "Doctor" Ghadiali, of Bombay, was fined 20,000 dollars and sent to Sing Sing for three years for selling a gadget called the "spectrochrome", which he claimed would cure anything by coloured lights. Yellow and magenta "cured" tuberculosis. A tartan beam, presumably, would cure everything.

My favourite phoney nostrum, however, is a device like a pencil, which costs only £150. Its modest inventor claims it will "absolutely cure bronchial trouble, toothache, sinus conditions, burns, injuries and all illnesses in general." I like that final claim. It reminds me of the man at the Socialist conference who rushed to the rostrum, after somebody had proposed to nationalise all the means of production, distribution and exchange in United Europe, and moved to add the words, "and the solar system". Old Kohebrahama was never quite so Napoleonic as that, though he did recite some ribald rhymes about Josephine. He destroyed my teeth but I forgive it him. May his gods rest his soul wherever it may be among the ghostly jungle drums. I wonder who is strumming his banjo now!

Ian Mackay

Good Gunnery

James II loved to experiment with artillery at a time when the firing of any gun was likely to do more damage to the person behind it than anyone in front of it. Oh, he would have loved Edinburgh's one o'clock gun. And he would have bestowed estates and a knighthood on the wee man who stands on Waverley Bridge every day with his gold watch in his hand, casting an anxious eye, first on the half-moon battery up at the Castle, then at the Nelson Monument on the Calton Hill away across the valley. There's a ball on top of the monument which drops at precisely one o'clock as a time signal to ships in the Firth of Forth. The seconds tick by, the gun fires, BANG!, the ball drops, and the old man snaps shut his watch-case.

"Damned good shooting," he says, and walks on.

Jock

I happened to visit Sir Compton Mackenzie in his home in Edinburgh only a day or two after the conclusion of the *Fanny Hill* pornography trial. He thought the verdict preposterous and greatly regretted the ban on publication. Sir Compton agreed with Marghanita Laski's view, expressed in evidence, that *Fanny Hill* was "a gay little book". And he sorrowed over the loss of his own copy, a privately-printed unexpurgated Victorian version.

Sir Compton's home was lined with books from floor to ceiling. They seemed to be everywhere, even in corridors and passageways. I remember him that day, flapping his hands towards the shelves and wagging his head sadly: "I used to have an excellent collection of the very best pornography, good stuff all of it, written by the most surprising people. But the books have been stolen one by one over the years and can't be replaced."

Sir Compton, who was the gentlest and kindest of men, seldom criticised his fellows, yet on this occasion he said: "You know, friends who steal your dirty books tell you three things about themselves.

"One, they're thieves – and they outrage the hospitality of my house.

"Two, they're cowards, because they make thieves of themselves rather than being seen to want to borrow a dirty book.

"And three, they're lechers, because they want the same from the books as I did."

I believe that most of Sir Compton's literary effects, including his library, was sold to a Texan university. I'm diverted by the thought that after Sir Compton died in 1972, so near to his ninetieth birthday, a copy of the *Fanny Hill* paperback was perhaps solemnly catalogued and shipped across the Atlantic.

A day or two after I had visited Sir Compton I met Jim Haines, the ebullient owner of the famous Edinburgh Paperback Bookshop who later created *International Times* and other extravagances. I told Haines Sir Compton's story and he immediately offered to give me two copies of the now banned *Fanny Hill* before the law seized them – one for me and one for Sir Compton, which was duly delivered.

Maybe it went to Texas. Maybe Sir Compton's friends got there first.

Behold the Hebrides

"Tell me," said the Board of Trade inspector to the Hebridean crofter, "I've always wondered if you have a word in the Gaelic which is equivalent to the Spanish, *mañana*?"

"Well, now," said the crofter, "There is no word in our language which conceives of such urgency."

Jock

"Come on!" roared the captain of a Hebridean ferry to the indolent harbour staff on the island of Barra, "Come on, there, and cast me off quickly, or I'll tow you and your silly wee island out into the Atlantic."

The Bydand Myths

A crofter in South Uist neglected his thatched roof so much that the rain poured in on top of his four-poster bed. So he thatched the roof of the bed and stayed dry until his chronic neglect caused that thatch to leak as well.

He caught such a serious cold that the island doctor had to call and attend to him. "Why don't you repair your roof, Donald, the real roof, instead of mucking about with the bed?" asked the doctor.

"Well now," said Donald, wheezing through his phlegm, "When the weather's bad it's too wet out there to mend it, and when it's not there's no need to bother, is there?"

Fred Macaulay

North of an uncertain line between Fort William in the west and Dingwall in the east the most common definition of a virgin is a girl who can run faster than her brother.

Jock

The earnest Scots writer, home on holiday from a recent success in Hollywood, was provoked on a television chat-show to describe his awful childhood in Glasgow – the squalor, the deprivation, the screaming poverty of his family's existence in the Gallowgate during the Depression. Another member of the panel, a less successful, less shrill, stay-at-home Scot, listened to this catalogue of misery and woe and said, *sotto voce*, "The Gallowgate? ... We used to go there for our summer holidays."

There is probably no phrase from those dark days between the wars so emotive as "the means test". The images of soup kitchens and dole queues are not quite so spectral as that of the Civil Servant, watered and fed, affronting the dignity of the poor and needy by prying into the most personal corners of their lives. A very humane ex-Civil Servant told me a story against his much-maligned colleagues.

A man from Paisley has applied for State assistance and the man from the Ministry is applying the means test. The applicant is shabby, unshaven, and in a poor physical state. The examiner is dapper, well-fed, and bright as a button. The perfect dramatic contrast for such a confrontation:

When did you last have a job?
Eighteen months ago.
Why did you stop working?
Paid off.
Have you been offered work and refused?
No.
Are you married?
Yes.
Children?
Yes.
How many?
Three.
Does you wife work?
No.
How much money do you have in the bank?
Two hundred and five thousand pounds, sixteen shillings and eight pence.
You must be joking!
Well, you started it!

Border farmers used to hire their workers on an annual agreement, sometimes engaging whole families – the father as ploughman or shepherd, the mother as help in the farmer's house, the children as casual farm labour. Hiring fairs were the occasion for a change if either party wanted out of the agreement. These fairs were holidays and after the conclusion of business there was much merrymaking, perhaps a dance, and the pubs full and overflowing. Willie Turnbull, a Border gamekeeper who paints pretty pictures of the life he leads near Jedburgh, illustrated the character of the hiring fairs with the story of the ploughman who was approached by the farmer:

"I hear you're thinking of a change."
"I am," said the ploughman.
"Would you think of coming to me?" asked the farmer, outlining his terms and conditions.
"I'll think about it," said the ploughman.
"Well, I'll just go to your last master," said the farmer, "and ask him what sort of character you have."
"Just do that," said the man, "and at the same time I'll have a word with your last ploughman and see what sort of character he gives you."
They parted agreeing to meet at the same spot an hour later. The

farmer was all smiles on his return. "Well, it seems you're a good workman, honest and true, a bit heavy on the drink at the end of the week, but they say you've never ploughed a crooked furrow in your life." The farmer paused, gave the ploughman a final look up and down as if he were a prize beast, "I think you can take it that you'll be working for me on Monday morning."

The ploughman hesitated for only a second. "I've been told about you, too," he said, "and it seems that you're a tight-fisted, black-hearted old rascal, never as good as your word, and I think you can take it that come Monday morning I'll be ploughing my straight furrows for somebody else."

The State of Israel, always in a precarious economic position decided to hire the best financial wizard that money could buy. Of course thousands applied for the job and after much weeding the short list was reduced to three – a French Jew, a German Jew, and a Scottish Jew. They were called to Jerusalem for the final interview.

The Frenchman, summoned first, was asked: "How much is two and two?"

There was no time even to draw breath. In a flash he answered: "Four. See in my head I can do it so quickly."

The German was asked the same question. Very deliberately, after first putting on his glasses, he scribbled in a notebook, tore out the page and waved it at his examiners. "The answer is four," he said solemnly, "I can confirm that, and here is documentary proof of my calculations."

When the Scotsman was asked the question he seemed troubled. He asked them to repeat it. "How much is two and two?" Then, looking the examining chairman straight in the eye he asked: "Are you buying or selling?"

With the exception of Raeburn and the elder William MacTaggart, the Scottish painters who have received most recognition outside Scotland and particularly in France, are the three so-called "colourists" – Hunter, Peploe, and Cadell. And they owe part of their success, certainly their posthumous recognition in their own country, to the late Dr Tom Honeyman, a great Glaswegian, who deserted medicine in favour of art-dealing and art gallery management.

Honeyman knew the "colourists" well. Hunter, a compulsive sketcher, survived the San Francisco earthquake. Until the end of his days Tom Honeyman was still on the trail of several Hunter canvases that were stolen from the painter's studio as he lay on his deathbed. Peploe seems to have been a shy ascetic, embarrassed about selling pictures, of the three far and away the most influential. F. C. B. Cadell most closely measured up to the public's romantic conception of how an artist should work and play.

Even in his student days at the Royal Scottish Academy he was unconventional and a bit of a wag. The president of the academy was due to visit the school one day and Cadell, like his fellows, busied himself at a life drawing. The great man went along the line of easels, criticising, offering advice, suggesting improvements.

When he came to Cadell's drawing he expostulated, "You'll never be an artist if you go on working with your left hand!" Cadell, all innocence, asked immediately, "What about Michelangelo?"

The president huffed and puffed but walked on without further comment.

A fellow student waited till the president's entourage was out of earshot then challenged Cadell: "I didn't know Michelangelo was left-handed."

"Neither did I," said Cadell. "And what's more important, neither did he," and with an airy wave of his charcoal at the departing dignitary he got on with his drawing.

The Auld Enemy

The English! My God, they ruffle my feathers. They strut this earth like medieval popes. They behave as if God has granted them the divine right to be smug. We've fought their wars for them, colonised the world for them, propped up their rotten Empire, and cleaned up the middens they've left behind from Belfast to Borneo. And in Whitehall and Westminster and all along their corridors of power they treat us as if we were savages, still painted in woad. A subject race of congenital idiots, a nation of Harry Lauders with curly sticks and wee daft dugs, and stags at bay, and flying haggises and tartan dollies and Annie Lauries and hoots mon Jock M'Kay ye'll be a' richt the nicht if ye can houghmagandie backwards.

Jock

Epitaph

When the time comes when I am not
Some friend no doubt will say "His head was hot."
While some fair charmer when the tale is told
Will sigh and murmur "And his feet were cold,"
And then I hope they'll walk off arm in arm
And say together "But his heart was warm."

Ian Mackay

Hypocrisy

Anybody who has read the report of a divorce case must be struck
by the fact that everybody in Court, from the Judge to the Usher,
places himself or herself in the correct posture for lying. They lie
to the jury, to the public, to themselves, and to God Almighty.

James Bridie

Holy Willie's Prayer

O Thou, wha in the heavens dost dwell,
Wha, as it pleases best Thysel',
Sends ane to Heaven, an' ten to Hell,
    A' for Thy glory,
And no for onie guid or ill
      They've done afore Thee!

I bless and praise Thy matchless might,
Whan thousands Thou hast left in night,
That I am here, afore Thy sight,
    For gifts an' grace,
A burnin' an' a shinin' light
      To a' this place.

What was I, or my generation,
That I should get sic exaltation!
I, wha deserv'd most just damnation,
        For broken laws
Sax thousand years 'fore my creation,
        Thro' Adam's cause.

When frae my mither's womb I fell,
Thou might hae plung'd me deep in Hell,
To gnash my gooms, to weep and wail
        In burnin' lakes,
Whare damnèd devils roar and yell,
        Chain'd to their stakes.

Yet I am here, a chosen sample,
To show Thy grace is great and ample;
I'm here a pillar o' Thy temple,
        Strong as a rock,
A guide, a buckler, an example
        To a' Thy flock!

O Lord, thou kens what zeal I bear,
When drinkers drink, and swearers swear,
And singin' there and dancin' here,
        Wi' great and sma':
For I am keepit by thy fear
        Free frae them a'.

But yet, O Lord! confess I must,
At times I'm fash'd wi' fleshly lust;
An' sometimes, too, inwardly trust,
        Vile self gets in;
But Thou remembers we are dust,
        Defil'd wi' sin.

O Lord, yestreen, thou kens, wi' Meg –
Thy pardon I sincerely beg;
O! may't ne'er be a livin' plaque
        To my dishonour,
An I'll ne'er lift a lawless leg
        Again upon her.

Besides I farther maun allow
Wi' Lizzie's lass, three times I trow –
But, Lord, that Friday I was fou,
        When I cam near her,
Or else thou kens thy servant true
        Wad never steer her.

May be Thou lets this fleshly thorn
Beset Thy servant e'en and morn,
Lest he owre proud and high should turn
    That he's sae gifted:
If sae Thy han' maun e'en be borne
    Until Thou lift it.

Lord, bless Thy chosen in this place,
For here Thou has a chosen race:
But God confound their stubborn face,
    An' blast their name,
Wha' bring Thy elders to disgrace
    An open shame!

Lord, mind Gawn Hamilton's deserts,
He drinks, an' swears, an' plays at cartes,
Yet has sae monie takin' arts,
    Wi' great and sma',
Frae God's ain priest the people's hearts
    He steals awa.

An' when we chasten'd him therefore,
Thou kens how he bred sic a splore,
As set the warld in a roar
    O' laughin' at us; –
Curse Thou his basket and his store,
    Kail an' potatoes!

Lord, hear my earnest cry and pray'r
Against the Presbyt'ry o' Ayr!
Thy strong right hand, Lord, mak it bare
    Upo' their heads!
Lord, visit them, an' dinna spare,
    For their misdeeds!

O Lord my God! that glib-tongu'd Aiken,
My vera heart and saul are quakin'
To think how we stood sweatin', shakin',
    An' pish'd wi' dread,
While he, wi' hingin' lip an' snakin',
    Held up his head.

Lord, in Thy day o' vengeance try him!
Lord, visit them wha did employ him,
And pass not in Thy mercy by them,
    Nor hear their pray'r;
But for Thy people's sake, destroy them
    An' dinna spare!

But, Lord, remember me and mine,
Wi' mercies temp'ral and divine,
That I for grace and gear may shine,
    Excell'd by nane,
An' a' the glory shall be Thine,
    Amen, Amen!

Robert Burns

Smiling Through

A great deal of what is called Scottish sentiment *is* funny. To anybody who knows the people who indulge in it, Wallacethebruceism, Charlieoverthewaterism, Puirrabbieburnsism, Bonniebonniebanksism, Myainfolkism, and Laymedoonandeeism, those not very various forms of Scottish Sentiment, are very comical indeed. The Scot himself, greeting heartily beneath his bonnie briar bush, has been known to smile through his tears.

James Bridie

Soupit the Poupit

A severe snow-storm in the Highlands, which lasted for several weeks, having stopped all communication betwixt neighbouring hamlets, snuff-takers were reduced to their last pinch. Borrowing and begging from all the neighbours within reach was resorted to, but this soon failed, and all were alike reduced to the extremity which unwillingly-abstinent sufferers alone know. The minister of the parish was amongst the unhappy number; the craving was so intense, that study was out of the question. As a last resort the beadle was despatched, through the snow, to a neighbouring glen in the hope of getting a supply; but he came back as unsuccessful as he went. "What's to be done, Jock?" was the minister's pathetic inquiry. John shook his head, as much as to say, that he could not tell, but immediately thereafter started up, as if a new idea had occurred to him. He came back in a few minutes crying, "Hae". The minister, too eager to be scrutinizing, took a long, deep pinch, and then said, "Whaur did ye get it?" "I soupit the poupit" (swept the pulpit) was John's expressive reply. The minister's superfluous sabbath snuff now came into good use.

Dean Ramsay

Sharp Wit

I feel that Charles Kirkpatrick Sharpe has himself become, as it were, a tradition of Edinburgh. His thin effeminate figure, his voice pitched *in alt* – his attire, as he took his daily walks on Princes Street, a long blue frock-coat, black trousers, rather wide below, and sweeping over white stockings and neat shoes – something like a web of white cambric round his neck, and a brown wig coming down to his eyebrows – had long established him as what is called a character . . . He had a quaint biting wit, which people bore as they could a scratch from a provoked cat. Essentially, he was good-natured, and fond of merriment . . . In jest upon his own peculiarity of voice, he formed an address-card for himself consisting simply of the following anagram:

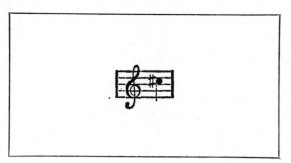

quasi dicitur C sharp.

Robert Chambers

Street Song

Sister, sister, I've been thinking
What on earth have you been drinking?
Looks like water
Smells like wine
O, my God, it's turpentine!

Light Fantastic

The dancing assemblies of Edinburgh were for many years, about the middle of the last century (eighteenth), under the direction and the dictatorship of the Honourable Miss Nicky Murray, one of the sisters of the Earl of Mansfield. Much good sense, firmness, knowledge of the world and of the histories of individuals, as well as a due share of patience and benevolence, were required for this office of unrecognised though real power; and it was generally admitted that Miss Murray possessed the needful qualifications in a remarkable degree, though rather more marked by good manners than good-nature ... The arrangements were of a rigid character, and certainly

tending to dullness. There being but one set allowed to dance at a time, it was seldom that any person was twice on the floor in one night. The most of the time was spent in acting the part of lookers-on, which threw great duties in the way of conversation upon the gentlemen. These had to settle with a partner for the year, and were upon no account permitted to change, even for a single night. The appointment took place at the beginning of the season, usually at some private party or ball given by a person of distinction, where the fans of the ladies were all put into a gentleman's cocked hat; the gentlemen put in their hands and took a fan, and to whomsoever the fan belonged, that was to be his partner for the season. In the general rigours of this system, which sometimes produced ludicrous combinations, there was, however, one palliative – namely, the fans being all distinguishable from each other, and the gentlemen being in general as well acquainted with the fan as the face of his mistress, and the hat being open, it was possible to peep in, and exercise, to a certain extent a principle of selection, whereby he was perhaps successfu in procuring an appointment to his mind.

Robert Chambers

Auld Alliance

I think it's a great pity that we haven't given the French as many words as we've taken from them – like an "ashet" for the tatties, or a "tassie" o' tea, and "gigot" chops. Just imagine what would have happened, like thon Edinburgh woman on a day-trip to Paris, who shouts out: "Oh, stop the bus, I want to get aff. I just have to skip intae Schiaperelli's for a new hankie." So she sails through the big revolving doors with a loud "bonjour, monsewer". And the manager's waiting for her. Your typical Frenchman. Black greasy hair. Wee pencil-line moustache. Black jacket and black striped trousers. And he doesn't just walk across the floor towards her. He oozes. And takes the elegant gloved Edinburgh hand and says, "Bonjour, hen!"

Jock

The Tight Fist

"Have you a shilling for the Lord's good work?" asks the Salvation Army lassie, just as auld Duncan is downing his dram in the village pub.

"Are you no' a bit young tae be in here?" says he.

"I'm eighteen," she says,

"Well, I'm eighty-two," says Duncan, so I'll be seein' Him afore you, and if ye dinna mind I'll just gie him the shilling masel!"

Jock

"If folk think I'm mean, then they'll no' expect too much, will they?"

Sir Harry Lauder

John Rafferty, the *Scotsman* newspaper's principal sports columnist, has travelled Europe with the great Celtic team of the past decade. Success has taken all but the worst elements of Celtic's support into a state of grace – they behave better, argue less, disdain all battles except those on the playing field. They drink as much, but are better-natured with it. Some years ago John Rafferty left me with this indelible image:

The supporters' plane is over the Bay of Biscay on its way home after a famous victory in the European Cup competition. The duty-free bottles were broached before the plane left the runway and are now nearly empty. Only the seat belts are keeping some of the supporters upright. The general hubbub of song and laughter dies away as a wee man teeters up the aisle, steering himself with the exaggerated precision of the practised drunk. In his hands he carries a brimming glass of whisky, balancing it as if his next breath depended on his not spilling a drop.

A voice rings out: "Heh, Bob! Where the hell'r ye gaun?"

The wee man daren't raise his head, but he manages to shake it scornfully. "Ye're a selfish lot," he says as he stumbles towards the crew cockpit, "ye've forgotten tae offer a drink tae the driver."

Gilbert Fisher's long term as director of Edinburgh's zoo saw several changes in the lay-out of the park, many of them directed towards giving the animals as much freedom as possible in a natural environment. Almost inevitably, a particularly bad-tempered brown bear saw a way out of his enclosure one morning when the zoo had few visitors. Keepers and attendants worked their way down the park's steep hillside looking for the bear. As Fisher and two keepers with a net turned a corner they saw him lumbering down the main roadway, heading straight for two old ladies who were making heavy weather of the climb.

The men considered creating a diversion and taking the bear by surprise but Fisher decided against it in case any sudden action should startle and anger the beast. They watched as the paths of bear and ladies crossed, all three taking each other for granted. As soon as the ladies were in the clear the keepers rushed the bear, netted him, and hauled him back to his enclosure.

Fisher ran up the hill after the ladies, intent on apology. They recognised him before he could open his mouth.

"Oh, it's you, Mr Fisher," said one of them, "I was just saying to my friend what a wonderful job you're doing here, giving the animals so much freedom."

Three Dedications

To all those people who find
themselves in possession of a
five-shilling watch which has
ceased to function, this book
    The Eye of the Needle
is savagely dedicated.

John MacGlashan

A man who is bandying his friends
about ought to bandy them gently.
My bandy acquaintances will
understand this, and forgive me.

Clifford Hanley

To
The
Old
Salt
Who
Knew
That
A
Passing
Vessel
Was
Scotch
Because
There
Were
No
Birds
Following
It

T. W. H. Crosland

Robert Burns bought a mare in Edinburgh "for over £4 Sterling" in 1787 and called her Jenny Geddes after the redoubtable lady who became a Scottish legend by throwing a stool at the head of the Episcopalian preacher in St Giles', Edinburgh, in 1637. Burns used the mare to carry him on a West Highland tour and, in a letter to a friend, told how, on the shores of Loch Lomond . . .

. . . by came a Highlandman at the gallop, on a tolerably good horse, but which had never known the ornaments of iron or leather. We scorned to be outgalloped by a Highlandman, so off we started, whip and spur. My companions though seemingly gaily mounted, fell sadly astern; but my old mare, Jenny Geddes, one of the Rosinante family, strained past the Highlandman in spite of all his efforts with the hair halter; just as I was passing him, Donald wheeled his horse, as if to cross before me to mar my progress, when down came his horse, and threw his breekless arse in a clipt hedge; and down came Jenny Geddes over all, and my Bardship between her and the Highlandman's horse. Jenny Geddes trode over me with such cautious reverence that matters were not so bad as might well have been expected; so I came off with a few cuts and bruises, and a thorough resolution to be a pattern of sobriety for the future.

Within a Month

There came to pass a day when the populations of the West Highlands of Scotland and Holland were mysteriously transferred to each other's countries.

Within the space of only a very few months wool and beef production in the Highlands was increased by several hundred per cent, the tourist trade boomed, fish farms occupied all the sea lochs, and Fort William became the electronics nerve-centre of Western Europe.

And within a month, within only four short and terrible weeks, Holland was flooded.

The Bydand Myths

What a Man was my First Boss!

When I was throwing away some old calendars the other night, I came across an entry which reminded me that if he had not died suddenly during the First World War, my earliest employer would have been ninety years of age today. And as he was a very great influence in my life – he colours my mind even now – I hope you will bear with me while I pay a tribute to his memory, even if you call me a sentimental old josser for doing so. He was an interesting chap and through him you may get a glimpse of that strange vanished era which seems farther away from us now than the days of Good Queen Bess. For, as we all know, Shakespeare, Donne and Drake are much nearer to us in word and spirit than Pinero, Hall Caine and Lord Charles Beresford.

In the second decade of this tormented century, when I was a freckled urchin in a chemist's shop in Wick, my employer was the most remarkable man in the town. In fact, he was in many ways the most remarkable man I have ever met, although since then, like Ulysses, I have seen many men and cities. His name was William Gow Miller, and his rosy cheeks and friendly eyes shone with benevolence and good cheer. He wore queer coloured suits, fancy waistcoats, flowing ties with blue and white dots on them, romantic feathered hats with green and vermilion cords and ribbons and he always carried a yellow silver-headed cane which with a flick of the wrist he could turn into a rapier.

There was a strange timeless look about him. As he strolled – for he could not be said to have walked – down the street he looked like one of the Cheeryble brothers dressed in Beau Brummel's fanciest suit. Every now and then he would emerge from the dispensary in green knickerbockers buttoned at the knee which, with his corded hat and yellow stick, gave him the look of a Tirolean yodeller. On such occasions he brightened up and glorified the dull grey northern town.

He loved Chianti, smoked perfumed cigars, carried little muslin sachets of lavender in his pockets, took cocaine like Sherlock Holmes by the needle, and adored Mr Asquith, whom he resembled when he was hatless among his jars and bottles. Though he died a bachelor he worshipped in a vague antiseptic sort of way a superb but disdainful siren who ran a hotel and wore feather boas all the year round. Nothing ever came of this, though she must have spent a fortune on sedatives and cosmetics making up to him. He lived with his sisters, two aged, arid but affectionate spinsters in a bleak house beside an even bleaker burn at the back of beyond.

For all that, his knowledge of the world, like Mr Weller's knowledge of London, was extensive and peculiar. Unlike Mr Weller's, it was expensive as well. For he lived a double life. From October to July he pounded away at his pills and powders and mixed his liniments and lotions in that queer *quant. suff.*, three-times-a-day-after-food world in which druggists live among their spirit lamps, sealing wax, orris root and alembics. But when summer came, he lived in a different world, on the Riviera, in the Engadine, in Madeira or the Costa Brava. Then he was the English milord in panama and white suit, a leisured sybarite dawdling from one luxurious resort to another, and living deliriously beyond his means. Early in August, when his annual supplies of castor oil and copaiba were safely delivered in big fat barrels, he went on to the Continent – he called it *Conteenong* – leaving the shop in charge of a Welsh student, myself and an English lad who was afterward devoured by a lioness in the Mountains of the Moon. He was away for two months, but every day we would get a glossy postcard from places like Bordighera and Seville. And now and then a packet of snapshots would arrive showing him in a barouche on the Promenade des Anglais, on a camel in front of the Sphinx, in a gondola at Torcello, sipping Pernod in the Cannebiere, standing on Vesuvius with a wisp of smoke behind him or knee-deep in water at Viareggio with a cross to mark the spot where Shelley's body was burnt.

Then one day in October he would be back so brown that his teeth shone like snow and everybody would feel happier. He brought little odds and ends for all of us; bright coloured little things that brought a whiff of magic and romance into our icy little lives. For weeks he would potter about with his Chianti flasks and his new pictures, some of which were considered by the local bailies to be distinctly naughty. How he would have done today I cannot imagine. For he was a *fin de siècle* character and was lucky enough to live in his own good time. God bless him, wherever he is with his funny waistcoats and his crazy hats. How Sir Max would have adored him!

Ian Mackay

Several of the McBrayne skippers, whose boats serve the Inner and Outer Hebrides, became legends in their own lifetimes. On a run across to Islay one of them was told that he had an English Commander R.N. (Retd.) on board, and could this privileged passenger please come on the bridge. The mate was at the wheel. The skipper straddled the bridge like Captain Bligh as the Commander ascended.

"Where are we now, Captain?" he asked, breathless from the clamber.

"About half-way there," said the skipper, biting fiercely on his pipe.

"Do you think I could see a chart? I've never sailed these waters before."

"We don't have a lot of use for charts," said the skipper.

"There's some in the locker," said the mate.

"Well see if you can find one that fits this part of the big wide ocean," said the skipper, relieving the mate at the wheel.

Donald the mate returned with a frayed and buckled chart and spread it out before the Commander.

"I'd say we'll be about here," said Donald, jabbing a finger in the middle of a marked channel.

The Commander studied the chart, looked up, checked back down again, and his face wore a worried frown as he carried the folded chart across to the skipper.

"According to this, I'd say we're heading straight for these rocks. What do you think, Captain?"

The skipper took the chart, studied it for only a moment, then handed it back to the Commander, saying:

"They may be rocks, and then again they may not be rocks. *I'd* say they're fly-shit, and we'll just hold our course for Islay as we always do, won't we Donald?"

The Bydand Myths

The Game Chicken

Bob Ainslie and I were coming up Infirmary Street from the High School of Edinburgh, our heads together, and our arms intertwisted.

When we got to the top of the street, and turned north, we espied a crowd at the Tron Church. "A dog-fight!" shouted Bob, and was off; and so was I, both of us all but praying that it might not be over before we got up. And is not this boy-nature? and human nature too? and don't we all wish a house on fire not to be out before we see it? Dogs like fighting, and boys are not cruel because they like to see the fight. They see three of the great virtues of dog or man – courage, endurance, and skill – in intense action. This is very different from a love of making dogs fight, and enjoying, and aggravating, and making gain by their pluck.

Well, Bob and I are up, and find it is not over: a small thorough-bred, white bull-terrier, is busy throttling a large shepherd's dog, unaccustomed to war, but not to be trifled with. They are hard at it; the scientific little fellow doing his work in great style, his pastoral enemy fighting wildly, but with the sharpest of teeth and great courage. Science and breeding, however, soon had their own; the Game Chicken, as Bob called him, working his way up, took his final grip of the other dog's throat – and he lay gasping and done for.

His master, a brown, handsome, big young shepherd from Tweeds-muir, would have liked to knock down any man: it was no use kicking the little dog; that would only make him hold the closer. Many were the means shouted out in mouthfuls, of the best possible ways of ending it. "Water!" but there was none near, and many cried for it who might have got it from the well at Blackfriar's Wynd. "Bite the tail!" and a large, vague, benevolent, middle-aged man, more desirous than wise, with some struggle got the bushy end of the other dog's tail into his ample mouth, and bit it with all his might. This was more than enough for the much-enduring, much-perspiring shepherd, who, with a gleam of joy over his broad visage, delivered a terrific facer upon our large, vague, benevolent, middle-aged friend – who went down like a shot.

Still the Chicken holds; death not far off. "Snuff! a pinch of snuff!" observed a calm, highly-dressed young buck, with an eye-glass in his eye. "Snuff, indeed!" growled the angry crowd, affronted and glaring. "Snuff! a pinch of snuff!" again observes the buck, but with more urgency; whereon were produced several open boxes, and, from a mull that may have been at Culloden, he took a pinch, knelt down and presented it to the nose of the Chicken. The snuff takes its course; the Chicken sneezes, and the other dog is free.

The young pastoral giant walks off with his dog in his arms – comforting him.

But the bull-terrier's blood is up, and his soul unsatisfied; he grips

217

the first dog he meets, and discovering she is not a dog, in a phrase, he makes brief amends, and is off. The boys, with Bob and me at their head, are after him: down Niddry Street he goes, bent on mischief; up the Cowgate like an arrow – Bob and I, and our small men, panting behind.

There, under the single arch of the South Bridge, is a huge mastiff, sauntering down the middle of the causeway, as if with his hands in his pockets: he is old, grey, brindled, as big as a little Highland bull, and has dewlaps shaking as he goes.

The Chicken makes straight at him, and fastens on his throat. To our astonishment, the great creature does nothing but stand still, hold himself up, and roar – yes, roar; a long, serious, remonstrative roar. How is this? Bob and I are up to them. He is muzzled! The bailies had proclaimed a general muzzling, and his master, studying strength and economy mainly, had encompassed his huge jaws in a home-made apparatus, constructed out of leather. His mouth was open as far as it could; his lips curled up in rage – a sort of terrible grin; his teeth gleaming, ready, from out of the darkness; the strap across his mouth tense as a bowstring; his whole frame stiff with indignation and surprise; his roar asking us all round, "Did you ever see the like of this?" He looked a statue of anger and astonishment, done in Aberdeen granite.

We soon had a crowd: the Chicken held on. "A knife!" cried Bob; and a cobbler gave him his knife: you know the kind of knife, worn away to a point, and always keen. I put its edge to the tense leather and then – one sudden jerk of that enormous head, a sort of dirty mist about his mouth, no noise – and the bright and fierce little fellow is dropped, limp, and dead. A solemn pause: this was more than any of us had bargained for. I turned the little fellow over, and saw he was quite dead: the mastiff had taken him by the small of the back like a rat, and broken it.

He looked down at his victim appeased, ashamed, and amazed; snuffed him all over, stared at him, and, taking a sudden thought, turned round and trotted off. Bob took the dead dog up, and said, "John, we'll bury him after tea." "Yes," said I, and was off after the mastiff. He made up the Cowgate at a rapid swing; he had forgotten some engagement. He turned up the Candlemaker Row, and stopped at the Harrow Inn.

There was a carrier's cart ready to start, and a keen, thin, impatient, black-a-vised little man, his hand at his grey horse's head, looking about angrily for something. "Rab, ye thief!" said he, aiming a kick at my great friend, who drew cringing up, and avoiding the heavy shoe with more agility than dignity, and watching his master's eye, slunk dismayed under the cart – his ears down, and as much as he had of a tail down too.

What a man this must be – thought I – to whom my tremendous hero turns tail! The carrier saw the muzzle hanging, cut and useless, from his neck, and I eagerly told him the story. The severe little man was mitigated, and condescended to say, "Rab, my man, puir Rabbie" – whereupon the stump of a tail rose up, the ears were cocked, the eyes filled, and were comforted; the two friends were reconciled. "Hupp!" and a stroke of the whip were given to the horse; and off went the three.

Bob and I buried the Game Chicken that night (we had not much of a tea) in the back-green of his house in Melville Street, number 17, with considerable gravity and silence.

John Brown

Richness Indeed

"If I was the Shah of Persia I'd be richer than he is."

"Dinnae be daft. You'd have just the same amount of money as he has."

"Aye, but I'd hae a wee job as well."

The Bydand Myths

An Abundance of Proverbs

" . . . there are current in society upwards of 3,000 proverbs, exclusively
Scottish . . . the Scots are wonderfully given to this way of speaking,
and as the consequence of that, abound with proverbs, many of which
are very expressive, quick, and home to the purpose; and, indeed, this
humour prevails universally over the whole nation . . . "

James Kelly [1721]

The Barbed Tongue

Our natural gift for epigrammatic expression blossoms when there is mischief – or better still, malice – in the air. Our tongues hone readily to a cutting edge or grow sarcastic barbs. My very gentle mother's everyday speech (not that she had anything special for Sunday) was strewn with sayings like:

> He's (usually my father) a hoose deil and a causey saint (a devil at home, a saint in the street).
> Ye (usually hungry me) cannae see green cheese but yer een reels (I would covet food in any condition).
> She (an uppity neighbour) thinks all her eggs hae twa yolks.
> He's (my father again) as black's the Earl o' Hell's waistcoat.

Inevitably, some of our proverbs are no more than Scottish adaptations of English or European folk maxims, but the authentic home-grown product attributed to us by scholars for centuries, is usually as recognisable as the thistle itself in a bed of violets.

> A blate (timid) cat makes a fine mouse.
> A bonny bride is soon buskit (dressed).
> A dog winna yowl if ye strike him with a bane.
> A tocherless (dowerless) dame sits long at hame.
> A toom (empty) purse makes a blate merchant.
> All are good lasses, but whence come the bad wives?
> All Stuarts are not sib (related) to the king.

> Bear wealth, poverty will bear itself.
> Better bairns greet (children cry) than bearded men.
> Better say Here it is than Here it was.
> Better sit still than rise up and fa'.
> Better wed over the mixen (dung-heap) than over the moor (marry one of your own rather than a stranger).
> Biting and scratching is Scots folk's wooing.
> Boys will be men.
> Bring a cow to the hall and she'll run to the byre.

> Cast not out the foul water till you bring in the clean.
> Come day, go day, God sent Sunday.
> Courtesy is cumbersome to them than ken it no'.
> Credit keeps the crown of the causeway.

Do on the hill as ye would do in the hall.
Do well and doubt nae man, do ill and doubt a' men.

Far fowls have fair feathers.
Fools and bairns should not see half-done work.
Fools are fain of flittin' (fond of moving house).
Fools make feasts, and wise fowk eat them; the wise make jests, and
    fools repeat them.

Gentility never boiled a pot.
Get a name as an early riser and you can lie in your bed all day.
Give a bairn his will and a whelp his fill, and none of these two will
    thrive.
Give a dog a bad name and hang him.
Glasses and lasses are brittle ware.
God help the poor, for the rich can help themselves.
God sends meat, but the de'il sends cooks.
Good will should be taken for part payment.

He loves me for little that hates me for naught.
He rises over early that is hanged ere noon.
He that cannot make sport should mar none.
He that comes first to the hill may sit where he will.
He that has two hoards will get a third.
He that is ill to himself will be good to nobody.
He that talks to himself speaks to a fool.
Him that has a muckle nose thinks ilka yin speaks o't.

If a man deceive me once, shame on him; if he deceive me twice,
    shame on me.
If the doctor cures the sun sees it; but if he kills the earth hides it.
If the laird slight the lady, so will all the kitchen boys.
If wishes were horses, beggars would ride.
If ye canna bite, dinna show yer teeth.
If ye wad sup wi' the deil, ye'll need a lang spoon.
It is needless to pour water on a drown'd mouse.
It is no sin to sell dear, but a sin to give ill measure.
It is not lost that a friend gets.
It's ill wark tae tak the breeks aff a Hielandman.

Kame sindle, kame sair (comb seldom, comb sore).

Likely lies in the mire when Unlikely gets over.

Maidens must be mild and meek, swift to hear and slow to speak.
Maidens should be mim (quiet) till they're married, and then they
    may burn kirks.

Many a man speirs the gate (asks the way) he knows full well.
Mickle (much) spoken, part spilt.

Naething to be done in haste but gripping of fleas.

Out of debt, out of danger.

Put your hand twice to your bonnet for once to your pouch.

Quick at meat, quick at work.

Right wrangs nae man.
Rue and thyme grow both in one garden.
Rule youth well, for age will rule itsel!

Scotsmen aye reckon frae an ill hour.
Set a stout heart to a stey brae (steep hill).
Show me the man, and I'll show you the law.

The day has eyes and the night has ears.
The deaf man aye hears the clink o' money.
The more mischief, the better sport.
The mother of mischief is no bigger than a midge's wing.
There is little for the rake after the besom (broom).
There is nane sae blind as them that winna see.
There is no medicine for fear.
There's no' much guile in a heart that's aye singing.
They are far behind that may not follow.
To a red man rede thy rede (give your counsel),
    With a brown man break thy bread,
    At a pale man draw thy knife,
    From a black man Keep thy wife.
            The red is wise, the brown trusty,
            The pale envious, and the black lusty.
Trust not a new friend nor an old enemy.

Unseen, unrued.

Want of wit is worse than want of wealth.
We can drink of the burn when we cannot bite of the brae.
We can live without our friends, but not without our neighbours.
We can shape coat and sark (shirt) for them, but we cannot shape
    their weird (fate).
We never miss the water till the well runs dry.
Wha teaches himself has a fool for a master.
What may be done at any time will be done at no time.
When all men speak, no man hears.

H

When I did well, I heard it never;
  When I did ill, I heard it ever.
When wine sinks, words swim.
When you are well hold yourself so.
When you christen the bairn you should know what to call it.
Whoredom and grace dwelt ne'er in one place.
Wilful waste makes woeful want.
Wink at wee faults, your ain are muckle.
Women and wine, game and deceit,
  Make the wealth small and the wants great.
Wood in a wilderness, moss in a mountain, and wit in a poor man's
  breast, are little thought of.

Ye never heard a fisher cry stinking fish.
You may ding the deil (beat the devil) into a wife, but you'll never
  ding him out of her.
You would do little for God if the devil were dead.

Dear Mortimer:

I know you don't want a cookery book. That other Scot, Elizabeth David, seems to have cornered the world market. It would be futile to pretend that we have made any impression on *haute cuisine*, but with the world tightening its belt maybe there's a place for some of our peasant dishes. So perhaps I should include one or two simple survival recipes.

Dear Gordon:

By all means. It would be interesting to know if Denis Law and Dave Mackay and Billy Bremner were brought up on a diet of sour milk, porridge, and haggis. Surely that could be one acceptable reason for the ferocity of their endeavour, their stamina, their animal hunger for the ball even in the eighty-ninth minute? Can you find out?

Vulgar Farin'

Buy my caller herrin'!
Though ye may ca' them vulgar farin',
Wives and mithers, maist despairin',
Ca' them lives o' men.

Lady Nairne

The Scottish Kitchen

"Do you like our Scots broth, Dr Johnson?"
"Ah! Very good for hogs, I believe."
"Then let me help you to a little more."

I was eighteen when I ate my first steak. It could have been camel or horse or iguana for all I knew, because it was served up to me in a Royal Air Force social club in Iraq. In the unlikely event of its being beef, the beast that provided it could have had little or no resemblance to the tender and tasty Aberdeen-Angus of my homeland.

My mother's "service" had included acting as cook to a minor figure in the Kailyaird school of Scottish literature. "Nothing fancy", she said, proud and without apology. She made exceptionally fine soups, as most Scotswomen do, particularly potato soup, with leek and carrots, that were best the day "they" were made, and lentil soup, thick and tangy with ham stock and onion, which was at its very thickest and best on the third day if it ever lasted that long.

Like all Scots housewives she relied on mince and tatties for at least one main meal of the week, sometimes with peas, occasionally with butter beans eking out the mince. She selected a cut of stewing steak at the butcher's, asked for it to be sliced before her eyes, and waited while the man took the meat into the back-shop and minced it for her.

Later I worked in that same shop and learned the trick of the trade. The sliced meat was put aside and the butcher brought out a fistful of prepared mince of inferior quality. But not all that inferior, because Scots mince is probably the best in the world.

It would be carrying chauvinism too ridiculously far to suggest that the ubiquitous chip is a peculiarly Scottish creation. The Scots, however, believe that they have a special relationship with the chip, comparable only with their belief in a similarly singular association with the Almighty.

Frenchmen slaver down their chins at the thought of fresh coffee and warm croissants. And when Italians get a whiff of the marsala and garlic in the saltimbocca they feel it jumping, literally, into their mouths.

But the chef has yet to be born who can dream up an aroma that turns on the stomach juices like the smell of fish and chips coming at you in waves round a street corner on a cold winter's night.

And the most succulent morsels – la crème de la crème, the crumbs from some heavenly table – are the wee crispy bits at the bottom of the bag.

Jock

231

Our seed potatoes feed hungry bellies all over the world. The privileged farmlands of East Lothian and Ayrshire breed seed of such vigour and purity that the market can seldom be satisfied. The names of the varieties are gastronomic poetry:

Arran Banner
Arran Comet
Arran Pilot
Arran Rose
Arran Viking
Edzell Blue
Duke of York
Kerr's Pink
Majestic
Pentland Dell
Pentland Falcon
Pentland Hawk
Pentland Ivory
Redskin

Long before the clever Italian immigrants set up their shops in every Scottish township, long before the itinerant vans steamed their way through the countryside, chips were an important element of Scottish working-class diet – in some sad cases the only hot food a child got in the day. And in eighteen- and nineteenth-century Edinburgh amongst the cries of the street vendors:

"Leddies, leddies, here are cresses!"
"Caller herrin', caller haddies, fresh and loupin' in the creel!"

"Wha'll buy syboes, wha'll buy leeks,
"Wha'll buy the bonnie lass wi' the red cheeks?"

the potato-seller sang out loud and clear:

"Potatoes all hot, all hot and sonsy peeryorries!"

All five hours of a Wagnerian opera taxed more than the minds of an over-dressed audience at one Edinburgh Festival. By the third interval the tummy-rumbles were adding a distracting bass pedal to the orchestral accompaniment. The Tollcross district of our spartan capital is as far removed from Glyndebourne's lawns as Holloway Prison from Kew

Gardens, and I will never forget the incongruity of a couple in full evening dress rushing back to the theatre while bolting down a fish supper and (that great Scottish delicacy) a white pudding supper, while hopping in and out of the traffic.

Oyster Song

The herring loves the merry moonlight,
   The mackerel loves the wind,
But the oyster loves the dredging-song,
   For he comes of gentle kind.

                  Sir Walter Scott

With the sea so much on Scotland's doorstep the freshest of cold-water fish is a precious birthright. Herring, the "silver darlings" of our seas, used to be cheap and plentiful. They are still delicious.

Herring Fried in Oatmeal

Winter herring are best, when they're at their smallest and sweetest. Allow two per person. Season coarse oatmeal with salt and black pepper and roll the fish in it, covering both sides. Melt two tablespoons of butter in a frying pan until it is bubbling hot but not burning, and fry the herring until golden brown on both sides. Drain and serve, ideally with new, boiled potatoes.

To the Chinaman his rice, the Italian his pasta, the Irish their potatoes. To the Scot, his oatmeal. As a matter of fact I know no Scot today who eats porridge – not the porage of the cereal packets – but many still do, savouring it with salt rather than sweetening it with sugar.

233

Field Kitchen

Under the flap of his saddle, each man carries a broad plate of metal; behind the saddle, a little bag of oatmeal. When they have eaten too much . . . sodden flesh, and their stomach appears weak and empty, they place this plate over the fire, mix with water their oatmeal, and when the plate is heated, they put a little of the paste upon it, and make a thin cake, like a cracknel or biscuit, which they eat to warm their stomachs; it is therefore no wonder that they perform a longer day's march than other soldiers.

Froissart's Chronicles

The redoubtable ladies of the Scottish Women's Rural Institutes, who do so much to keep the highways and byways of folk-tradition free of foreign weeds and undesirable undergrowth, publish and frequently revise a Scottish cookery book. My 1950 edition gives no fewer than twenty-eight recipes under a special section, "oatmeal dishes". But the 1968 edition carries no such section, although they give a nod to the passage of time by the addition of a special chapter on "Deep Freezing".

My own dislike of porridge is psychological as much as anything else. Long before refrigerators or deep-freeze cabinets, before even an airy pantry was obligatory in new houses, we were told about peasants in the rural hinterland who made a big batch of porridge at the one stirring, poured it into a drawer, and cut off a rubbery slice when required.

Oatcakes (thin), as distinct from bannocks (thick), I am never able to resist, particularly with cheese, and especially if the oatcakes are crisp and well-fired to a nutty flavour.

Oatcakes Thin

Mix one cup of oatmeal, a pinch of bicarbonate of soda, and a quarter teaspoonful of salt. Rub in a teaspoonful of melted fat. Add enough hot water to make a stiff dough. Roll out as thin as possible, working quickly and dusting frequently with dry oatmeal. Bake one side on the traditional girdle (or on the plate of an electric cooker!) till the edges begin to curl, toast the other side in front of the fire or under a hot grill.

The Miller's Kitchen

Merry may the maid be
   That marries the miller:
For foul day and fair day
   He's aye bringin' till her;
He's aye a penny in his purse
   For dinner and for supper;
And gin she please, a good fat cheese
   And lumps o' yellow butter.

Behind the door a bag o' meal,
   And in the kist was plenty
Of good hard cakes his mither bakes,
   And bannocks were na scanty.
A good fat sow, a sleaky cow
   Was standin' in the byre;
While lazy puss with mealy mouse
Was playing at the fire.

In winter, when the wind and rain
   Blows o'er the house and byre,
He sits beside a clean hearth-stane
   Before a rousing fire;
With nut-brown ale he tells his tale,
   Which rows him o'er fu' nappy
Wha'd be a king – a petty thing,
   When a miller lives sae happy?

Sir John Clerk of Penicuik

The New Markets

The opening in 1826 of an establishment called the New Town Markets at Stockbridge recalled some curious, though not distant, recollections of Edinburgh. It was only about fifteen or twenty years before that our only fish market was in the Fishmarket Close, a steep, narrow, stinking ravine. The fish were generally thrown out on the street at the head of the close, whence they were dragged down by dirty boys or dirtier women, and then sold unwashed – for there was not a drop of water in the place – from old, rickety, scaly, wooden tables, exposed to all the rain, dust and filth; an abomination the recollection of which greatly impaired the pleasantness of the fish at a later hour of the day . . . I doubt if there was a single fish shop in Edinburgh so early as the year 1822.

Our vegetables had to pass through as bad a process. They were entirely in the hands of a college of old gin-drinking women, who congregated with stools and tables round the Tron Church. A few of the aristocracy of these ladies – the burgo-mistresses, who had established a superior business – the heads of old booths – marked their dignity by an awning of dirty canvas or tattered carpet; and every table had its tallow candle and paper lantern at night. There was no water here, either, except what flowed down the gutter, which, however, was plentifully used. Fruit had a place on the table, but kitchen vegetables lay bruised on the ground. I doubt if there was a fruit shop in Edinburgh in 1815.

Henry Thomas Cockburn

Battered Barley

Though broth was so commonly used, the barley, a principal ingredient, was ill-prepared, and of the coarsest quality. It was not milled or scaled, but bruised or beaten in a trough, something like an apothecary's mortar, and called the knocking stone, which was at that time an indispensable article in every kitchen. After being then winnowed in what was called a wecht or sieve, and rubbed with a coarse cloth, the barley was ready for use. The knocking of the barley formed a material part of the cook's daily work.

Thomas Somerville

Scotch Broth

One runner of beef or a good fresh marrow bone, which makes as good broth as either beef or mutton, 5 quarts cold water, 1 cupful well-washed pearl barley. When water is hot, put in beef and barley, and salt to taste; skim well; chop up six Brussels sprouts, 1 small cabbage or savoy, 1 small head of curley [sic] greens, and 3 leeks; cut in dice 1 good slice of swede turnip and 1 carrot; put in other 2 slices of turnip whole, and mash well afterwards as a vegetable. Let the broth boil for a few minutes after vegetables are added with lid off [sic]. Cook thoroughly and slowly, and skim now and again; attention to this makes such a difference to flavour. Boil 3 hours, taking meat out when cooked 2 hours, and re-heating at the last. Then 15 minutes before ready add 1 carrot grated and a good tablespoonful minced parsley. Lift meat on to a hot dish, and serve with a little broth round it. (If broth is for persons of weak digestion, scald vegetables before adding to broth by covering them for 10 minutes with boiling water.)

S.W.R.I. Cookery Book
(1950 edition)

"You never ate it before?"

"No, sir," replied Johnson, "but I don't care how soon I eat it again."

James Boswell

Clever Dug !

In the kitchen, the utensils were few and clumsy. I do not remember to have seen a roasting-jack in my early life. The spit was turned by one of the servants, and sometimes by a dog trained for that cruel service. The dog was made to turn a large wooden wheel in a box attached to the spit. The dogs, I have heard, used to hide themselves or run away when they observed indications that there was to be a roast for dinner.

Thomas Somerville

Passionate Pies

Green peas, mutton pies,
Tell me where my Jeannie lies,
And I'll be with her ere she rise,
And cuddle her to my bosom.

I love Jeannie over and over,
I love Jeannie among the clover;
I love Jeannie, and Jeannie loves me,
That's the lass that I'll go wi!

Traditional

Next to oatmeal, and broth, and mince and tatties, and chips (and together only if you're a specific type of Glaswegian), the pie has to be given high place on any list of Scottish fare. They can be filled with beef mince or mutton mince or such a minced mixture as to defy definition, but they must be round, fit the palm of the hand, tasty, and their juices must be contained and not absorbed by crisp short pastry. They fail all consumer tests if, when eaten warm from the hand, the gravy doesn't dribble down one's chin.

They were our Saturday meal before the war, and I bought a dozen of the best pies in the world and carried them home by train. They were made by a baker called Todd at Ardmillan and were justly famous all over Edinburgh. To the best of my recollection I never delivered more than nine.

My friend Alan Sharp, who fills his Hollywood film scripts with improbable Greenockians, travels from Sunset Boulevard, where he lives, fifteen miles up the Californian coast to Santa Monica where he has found a shop which sells "shell" pies – impostors certainly, but pies nevertheless. A year or two ago he had been visiting me in Edinburgh and was on his way to London and a big dinner that night in the Dorchester. On our way to the station, with the diesel heart of the "Flying Scotsman" already pounding at Waverley, he stopped off at a Hanover Street baker's shop to buy a dozen pies for the journey.

Bellgutsin' and Gormandizing

In speaking of minutiæ of manners characteristic of the times, the fashion of pressing people to eat must not be omitted. As it originated

Holyrood Palace. A few years ago I was told the story in Moscow, same story but different dramatis personæ.

Baxter's plain scones made him famous all over old Edinburgh. They were so light and tasty that the populace scarcely missed the rich Mayue bread which, by decree, could be made only on four great feast days of the year.

The fame of Baxter spread to the Palace of Holyrood and the king commanded that these celebrated scones should grace his table. They were so appreciated that a permanent order was lodged, the equivalent of a royal warrant, and Baxter prospered. He became a burgess of the town, an employer of many people, and began to entertain ambitions well above his station.

Then one mid-morning an armed guard called at the bakehouse and summoned Baxter to the king. He was half fearful and half elated; could he expect a royal rebuke or some tangible expression of his majesty's continued satisfaction?

When he arrived at the palace he was conducted straight to the royal dining room. The king sat back from the table, his face black as thunder. A servant, knife still in hand, stood above what was unmistakably one of Baxter's large round scones, sliced through the middle.

"Is this your scone?" growled the king.

"Sire, of that there can be no doubt."

"Then it will be your beetle or cockroach in your scone," said the king, and he swung the scone round to expose a black object snug in the snow-white dough.

Baxter did not hesitate for the blink of an eye. He stepped forward, plucked out the black object with his fingers, popped it into his mouth, chewed it ostentatiously, and swallowed with relish.

"That was no beetle, sire. It was a big currant, a 'raysin of Corinth', which must have strayed into the dough by mistake. I am sorry if it has caused your majesty any distress."

He then left the chamber, and continued to prosper, as any clever and brave business man deserves.

The Chieftain

Finally, that object of such universal ignorance, ribaldry, fear and fun – the haggis.

There were several Scotch dishes, two soups and the celebrated "Haggis", which I tried last night and really liked very much. The Duchess [of Atholl] was delighted with my taking it.

Queen Victoria

Letter to Margaret Morris
19th October, 1915. Edinburgh.

Dear Gosse ... My God, let me have artists for friends – I mean people who feel, even if they're grocers, coal-heavers, anything you like except people devoid of time, colour and sound. The man I called on, on Sunday night, was discussing painting and has a real feeling for it. I mentioned Burns (of course) and he told me he was at a Golf Club dinner and a butcher who was a great admirer of Burns recited "Address to a Haggis". He put so much into it that he nearly collapsed at the end.

Being a squeamy veg, of course you'll think that most ludicrous and disgusting. I think it splendid and inspiring. The man making haggis, selling haggis and reciting the haggis address with real feeling of sympathy with Burns's understanding and sympathy, seems to me to be really getting near the real thing. I'm sorry you can't see it. Think of this disgusting person, a dealer in meat! Worse still, a dealer in tripes – that is, entrails, innards or guts. A maker of haggises, or haggi. That is, a person who stuffs intestines of animals with chopped livers, in fact the large and small stomach-bags of sheep, stuffing them with a mixture of lights, liver, heart and oatmeal, Jamaica peppers and black peppers and salt and the juice the pluck was boiled in, stirred into a consistency and stuffed into the large stomach-bag, sewn up with a needle and thread and boiled for hours and prodded from time to time with a large needle – to let out the gas and keep it from bursting. Imagine him over a cauldron of boiling haggises, watching them and prodding them with a needle, moving them about rhythmically while Burns's words run in his head and at moments of intense emotion, at the *sight* of their fullness of form and the *knowledge* of their fullness of food, of real food that nourishes both through feeling and fact – at these moments, feeling the continuity of idea that comes from having conceived created and completed the work – at these moments this frightful person will get into the fourth dimension, so to speak, and recite with the fullness of emotion derived from this comprehensive experience, marking the rhythm with the needle, and punctuating the time with prods.

J. D. Fergusson

Fair fa' your honest sonsie face,
Great chieftain o' the puddin'-race!
Aboon them a' ye tak your place,
    Painch, tripe, or thairm:
Weel are ye wordy o' a grace
    As lang's my airm.

Robert Burns

The world neither mocks nor shuns Genoese salame or mortadella from Bologna, garlicky wurst or multi-hued polony from a dozen European cuisines. Are there sausage-shoots in Cumberland when there is a full moon and the wind is in the west? Ah, sweet mysteries of Scottish life – the contents of the haggis and what we wear under the kilt. I know no-one who makes it at home today, but all Scottish butchers sell it, many of us eat and enjoy it, and that enterprising firm of Speyside purveyors can it and ship it all over the world. The following is neither recipe nor deterrent and is offered merely as inventory:

Sheep or lamb's stomach bag, oatmeal, suet, liver, stock, minced heart and lights of a sheep, onion, cayenne pepper, Jamaica pepper, salt. And, ideally, mashed potatoes and turnips on the side, *all washed down between mouthfuls with neat whisky.*

But First, the Blessing

The bursars, or students residing within the college [United College, St Andrews] and entitled to be maintained by the institution, dined together daily in the common hall. The fare was mean, consisting generally of rabbits from a warren in the neighbourhood. The bursars had often grumbled, but as a professor presided at table, none ventured openly to complain. Each bursar asked the blessing by turns. It was Fergusson's [the poet, Robert Fergusson] turn. He rose up reverently, and repeated the following:

For rabbits young and for rabbits old,
For rabbits hot and for rabbits cold,
For rabbits tender and for rabbits tough,
Our thanks we render, for we've had enough.

Rev. Charles Rogers

Grace be here, an' grace be there,
   An' grace be roon the table;
Let ilka ane tak' up their spoon
   An' eat as muckle's they're able.

Robert Burns

Some hae meat, and canna eat,
   And some wad eat that want it,
But we hae meat and we can eat,
   And sae the Lord be thankit.

Traditional

Bless the fish for Peter's sake,
   He gruppit fish himsel';
Bless the sheep for David's sake,
   He herdit sheep himsel';
Bless the soo for Satan's sake,
   He was aince a soo himsel'.

Traditional

And a Last Word

Oh Lord, who blessed the loaves and fishes,
Look doon upon these twa bit dishes,
And though the tatties be but sma',
Lord, mak them plenty for us a';
But if our bellies they do fill,
'Twill be another miracle.

Anonymous

Dear Gordon:

You know, I'm almost beginning to like what I read about the Scots. What a curiously enigmatic but stimulating mixture. Bombast and insecurity, cunning and naivete, industry and indolence, conservatism and radicalism, honesty and sophistry, romanticism and materialism – all buttressed and shored-up by those powerful piers, hypocrisy and an infinite capacity for self-delusion. Is that true and fair, or more likely, true but unfair? Surprisingly, you have untold friends all over the world, and fewer enemies than the English. Keep up the good work.

Dear Mortimer:

With President Amin for a friend, who needs enemies? You are too kind. Too damnably, patronisingly, condescendingly, typically English kind. As Hugh McIlvanney says:

"It is no accident that probably the highest art form achieved by the Scottish people is the lament."

He didn't add that the bagpipes are *never* played from a kneeling position.

The Nation's Obsession

"Never mind the ba', get on with the game."

The Fut-Ball

Scotland's obsession with the game of football was best illustrated by Bill Shankly, that glorious Sam Goldwyn of Liverpool, when he told guests at a dinner:

"I'm disturbed by your attitude to the game. Some of you seem to regard it as a matter of life and death. I can assure you, it's much more serious than that."

Shankly, who once played for a very minor Scottish team called Glenbuck Cherrypickers, is also alleged to have put his head round the door of the visitors' dressing-room after a goalless game and announced: "The better team drew."

Mirror Image

When I was in Mexico for the World Cup I thought England played very well against Brazil, but it would have been impossible for me to identify with them and support them. I think they played well enough against Brazil for me not to be actively pleased when they got beaten by Germany because so did Scotland, and one sees such levelling notions wherever one can find them. I go to watch Chelsea, for instance, and it's quite nice to see people playing football at that level, but it doesn't really involve me. Very often Scotland play infinitely worse than Chelsea, but one is totally committed to Scotland.

Football is the process which takes all those diverse elements of Scottishness which, in their real form, involve psychology and history and sociology, and it nutshells them, so when you see a Scottish football team play they play exactly like Scotsmen. They've not just got blue jerseys on, they've got all that complex inferiority/superiority thing going, they play in a certain kind of very fragile, arrogant, aesthetic way, and you realise that you're looking at your own image when you see a Scottish football team playing with all its defects and its enormous richness as well. To that extent it is very easy to identify, to commit, and there's a constant reminder, in a way a very pungent reminder, of your origins.

Alan Sharp

251

Matrons Win

In the ancient burgh of Musselburgh, on Shrove Tuesday, there used to be a standing match at football between the married and unmarried fishwomen, in which the former were always victorious. No doubt the knowledge that their victory would reflect honour on their "gudemen and bairns" would nerve the arm and impart vigour to the stroke of the Musselburgh matrons on the occasion of these animated contests.

E. J. Guthrie

Poetry is where you find it, like the man on the terracing who spoke into the tape recorder as if he were addressing the world:

Life's no' much o' a bed o' cherries, or a bowl o' roses either, if it comes to that. Eh? Oh, there's ay somethin', isn't there? Nae work. Or too much work. And at five o'clock every Saturday there's aye the wan home win, the bum banker, that bursts the bloody coupon. A' the same, Ah canna say Ah've hud a bad life. Ah'm no' complainin'. No' really. No' when ye consider the blessin's, when ye think o' the advantage, ye know, the sheer privilege, aye that's the word, the *privilege* of wakin' up every mornin', just *knowin'* that ye're a Celtic supporter.

My son and I were standing on the terraces at Tynecastle, home of Heart of Midlothian, awaiting the kick-off in an early-season game with Rangers. The pitch, after a wet summer, was in exceptional condition. A Rangers supporter in front of us fidgeted around, obviously looking for a friend. At five-to-three the friend arrived and they settled down.

"Fine-looking pitch."

"Aye, so it is."

"Quite big, too."

"Aboot the same as ours."

"Would you look at that grass, it's sae green."

"In great nick."

"Course, it's nae wunner."

"Why no'?"

"The Hearts defence shites on it every Saturday."

At Easter Road, at the other end of the town, where, I confess, my own loyalties lie, Pat Stanton is captain and loyal servant of Hibernian. He was having an off-day.

"Haw, see you Stanton," shouted one of his most unreasonable critics, "it's time ye got off the wee heavies."

I should explain that the wee heavy is a potent Scottish beer that packs the biggest punch in the smallest possible bulk.

"He doesn't drink," shouted a man at the back for whom Stanton will never put a foot wrong.

"Haw, see you Stanton," continued the original critic, not faltering in his stride, "it's time ye got *on* the wee heavies!"

Kings Lose

Each individual noble was a law unto himself, and the Scottish Kings were by no means successful in substituting archery for football and golf. Football was prohibited in 1424, 1451, 1471, and 1491; but the very repetition of the enactments is proof of their inefficiency.

T. F. Henderson

He was a braw gallant
    And he played at the ba';
And the bonnie Earl of Moray
    Was the flower amang them a'.

Traditional

About twenty of her [Mary Queen of Scots] retinue played at football before her the space of two hours, very strongly, nimbly, and skilfully, without any foul play offered.

Sir Francis Knollys

Naked Punters

You go up to Hampden and have all sorts of external wrappings torn away. You may be living in London or Los Angeles, but there you are, up there with all the punters and wanting the same thing as they want. They want to see Scotland winning and you are as powerless as they are to produce that much-desired end result.

You're in a very vulnerable naked position and you become indebted to the people on the pitch if they make this happen for you. In our lives we tend to protect ourselves from that kind of situation. It's not customary to put yourself in a position where you may lose everything. Every time I support Scotland, every time I go to watch them I put myself in that position.

At the end of the night it might be disaster – like at Hamburg when they beat us 3-2. That was bloody disaster. I was standing there greetin', and this German woman kept putting her arms round me and saying whatever they say for victory, and all I could say was that I wasn't even on her side, it was Scotland I was supporting, and I was destroyed.

Then when we played Italy that time in the World Cup, and it was the eighty-ninth minute, and all that same old Scottish story, and Baxter gave it to Billy Bremner and Billy Bremner gave it back to Baxter and Baxter gave it to Greig, and he kicked it in the bag, and the net went all that silvery way, and everybody just wept. I was kissing people I didn't know.

Alan Sharp

I wot there is nocht ane among you all
More finelie can play at the fut-ball.

Sir David Lindsay

Those who, by a long parade of "accidents", attempt to frown the
pastime down as brutal and demoralising are merely doing their
little best to make it both. And, after all, is it as now played exceptionally dangerous? Minor accidents are common enough; but so far
as loss of life is concerned, is football as perilous as hunting, shooting,
riding, yachting, bathing, or even doing nothing? Is it very much more
deadly than crossing a crowded London street? or is it anything like
so hazardous as railway travelling?

T. F. Henderson [1893]

Sans Sight, Sans Teeth

I thought the greatest moment of my life was this year [1974] on the
rain-soaked terraces of Hampden when that second goal went in and
we'd beaten the white-shirted swines.

Oh, I tell you, I was standing with my brother and he lost his
glasses, his hat, his cigarettes. I think his false teeth fell out on the
terracing, and we were scrabbling around trying to retrieve all his
gear, and men, grown men were greetin' like ... this wee fellow
next to me in a big tartan tammy, I threw him in the air. "We've done
it," I was shouting, "we've done it," and there was no way they were
going to get two goals back.

And he said, as he was sort of coming down – well, I exaggerate a
trifle, but I did chuck him up – he said: "I'm from Shepherds Bush,
mate." I said, "Well, what are you wearing that thing for?" And he
said, "It's only for protection, to get into the grounds."

I think it's the greatest game. There's nothing artificial about it.
Ever since I could walk we went to Love Street, Paisley, every
Saturday – the first team one Saturday, the ham-and-eggs the second
Saturday. In all of my life I would feel on a Saturday afternoon that
if you weren't going to a game, you were like a deviate or pervert.
Even in London – which is sometimes a poor apology but still a game
– if I'm walking about the streets on a Saturday, I look at all the
men, thinking, "there's something wrong with him".

255

If one has to rationalise it, I suppose Hampden is the one place where Scotland actually *meets*. I presume it would be the same for a rugger fan at Murrayfield. But Hampden is the one place. Scotland is all there, and there are eleven men who actually represent Scotland.

It's a bit silly, of course. The last time I lost a good leather coat, a sixty-quid coat that I got at a sale and it was going to do me for ten years. Gone! A leather coat gone, and I had to explain it to the wife.

But, you know, you throw your sixty-quid coats about when Scotland are beating the white-shirted swines.

Gordon Williams

Follow, Follow

In the good old times, the parishioners of Menzie were in the habit of assembling on the green on Sunday morning, to play at football. On these occasions, their clergyman, Mr Chalmers, who experienced great difficulty in getting his people to attend church, occasionally took part with them in the game. He thus gained their affections, and in a short time, prevailed upon them to attend him to church, and to listen to his instructions.

E. J. Guthrie [1885]

Dear Mortimer:

You were asking if porridge or Burns or Robert the Bruce or whatever had produced the *character* of the Scot, that quality you admired so much on the football fields of the world. You seem to forget that as a race we were moulded by the Calvinist credo and put in possession of the dream of perfection. What else do you expect from a people who, despite centuries of poverty, despite corrupt kings and lairds and bureaucrats, despite the abject precariousness of their lives, were taught to believe that they were the Chosen of God, the Blessed Elect, and among whom would take place the first true theocracy, the setting up of the Kingdom of Heaven on earth?

Dear Gordon:

Yes. I suppose that's what these dreadful barbarians who follow Glasgow Rangers mean when they chant WE ARE THE PEOPLE. And I suppose that's also the reason why they scale the fences and jump the moats and sweep across the playing fields of Europe like the hordes of Genghiz Khan. They may be the chosen, but isn't it a bit difficult to like them? Do they have mothers?

I

Many Are Called

An atheist is a man who has no invisible means of support.

John Buchan

A Scot is a man who keeps the Sabbath – and every other doggone thing he can lay his hands on!

American folk saying

Few Are Chosen

I shall say nothing of the terrible Scotch Sunday, beside which London's is a positive jollification. This day, consecrated to the honour of heaven, is the nearest thing to hell that I have ever seen on earth. Said a Scotchman to a French friend as they were returning from church: "Not quite so fast, or people will think we are taking a walk!"

Stendhal

The Twenty-third Pschalme

The Lord maist hie
I know will be
A shepherd to me;
I cannot lang have stress nor stand in neid;
He makes my lair
In fields maist fair,
Where without care,
Reposing at my pleasure, safely feid.
He sweetly me convoys,
Where naething me annoys,
But pleasure brings.
He brings my mynd
Fit to sic kynd,
That force, or fears of foe cannot me grieve.
He does me leid,
In perfect freid,
And for his name he never will me lieve.
Though I wald stray,
Ilk day by day,
In deidly way,
Yet will I not dispair; I fear none ill,
For why thy grace
In every place
Does me embrace,

261

Thy rod and shepherd's crook me comfort still.
In spite of foes
My table grows,
Thou balms my heid with joy;
My cup overflows.
Kyndness and grace,
Mercy and peice,
Shall follow me for all my wretched days,
And me convoy,
To endless joy,
In heaven where I sall be with thee always.

Alexander Montgomerie

The Protestant Curse

Four hundred years of bloody bigotry bitten deep into the bone. Centuries of self-righteousness and extreme unctuousness. Slavering hypocrisy and unrepenting smugness. The rape of logic and the murder of reason. Blindness, deafness, and beggared imagination . . . To think that in this age of penicillin and streptomycin there's no anti-biotic to cure such a pox of the mind.

Knox

Oor Wee Schule

Oor wee schule's a great wee schule,
It's made o' bricks an' plaster;
The only thing that's wrang wi' it's
The baldy-heided master.
He goes to the pub on Saturday,
He goes to the Kirk on Sunday,
He prays tae the Lord tae gi'e him strength
Tae murder the bairns on Monday.

Children's Street Song

Religiously Unemployed

In Edinburgh two men have just been taken up for whistling in the street on Sunday, and in Glasgow a barber has been sent to jail for having dared to shave three men on that same day! Owing to the zeal with which these pious regulations are enforced you see the populace, driven from home by sheer boredom, thronging the pavements like citizens forced from their firesides by some public calamity. Their spiritual guides forbid not merely work for gain, but anything whatsoever in the nature of amusement. In other countries on holy days, the crowds in public places are out for recreation; but in Scotland all you see is a lot of people, religiously unemployed, wandering aimlessly about the town, and going home after a long "day of rest" thanking heaven that they will be back at work again on the morrow. Relaxation has been made so painful that fatigue comes as a blessed relief.

Marquis de Custine [1822]

Keeping it Holy

This business of an early train which desecrates the Sunday is very like that of champagne on the table of a Turk – it passes under another name. This Sunday train is really a Saturday evening train. The thing works as follows. The Great Northern Railway, which traverses England and Scotland from head to foot, runs a daily express which leaves London in the evening; now if a traveller boards it in London on a Saturday evening with the intention of going to Perth and Aberdeen *via* Edinburgh, this is entirely in accordance with prevailing law and custom; even the church-mindedness of a Scot can hardly object to it. After all, it isn't the traveller's fault that the express doesn't go faster than it actually does, and consequently the Saturday has to borrow a bit of Sunday. It is only the act of making use of the train after it has actually touched Scottish soil that is frowned upon.

Theodor Fontane [1860]

Best Dirty Bits

By the age of ten I was already locally famous for my concordance to the bible's best dirty bits. It was easy to work out what they were up to in Sodom, but what did they do in Gomorrah? . . . I think I hated the sepulchral Sundays more than anything else. The silence and the stillness – it was eerie, and more than just an absence of movement and noise. These empty streets and evacuated parks. The whole world holding its breath. The totally wasted void of Sunday itself and a yawning chasm till Monday. And being scrubbed, raw and squeaky-clean, on Saturday night. Being nipped and nudged for fidgeting during the itchy sermons. And worst of all, condemned to balancing a cup of tarry tea on my granny's parlour sofa, with the black horsehair nibbling at my bare thighs like a regiment of hungry ants.

Knox

Sorrowing Sinners

Though the Scots have no absolution, they have something very like it – a superstitious reliance upon the efficacy of going to church. Many of them may be said to pass half their lives there; for they go without ceasing, and looking as sorrowful at the time as if they were going to bury not only their sins but themselves.

Edward Topham

The Soporific Saints

I learned afterwards that on Sunday in Scotland one must not sing, whistle, dance or play, but one may drink, yawn and sleep, since when I have done my best to conform to the custom of the country. Presently I asked my worthy landlady to lend me a book, and she let me have a volume of the *Lives of the Presbyterian Saints*, which were not of much use to me, as they rival our own *Lives of the Saints* in soporific quality.

To show her that I knew as well as she did that it was Sunday I asked her if there was a Catholic chapel in the town. "Catholic!" she repeated, "Catholic!" – making such a face that you would think she had seen the Devil – "Catholic!" and left my room without another word. That made me want more than ever to find out if there was really a chapel in the town, and accordingly I went out and without much trouble was directed to one, where I had the pleasure of hearing an eloquent sermon in Gaelic, of which unfortunately I didn't understand a word but "the Virgin Mary".

The Chevalier de Latocnaye

Insidious Rome

This puts me in mind of a story I was told by an English lady, wife of a certain lieutenant-colonel, who dwelt near a church in the low-country on your side Edinburgh. At first coming to the place, she received a visit from the minister's wife, who, after some time spent in ordinary discourse, invited her to come to kirk the Sunday following. To this the lady agreed and kept her word, which produced a second visit; and the minister's wife then asking her how she liked their way of worship, she answered – Very well, but she had found two great inconveniences there, viz. that she had dirtied her clothes, and had been pestered with a great number of fleas. "Now", says the lady, "if your husband will give me leave to line the pew, and will let my servant clean it against every Sunday, I shall go constantly to church."

"Line the pew!" says the minister's wife; "troth, madam, I cannot promise for that, for my husband will think it *rank papery*."

Edward Burt

Yin o' Yon

In Scotland, it's funny, isn't it, you're either a *staunch* Protestant or a *devout* Catholic! I wonder why you're never a *devout* Protestant or a *staunch* Catholic . . . ?

Billy Connelly

265

Decent by Turn

M. C. Nodier and his friends, said the consul, arrived here one Sunday morning. They had the misfortune to lose almost all their hats on the way; they had only one remaining among four. The observation of the Sabbath is so strict in Edinburgh that they could not get any hatter to open shop till late in the day; and in order to lose no time, each of the party in his turn wore the preserved hat, and took a solitary walk through the town!

Amedée Pichot [1822]

Ring Out, Wild Bells

... that surprising clamour of church bells that suddenly breaks out upon the Sabbath morning, from Trinity and the sea-skirts to Morning-side on the borders of the hills. I have heard the chimes of Oxford playing their symphony in a golden autumn morning, and beautiful it was to hear. But in Edinburgh all manner of loud bells join, or rather disjoin, in one swelling, brutal babblement of noise ... Indeed, there are not many uproars in this world more dismal than that of the Sabbath bells in Edinburgh.

Robert Louis Stevenson

Walking to Church

They hardly ever wear shoes ... but on Sunday; and then, being unused to them, when they go to church they walk very awkwardly; or, as we say, like a cat shod with walnut-shells.

Edward Burt

Highland Service in 1809

The minister gave out the psalm; he put a very small dirty volume up to one eye, for he was near sighted, and read as many lines of the old version of the rhythmical paraphrase (we may call it) of the Psalms of David as he thought fit, drawling them out in a sort of sing-song. He stooped over the pulpit to hand his little book to the precentor, who then rose and calling out aloud the tune – "St George's tune", "Auld Aberdeen", "Hondred an' fifteen", etc. – began himself a recitative of the first line on the key-note, then taken up and repeated by the congregation; line by line, he continued in the same fashion, thus doubling the length of the *exercise*, for really to some it was no play – serious severe screaming quite beyond the natural pitch of the voice, a wandering search after the air by many who never caught it, a flourish of difficult execution and plenty of the *tremolo* lately come into fashion. The dogs seized this occasion to bark (for they always came to the kirk with the family), and the babies to cry. When the minister could bear the din no longer he popped up again, again leaned over, touched the precentor's head, and instantly all sound ceased. The long prayer began, everybody stood up while the minister asked for such blessings as he thought best ... The prayer over, the sermon began; that was my time for making observations ... Few save our own people sat around; old grey-haired tough-visaged men that had known my grandfather and great-grandfather, black, red, and fair hair, belonging to such as were in the prime of life, younger men, lads, boys – all in the tartan. The plaid as a wrap, the plaid as a drapery, with kilt to match on some, blue trews on others, blue jackets on all. The women were plaided too, an outside shawl was seen on one, though the wives wore a large handkerchief under the plaid, and looked picturesquely matronly in their very high white caps ... The wives were all in homespun, home-dyed, linsey-woolsey gowns, covered to the chin by the modest kerchief worn outside the gown. The girls who could afford it had a Sabbath day's gown of like manufacture and very bright colour, but the throat was more exposed, and generally ornamented with a string of beads, often amber; some had to be content with the best blue flannel petticoat and a clean white jacket, their ordinary and most becoming dress, and few of these had either shoes or stockings; but they all wore the plaid, and they folded it round them very gracefully. They had a custom in the spring of washing their beautiful hair with a decoction of the young buds of the birch trees. I do not know if it improved or hurt the hair, but it agreeably scented the kirk, which at other times was wont to be overpowered by the combined odours of snuff and peat reek, for the men snuffed immensely during the delivery of the English sermon; they fed their noses with quills fastened by string to the lids of their mulls, spooning up the snuff in quantities and without waste. The old women snuffed too, and groaned a great deal, to express their mental sufferings, their grief for all the backsliding supposed to be thundered at from the pulpit; lapses from faith was their grand self-accusation, lapses from virtue were, alas! little commented on; temperance and chastity were not in the Highland code of morality ... There was no very deep religious feeling in the Highlands up to this time. The clergy were reverenced in their capacity of pastors without this respect extending to their persons unless fully merited by propriety of conduct. The established form of faith was determinately adhered to, but the *kittle questions*, which had so vexed the Puritanic south, had not yet troubled the minds of their northern neighbours. Our mountains were full of fairy legends, old clan tales, forebodings, prophecies, and other superstitions, quite as much believed in as the Bible. The Shorter Catechism and the fairy stories were mixed up together to form the innermost faith of the Highlander, a much gayer and less metaphysical character than his Saxon-tainted countryman.

Elizabeth Grant

The seats [in Glasgow Cathedral] are so closely packed that any person who could remain there during time of service must have an invincible nose. I doubt even whether any incense could overcome so strong and concentrated an odour of humanity.

Robert Southey [1819]

Good Example

Were I asked what there was in my father's teaching and training that did us all so much good, I would say, both in regard to him and my beloved mother, that it was love and truth. They were both so real and human. No *cranks, twists, crotchets, isms,* or systems of any kind, but loving, sympathising; giving a genuine *blowing up* when it was needed, but passing by trifles, failures, infirmities, without making a fuss. The liberty they gave was as wise as the restraint they imposed. Their home was happy, intensely happy. Christianity was a thing taken for granted, and not enforced with scowl and frown. I never heard my father speak of Calvinism, Arminianism, Presbyterianism, or Episcopacy, or exaggerate doctrinal differences, in my life. I had to study all these questions after I left home.

Dr Norman Macleod

Following Ahint

Tradition tells of an old minister . . . not of the brightest parts it may be supposed, who, in discoursing from some text in which the word "follow" occurred, informed his audience that he would speak of four different kinds of followers: "First," said he, "my friends, there are followers ahint; secondly, there are followers afore; thirdly, there are followers cheekie for chow, and sidie by sidie; and last o' a', there are followers that stand stane-still."

John Jamieson

I'll tell you a sermon that was preached by a Presbyterian minister in Kirkintilloch about a hundred years ago. He must have been having some trouble with the fornicators. He said: "The birds of the air hae their season, the fishes in the sea hae their season, the beasts of the field hae their season, but the lasses o' Kirkintilloch are *aye* in season."

Bruce Marshall

The reward of dancers is to drink in hell.

John Knox

To the Tune "Crimond"

I wish I were a brewer's horse
Three quarters of the year;
I'd turn my head where tail should be
And drink up all the beer.

Traditional Precentor Rhyme

The Meenister

Grangemouth was my idea of hell. It lay across the water from the village where I was born, and the flames from the refinery, long tongues of purple and orange, licked the whole sky alight at night. I used to think that Mr McPherson, the minister, conjured the fire to punish us when we told lies and stole the new jam. When we saw him in the streets, or when he came to the school and drew the Sea of Galilee on the blackboard, he was pink and fluffy, like a Disney dwarf who smelled of camphor and peppermint . . . He was soft and gentle and kind of easy, like a good uncle. But on Sundays, especially winter days, when we huddled together in the pews to keep warm and it was as dark as inside the whale's belly, Mr McPherson spoke about the woman astride the scarlet beast with seven heads and ten horns. And about eating the flesh of horses and captains and mighty men. And the filthiness and abominations of desolation. And fornication and fornication and fornication, and the wrath of so many murdering angels. And nakedness and shame. You could feel the sulphur and brimstone lapping and bubbling round your ankles and the fumes of it catching at your throat. And if you had the courage to open your eyes and look up at Mr McPherson the cuddly wee man had changed into a big black devil ten feet tall, red in the eye, and spitting fire, his tufty hair sticking up behind his ears like horns, and his Geneva bands forking the air like the tongue of the serpent.

Knox

Fartality

Mr Robert Blair, that famous Presbyterian preacher at St Andrews, was very much thought of for his familiar way of preaching. He preached often against the observation of Christmas, and once in this Scotch jingle, "You will say, Sirs, 'Good old Youle-day'. You will say, 'It is a brave Haly-day'; I tell you, It is a brave Belly-day. You will say, 'These are bonny formalities'; but I tell you, they are bonny fartalities."

Anonymous: *The Scotch
Presbyterian Eloquence*

Unanswered Prayer

There was aince an auld body o' Sydney
Wha suffered from pains in the kidney.
  He prayed to the Lord
  That he might be restored,
And He promised He would – but He didnae!

Anonymous

Special Pleading

The sermons were by no means bad, though from constant repetition they grew tiresome . . . A violent Tory, detesting the House of Hanover, yet compelled to pray for the reigning family, he cut the business as short as possible – "God bless the King, and all the Royal Family; as Thou hast made them great make them GOOD", with great emphasis, and then he hurried on to more agreeable petitions.

Elizabeth Grant

Up the Creek

O melancholy Brothers, dark, dark, dark!
O battling in black floods without an ark!

James Thomson

The Exorcist

There was in the countrie of Mar a young gentlewoman of excellent beautie, and daughter unto a nobleman there, refusing sundrie wealthie marriages offered to her by her father, and other friends. At length she prooved with child, and being rigorouslie compelled by her parents to tell who was the father, she confessed that a certain young man used nightly to come unto her, and kept her companie, and sometimes in the day also, but how or from whence he came, or by what meanes he went awaie, she was not able to declare. Her parents, not greatlie crediting her words, laid diligent watch, to understand what he was that had defiled their house; and within three days after, upon signification given by one of their maidens, that the fornicator was at that very instant with their daughter, incontinentlie thereupon, making fast the doors, they enter the chamber with a great manie of torches and lights, where they find in their daughter's armes a foul monstrous thing, verie horrible to behold. Here a number coming hastilie in, to behold this evil favoured sight, amongst others, there was a priest of verie honest life, not ignorant (as was thought) in knowledge of holie scripture. This priest (all other being afraid), and some of them running their waies, began to recite the beginning of St John's Gospell, and coming to these words, *Verbum caro factum est*, suddenlie the wicked spirit, making a very sore and terrible roaring noise, flue his waies, taking the roofe of the chamber away with him, the hangings and coverings of the bed being also burnt therewith. The gentlewoman was yet preserved, and within three or four daies after was delivered of such a mishapen thing, as the like before had not beene seene, which the midwives and women, such as were present at her labour, to avoid the dishonour of her house, immediately burnt in a great fire, made in the chamber for the same intent.

Raphael Holinshed [1577]

A Bible Story

> And Jacob made for his wee Josie,
> A tartan coat to keep him cosie;
> And what for no? – there was nae harm
> To keep the lad baith saft and warm.

Samuel Colvill

The Father's Gift

One Mr John Hepburn, lecturing on the second psalm, told "That there was a dialogue betwixt the Father and the Son in heaven. The Son said, Father, will you give me my portion now? Your portion, Son, says the Father, indeed shall you; thou hast been a dutiful son to me, thou never angered me in thy days; what portion will you have, Son? Will you give me poor Scotland, saith the Son? Scotland, said the Father, truly thou shall get poor Scotland, and he proved that it was Scotland he sought, from ver. 8. I shall give thee the outmost part of the earth for a possession. Now, Sirs, Scotland is the outmost part of the earth, and therefore it was given to the Son for a patrimony."

Robert Calder

The Readers

Perhaps the prejudice against read sermons lingered longer in Scotland than in any other district. Until very recently [1880] the use of any manuscript would have been fatal to the cordial acceptance of any candidate.

"He's a grand preacher," whispered an old spinster to her sister on hearing a young minister for the first time. "Whist! Bell," was the reply; "he's readin'" "Readin', is he?" said the eulogist, changing her tone; "paltry fellow; we'll gang hame, Jenny, and read our Book." In 1762 Dr Blacklock, the well-known poet, was presented by the Earl of Selkirk to the living of Kirkcudbright. He was afflicted by the loss of sight, but when he was preaching one of his trial discourses, an old woman who sat on the pulpit stairs inquired of a neighbour whether he was a reader. "He canna be a reader," said the old wife, "for he's blin'." "I'm glad to hear it." said the ancient neighbour; "I wish they were all blin'!"

Paxton Hood

Warm Welcome

If in the remote depths of a French province a traveller were to halt at a country clergyman's house he would find, I suppose, a human being, but no more. Here I was received as an honoured guest. My host talked to me on all sorts of topics with the courtesy and address of a man of the world, and in addition gave me some valuable information about my itinerary even to the most distant parts.

The Chevalier de Latocnaye

Jacob, Good or Bad?

He now called up the Bible class, and Malcolm sat beside and listened. That morning they had read one of the chapters in the history of Jacob.

"Was Jacob a good man?" he asked as soon as the reading, each of the scholars in turn taking a verse, was over. An apparently universal expression of assent followed; halting in its wake, however, came the voice of a boy near the bottom of the class: "Wasna he some double, sir?" "You are right, Sheltie," said the master; "he *was* double. I must, I find, put the question in another shape: was Jacob a bad man?"

Again came such a burst of "yeses" that it might have been taken for a general hiss. But limping in the rear came again the half dissentient voice of Sheltie: "Pairtly, sir."

"You think then, Sheltie, that a man may be both bad and good?"

"I dinna ken, sir; I think he may be whiles ane and whiles the other, and whiles maybe it wad be ill to say which. Our colly's whiles in twa minds whether he'll do what he's telled or no."

"That's the battle of Armageddon, Sheltie, my man. It's aye raging, as gun roared or bayonet clashed. Ye maun up and do your best in't, my man. Gien ye die fechting like a man, ye'll flee up with a quiet face and wide open een; and there's a great One that will say to ye, 'Weel done, laddie!' But gien ye gie in to the enemy, he'll turn ye into a creeping thing that eats dirt; and there'll no be a hole in a' the crystal wa' of the New Jerusalem near enough to let ye creep through."

"I reckon, sir," said Sheltie, "Jacob hadna foughten out his battle."

"That's just it, my boy. And because he would not get up and fight manfully, God had to take him in hand. Ye've heard tell of generals,

274

when their troops were rinnin' awa', having to cut this man down, shoot that ane, and lick another, till he turned them a' right face about, and drave them on to the foe like a spate. And the trouble God took wi' Jacob was not lost upon him at last."

"An' what came o' Esau, sir?" asked a pale-faced maiden with blue eyes. "He wasna an ill kind o' a chield, was he, sir?"

"No, Mappy," answered the master; "he was a fine chield as you say, but he needed mair time and gentler treatment to make onything o' him. Ye see he had a guid heart, but was a duller kind o' creature a'thigether, and cared for naething he couldna see or handle. He never thought muckle about God at a'. Jacob was another sort – a poet kind o' man, but a sneck-drawing creature for a' that. It was easier, however, to get the slyness out o' Jacob than the dullness out o' Esau. Punishment telled upon Jacob like upon a thin-skinned horse, whereas Esau was mair like the minister's powny, that can hardly be made to understand that ye want him to gang on."

George MacDonald

Parish Visits

A poor old deaf man resided in Fife; he was visited by his minister shortly after coming to his pulpit. The minister said he would often call and see him; but time went on, and he did not visit him again until two years after, when, happening to go through the street where the deaf man was living, he saw his wife at the door, and could therefore do no other than inquire for her husband. "Weel, Margaret, how is Tammas?" "None the better o' you," was the rather curt reply. "How! how! Margaret?" inquired the minister. "Oh, ye promised twa year syne to ca' and pray once a fortnight wi' him, and ye hae ne'er darkened the door sin' syne." "Weel, weel, Margaret, don't be so short; I thought it was not so very necessary to call and pray with Tammas, for he is so deaf ye ken he canna hear me." "But, sir," said the woman with a rising dignity of manner, "the Lord's no deaf!" And it is to be supposed the minister felt the power of her reproof.

Paxton Hood

Here and There

I've got only one big grumble about Scotland. Why are the places so far apart

Aidan Smith

Edinburgh

Throned on crags, Edinburgh takes every eye; and not content with supremacy in beauty, she claims an intellectual supremacy also. She is a patrician amongst British cities, "A penniless lass wi' a lang pedigree." She has wit if she lacks wealth: she counts great men against millionaires. The success of the actor is insecure until thereunto Edinburgh has set her seal. The poet trembles before the Edinburgh critics. The singer respects the delicacy of the Edinburgh ear. Coarse London may roar with applause: fastidious Edinburgh sniffs disdain, and sneers reputations away. London is the stomach of the empire – Edinburgh the quick, subtle, far-darting brain.

Alexander Smith

The Elastic Street

I was about in the afternoon with Baxter; and we had a good deal of fun, first rhyming on the names of all the shops we passed, and afterwards buying needles and quack drugs from open-air vendors, and taking much pleasure in their inexhaustible eloquence. Every now and then as we went, Arthur's Seat showed its head at the end of a street. Now, today the blue sky and the sunshine were both entirely wintry; and there was about the hill, in these glimpses, a sort of thin, unreal, crystalline distinctness that I have not often seen excelled. As the sun began to go down over the valley between the new town and the old, the evening grew resplendent; all the gardens and low-lying buildings sank back and became almost invisible in a mist of wonderful sun, and the Castle stood up against the sky, as thin and sharp in outline as a castle cut out of paper. Baxter made a good remark about Princes Street, that it was the most elastic street for length that he knew; sometimes it looks, as it looked tonight, interminable, a way leading right into the heart of the red sundown; sometimes again, it shrinks together, as if for warmth, on one of the withering, clear east-windy days, until it seems to lie underneath your feet.

Robert Louis Stevenson

Like Being in Love

The Castle looks down upon the City as if out of another world; stern with all its peacefulness, its garniture of trees, its slopes of grass ... From George Street, which crowns the ridge, the eye is led down sweeping streets of stately architecture to the villas and woods that fill the lower ground, and fringe the shore; to the bright azure belt of the Forth with its smoking steamer or its creeping sail; beyond, to the shores of Fife, soft blue, and flecked with fleeting shadows in the keen clear light of spring, dark purple in the summer heat, tarnished gold in the autumn haze; and farther away still, just distinguishable on the paler sky, the crest of some distant peak, carrying the imagination into the illimitable world. Residence in Edinburgh is an education in itself. Its beauty refines one like being in love. It is perennial, like a play of Shakespeare's. Nothing can stale its infinite variety.

Alexander Smith

Purgatorio . . .

Edinburgh pays cruelly for her high seat in one of the vilest climates under heaven. She is liable to be beaten upon by all the winds that blow, to be drenched with rain, to be buried in cold sea fogs out of the east, and powdered with the snow as it comes flying southward from the Highland hills. The weather is raw and boisterous in winter, shifty and ungenial in summer, and a downright meteorological purgatory in the spring. The delicate die early, and I, as a survivor, among bleak winds and plumping rain, have been sometimes tempted to envy them their fate. For all who love shelter and the blessings of the sun, who hate dark weather and perpetual tilting against squalls, there could scarcely be found a more unhomely and harassing place of residence.

Robert Louis Stevenson

... E Paradiso

The chief scene where these winds exert their influence, is the New Bridge [the North Bridge], which, by being thrown over a long valley that is open at both ends, and particularly from being ballustraded on each side, admits the wind in the most charming manner imaginable; and you receive it with the same force you would do, were it conveyed to you through a pair of bellows. It is far from unentertaining for a man to pass over this bridge on a tempestuous day. In walking over it this morning I had the pleasure of adjusting a lady's petticoats which had blown almost entirely over her head, and which prevented her disengaging herself from the situation she was in: but in charity to her distresses, I concealed her charms from public view. One poor gentleman, who was rather too much engaged with the novelty of the objects before him, unfortunately forgot his own hat and wig, which were lifted up by an unpremeditated puff, and carried entirely away.

Edward Topham

Haughty Junos

The ladies of Edinburgh possess a more graceful deportment than those of London; they are at once slenderer and more fragile. Up to the present time I have found among them fewer laughing Hebes than haughty Junos and stately-walking Dianas ... To grace of figure the young ladies of Edinburgh add, for the most part, the charm of some agreeable talents. There are few of them who are not musicians, and who are deficient in extraordinary skill in the labours of the needle; there are few of them also unacquainted with French.

Amedée Pichot [1822]

To Mrs Sitwell . . .

. . . Last night it blew a fearful gale; I was kept awake about a couple of hours, and could not get to sleep for the horror of the wind's noise; the whole house shook; and, mind you, our house *is* a house, a great castle of jointed stone that would weigh up a street of English houses; so that when it quakes, as it did last night, it means something. But the quaking was not what put me about; it was the horrible howl of the wind round the corner; the audible haunting of an incarnate anger about the house; the evil spirit that was abroad; and, above all, the shuddering silent pauses when the storm's heart stands dreadfully still for a moment. O how I hate a storm at night! They have been a great influence in my life, I am sure; for I can remember them so far back – long before I was six at least, for we left the house in which I remember listening to them times without number when I was six. And in those days the storm had for me a perfect impersonation, as durable and unvarying as any heathen deity. I always heard it, as a horseman riding past with his cloak about his head, and somehow always carried away, and riding past again, and being baffled once more, *ad infinitum*, all night long. I think I wanted him to get past, but I am not sure; I know only that I had some interest either for or against in the matter; and I used to lie and hold my breath, not quite frightened, but in a state of miserable exaltation . . .

Robert Louis Stevenson

Flowers of Edinburgh

Being a stranger, I was invited to sup at a tavern. The cook was too filthy an object to be described; only another English gentleman whispered me and said, he believed, if the fellow was to be thrown against the wall, he would stick to it.

Twisting round and round his hand a greasy towel, he stood waiting to know what we would have for supper, and mentioned several things himself; among the rest, a *duke*, a *fool*, or a *meer-fool*. This was nearly according to his pronounciation; but he meant a duck, a fowl, or a moor-fowl, or grouse.

We supped very plentifully, and drank good French claret, and were very merry till the clock struck ten, the hour when everybody is at

280

liberty, by bent of the city drum, to throw their filth out at the windows. Then the company began to light pieces of paper, and throw them upon the table to smoke the room, and, as I thought, to mix one bad smell with another.

Being in my retreat to pass through a long narrow *wynde* or alley, to go to my new lodgings, a guide was assigned to me, who went before me to prevent my disgrace, crying out all the way, with a loud voice, "Hud your haunde". The throwing up of a sash, or otherwise opening a window, made me tremble, while behind and before me, at some little distance, fell the terrible shower.

Well, I escaped all the danger, and arrived, not only safe and sound, but sweet and clean, at my new quarters; but when I was in bed I was forced to hide my head between the sheets; for the smell of the filth, thrown out by the neighbours on the back side of the house, came pouring into the room to such a degree I was almost poisoned with the stench.

Edward Burt

Videlicet, S.N.P.

York was, London is, but Edinburgh shall be
The greatest o' the three.

Thomas the Rhymer
(13th century)

The Winter Loch

Duddingston, our big loch, is bearing; and I wish you could have seen it this afternoon, covered with people, in thin driving snow flurries, the big hill grim and white and alpine overhead in the thick air, and the road up the gorge, as it were into the heart of it, dotted black with traffic. Moreover, I *can* skate a little bit; and what one can do is always pleasant to do . . . If you had seen the moon rising, a perfect sphere of smoky gold, in the dark air above the trees, and the white loch thick with skates, and the great hill, snow-sprinkled, overhead! It was a sight for a king . . . The little booths that hucksters set up round the edge were marked each one by its little lamp. There were some fires too; and the light, and the shadows of the people who stood round them to warm themselves, made a strange pattern all round on the snow-covered ice. A few people with lit torches began to travel up and down the ice, a lit circle travelling along with them over the snow . . . The walk home was very solemn and strange. Once, through a broken gorge, we had a glimpse of a little space of mackerel sky, moon-litten, on the other side of the hill; the broken ridges standing grey and spectral between; and the hilltop over all, snow-white, and strangely magnified in size.

Robert Louis Stevenson

Tak' Heed!

These sentences have, I hear, given offence in my native town, and a proportionable pleasure to our rivals of Glasgow. I confess the news caused me both pain and merriment . . . To the Glasgow people I would say only one word, but that is of gold: *I have not yet written a book about Glasgow.*

Robert Louis Stevenson

A Border Burn

Oh, Tam! Gie me a Border burn
That canna rin without a turn,
And wi' its bonnie babble fills
The glens among oor native hills . . .
Ay, penter lad, thraw to the wund
Your canvas, this is holy grund;
Wi' a' its higher airt acheevin',
That picter's deid, and this leevin'!

J. B. Selkirk

282

Scott Country

We had a day's journey before us along the banks of the Tweed, a name which has been sweet to my ears almost as far back as I can remember anything. After the first mile or two our road was seldom far from the river, which flowed in gentleness, though perhaps never silent; the hills on either side high and sometimes stony, but excellent pasturage for sheep. In some parts the vale was wholly of this pastoral character, in others we saw extensive tracts of corn ground, even spreading along whole hill-sides, and without visible fences, which is dreary in a flat

country; but there is no dreariness on the banks of the Tweed, – the hills, whether smooth or stony, uncultivated or covered with ripe corn, had the same pensive softness. Near the corn tracts were large farm-houses, with many corn-stacks; the stacks and house and outhouses together, I recollect, in one or two places upon the hills, at a little distance, seemed almost as large as a small village or hamlet. It was a clear autumnal day, without wind, and being Sunday the business of the harvest was suspended; and all that we saw and felt and heard combined to excite one sensation of pensive and still pleasure.

Dorothy Wordsworth

Valley of Yarrow

I repeatedly walked through that country up to Edinburgh and down by myself in subsequent years, and nowhere remember such affectionate, sad, and thoughtful, and in fact, interesting and salutary journeys. I

283

have had days clear as Italy ... days moist and dripping, overhung with the infinite of silent grey – and perhaps the latter were the preferable in certain moods. You had the world and its waste imbroglios of joy and woe, of light and darkness, to yourself alone. You could strip barefoot if it suited better, carry shoes and socks over shoulder, hung on your stick; clean shirt and comb were in your pocket; *omnia mea mecum porto.* You lodged with shepherds who had clean solid cottages; wholesome eggs, milk, oatmeal, porridge, clean blankets to their beds, and a great deal of human sense and unadulterated natural politeness. Canty, shrewd, and witty fellows, when you set them talking; knew from their hill tops every bit of country between Forth and Solway, and all the shepherd inhabitants within fifty miles, being a kind of confraternity of shepherds from father to son. No sort of peasant labourers I have ever come across seemed to me so happily situated, morally and physically well-developed, and deserving to be happy, as those shepherds of the Cheviots. *O fortunatos nimium!* But perhaps it is all altered not a little now, as I sure enough am who speak of it!

Thomas Carlyle

A Proclamation

Hoys, Yes! That's ae time! Hoys, Yes! That's Twae times! Hoys, Yes! That's the third and last time!

This is tae gi'e notice!

That there's a muckle Fair to be hadden in the Muckle Toon o' the Langholm, on the 15th day of July, auld style, upon His Grace the Duke o' Buccleuch's Merk Land, for the space o' eight days and upwards; and a' land-loupers, and dub-scoupers, and gae-by-the-gate swingers, that come here tae breed hurdums or durdums, huliments or buliments, hagglements or bragglements, or tae molest this public Fair, they shall be ta'en by order o' the Bailie an' the Toon Cooncil, and their lugs shall be nailed tae the Tron wi' a twal-penny nail; and they shall sit doon on their bare knees and pray seeven times for the King, thrice for the Muckle Laird o' Ralton, and pay a groat tae mee, Jamie Ferguson, Bailie o' the aforesaid Manor, and Aw'll away hame an' hae a barley banna' an' a saut herrin' tae my denner by way o' auld style.

Huzza! Huzza! Huzza!

Traditional: Langholm Common Riding

Glasgow

City! I am true son of thine;
Ne'er dwelt I where great mornings shine
   Among the bleating pens;
Ne'er by the rivulets I strayed,
And ne'er upon my childhood weighed
   The silence of the glens.
Instead of shores where ocean beats,
I hear the ebb and flow of streets.

Black labour draws his weary waves
Into their secret moaning caves;
   But with the morning light
That sea again will overflow
With a long, weary sound of woe,
   Again to faint in night.
Wave am I in that sea of woes,
Which, night and morning, ebbs and flows.

Draw thy fierce streams of blinding ore,
Smite on thy thousand anvils, roar
   Down to the harbour bars;
Smoulder in smoky sunsets, flare
On rainy nights, when street and square
   Lie empty to the stars.
From terrace proud to alley base
I know thee as my mother's face.

Alexander Smith

The Pretty Town

Glasgow is, to outward appearances, the prettiest and most uniform town that I ever saw, and I believe there is nothing like it in Britain. It has a spacious *carrifour*, where stands the cross, and going round it, you have, by turns, the view of four streets, that in regular angles proceed from thence.

Edward Burt

285

Perfect Bee-Hive

I am so far happy as to have seen Glasgow, which to the best of my recollection and judgment, is one of the prettiest towns in Europe; and, without all doubt, it is one of the most flourishing in Great Britain. In short, it is a perfect bee-hive in point of industry. It stands partly on a gentle declivity; but the greatest part of it is in a plain, watered by the river Clyde. The streets are straight, open, airy, and well paved; and the houses lofty and well built of hewn stone . . . Our landlord showed us everything, and introduced us to all the world at Glasgow, where, through his recommendation, we were complimented with the freedom of the town. Considering the trade and opulence of this place, it cannot but abound with gaiety and diversions. Here is a great number of young fellows that rival the youth of the capital in spirit and expense; and I was soon convinced, that all the female beauties of Scotland were not assembled at the hunter's ball in Edinburgh. The town of Glasgow flourishes in learning as well as in commerce. Here is a university, with professors in all the different branches of science, liberally endowed and judiciously chosen.

Tobias Smollett [1771]

Still Flourishing?

Nowhere else in Europe can one witness the destruction of a town environment through such an orgy of philistine barbarity, which only mirrors the fact that nowhere else in Europe can one find the equivalent of Glasgow's decadent and corrupt political situation which is the fundamental cause of the tragedy.

The magnificence of much of the Glasgow townscape was created by commercial and industrial interests who were no less out for profits than the "developers" of today, but at least they insisted on certain accepted standards of quality in the buildings they erected, and they did employ native architects and builders trained in the relatively homogeneous Scottish tradition.

Even allowing for the fact that a large number of the creators of the new Glasgow are this time based in the South of England, what sort of an architect is it who designs a building which bears no relation whatever to its surroundings in scale, design and visible materials? Above all, what sort of a planning authority is it whose members are so deficient in good taste and basic cultural education as to permit him to do so? Or am I mistaking the function of such an authority? . . .

Having stayed and travelled in a dozen or so continental countries, I have no hesitation in stating that the industrial revolution, together with a more recent rootless materialism, and the increasing lack of any sort of moral faith, have created more havoc in Scotland than all the destruction of two world wars in Central Europe . . .

Material prosperity is necessary, but it is no substitute for moral values, and all the oil in the Scottish seas will avail us nothing if the way of life it produces is not worth living.

Dr. James Wilkie
(Vienna, 1975)

Fashionable Dead

James Hodge, who lives in the first close above the Cross, on the west side of the High Street, continues to sell burying crapes, ready made; and his wife's niece, who lives with him, dresses dead corpses at as cheap a rate as was formerly done by her aunt, having been educated by her and perfected at Edinburgh, from whence she has lately arrived, and has brought with her the newest and latest fashions.

Glasgow Advertisement, 1747

Get Well Soon

As he lay in hospital recuperating after severe surgery a Provost of Glasgow is said to have received a message from the City Chambers, saying: "At it's meeting today the entire Corporation wished you a speedy recovery by a vote of 62 to 47."

The Bydand Myths

The Banker's Pittance

Robin Carrick was one of the earliest bankers of Glasgow; he came to Glasgow a poor boy; he became the chief and leading partner of the old Ship Bank; he lived and he died a grim, penurious old bachelor, and left not a penny to any benevolent institution in the city in which all his wealth had been accumulated; but, on one occasion, the old miser was waited on by a respectable deputation of three fellow-citizens, for a subscription to the Royal Infirmary, then in its infancy; he was requested to head the subscription, and, to their mortification and surprise, he would only put down his name for two guineas; and when they earnestly besought him to increase his miserable pittance, he talked even of drawing it back. He told them he could not really even afford that sum, bowed them out of the room, encased with hoards of money, represented by bills and other documents.

The deputation then proceeded to Mr M'Ilquham, one of the great early manufacturers of Glasgow, to ask his help. He looked down the list of subscribers, but exclaimed, "Bless me, what's this? Banker Carrick only *two guineas*!" They told the manufacturer that the banker had said he really could not afford any more. "What's that you say? Jamie" – to his faithful cash-keeper and confidant, James Davidson – "Jamie, bring me the bank-book, and a cheque, and the ink-bottle, and a pen," and he wrote a cheque on the Ship Bank for £10,000. Some reports give a much larger sum; no matter, it was large. "Now, Jamie, run down as fast as your legs will carry you to the bank and bring that money to me."

The cheque was presented. Old Robin stared. "Go back," said he, "there's some mistake." And presently he came running into M'Ilquham's counting-house in a high state of fever. "What's wrong wi' ye the day?" said the banker. "Nothing in the least degree wrong. I only suspect there's surely something very far wrong with yourself and the bank; for my friends, these douce gentlemen sitting there yonder, have assured me that, in your own premises, and out of your own mouth, you declared you could only *afford* them scrimp two guineas for the purpose; and, if that is the case, I think it is high time I remove some of my deposits out of your hands."

With some reluctance Robin had to put down his name for fifty guineas before Mr M'Ilquham would cancel his cheque for £10,000.

Paxton Hood

Kiss'd Yestreen

Kiss'd yestreen, and kiss'd yestreen,
Up the Gallowgate, doun the Green:
I've woo'd wi' lords, and woo'd wi' lairds,
I've mool'd wi' carles and mell'd wi cairds,
I've kiss'd wi' priests – 'twas done i' the dark,
Twice in my goun and thrice in my sark;
But priest, nor Lord, nor loon can gie
Sic kindly kisses as he gave me.

Anonymous

Liberated Lady

Brown, Mrs, was an extensive and well-known dealer in cotton and cotton yarn. Her history is interesting. On the death of her husband, a respectable shoemaker, she consulted David Dale, Esq., whether to continue the business or sell off. He recommended her to wind up; but as there remained a large stock of leather on hand, and of boots and shoes, Mr Dale suggested that she should work up the leather into shoes, and then export these to America on adventure. She was afraid of the risk, but Mr Dale kindly said, if she liked, he would "run halves". This was agreed to, and the whole stock of leather converted into shoes, and consigned to an American house. Mr Dale further advised that the proceeds should be remitted home in cotton. When this cotton arrived Mary again applied to Mr Dale for advice about its disposal. He recommended a cotton broker; but this thrifty woman replied, "Na, na; I'll sell it mysel' and save the commission." Accordingly, with a stout leather purse at her side filled with samples, she went through the cotton purchasers, and sold her stock to such advantage that she immediately commenced the business of a cotton broker, and soon became the first in the line. She passed more value through her hands than perhaps any woman in Scotland. But like many other speculators *at first*, she got into difficulties and was sequestrated in 1794. Mary did not care a pin for the society of women, but delighted to meet with merchants who could talk to her about the long and short pile of cotton, of Pernams, Surats, Surinams, Brazils, Georgias, &c., eschewing all conversations of her sex about flounces, tucks, bowknots, and trimmings.

Notes to *Jones's Directory*

K

A Glasgow Deal

O the bonnie wee barra's mine,
It disnae belong to O'Hara;
The fly wee bloke,
He stuck tae my rock,
Sae I'm gonna stick tae his barra!

Traditional Street Song

Blackballed

A well-known and very able practitioner, but not less remarkable for a capricious and troublesome temper, sought admission into the Medical Club of Glasgow. By the laws of the club one black ball was sufficient for exclusion; the gentleman who had proposed his professional brother fearing, perhaps, that the fervour of his eloquence might permit this anti-social element to slip in, and thereby injure the harmony of the fraternity, resolved to sacrifice friendship at the shrine of duty, and, as the ballot-box came round, he slipped in a black ball. But what was the surprise of all present when, on opening the repository of the silent voices of the club, it was found they were *all* of the same colour, and all *black*!

Paxton Hood

Burns Country

Travelled through the vale of Nith, here little like a vale, it is so broad, with irregular hills rising up on each side . . . There is a great deal of arable land; the corn ripe; trees here and there – plantations, clumps, coppices, and a newness in everything. So much of the gorse and broom rooted out that you wonder why it is not all gone, and yet there seems to be almost as much gorse and broom as corn; and they grow one among another you know not how. Crossed the Nith; the vale becomes narrow, and very pleasant; cornfields, green hills, clay cottages, the river's bed rocky, with woody banks. Left the Nith about a mile and a half, and reached Brownhill, a lonely inn, where we slept. The view from the windows was pleasing . . . It is an open country – open yet all over hills. At a little distance were many cottages among trees, that looked very pretty. Brownhill is about seven or eight miles from Ellisland. I fancied to myself, while I was sitting in the parlour, that Burns might have caroused there, for most likely his rounds extended so far.

Dorothy Wordsworth

Stirling

From the field of Bannockburn you obtain the finest view of Stirling. The Ochils are around you. Yonder sleeps the Abbey Craig, where, on a summer day, Wight Wallace sat. You behold the houses climbing up, picturesque, smoke-feathered; and the wonderful rock, in which the grace of the lily and the strength of the hills are mingled, and on which the castle sits as proudly as ever did rose on its stem. Eastward from the castle ramparts stretches a great plain, bounded on either side by mountains, and before you the vast fertility dies into distance, flat as the ocean when winds are asleep. It is through this plain that the Forth has drawn her glittering coils – a silvery entanglement of loops in the opposite direction, and the aspect of the country has entirely changed. It undulates like a rolling sea. Heights swell up into the blackness of pines, and then sink away into valleys of fertile green. At your feet the Bridge of Allan sleeps in azure smoke. Beyond are the classic woods of Keir; and ten miles farther what see you? a multitude of blue mountains climbing the heavens! The heart leaps up to greet them – the ramparts of a land of romance, from the mouths of whose glens broke of old the foray of the freebooter; and with a chief in front, with banner and pibroch in the wind, the terror of the Highland war. Stirling, like a huge brooch, clasps Highlands and Lowlands together.

Alexander Smith [1865]

The Trossachs

What exactly *are* the Trossachs? They are a pass, a gorge, a hollow way
that stretches out beside a little river between the two masses of rock,
those of Ben A'an and Ben Venue, which stand like watchmen next to
Loch Katrine with their broad backs stretching to Loch Achray . . . As
a picture the whole thing is quite perfect, and Walter Scott knew very
well what he was doing when he made Ellen Douglas put her boat
ashore and made the King step forth from the undergrowth by the
lakeside just at this particular point. The place seems positively to
compel the poet to speak in a romantic vein, and no maiden could here
step ashore from the lake without being immediately taken for the
Lady of the Lake herself.

Theodor Fontane [1860]

The rocky summits, split and rent,
Form'd turret, dome, or battlement,
Or seem'd fantastically set
With cupola or minaret,
Wild crests as pagod ever deck'd,
Or mosque of Eastern architect.
Nor were these earth-born Castles bare,
Nor lack'd they many a banner fair;
For, from their shiver'd brows display'd,
Far o'er the unfathomable glade,
All twinkling with the dewdrops sheen,
The brier-rose fell in streamers green,
And creeping shrubs, of thousand dyes,
Waved in the west-wind's summer sighs.
Aloft, the ash and warrior oak
Cast anchor in the rifted rock;
And, higher yet, the pine-tree hung
His shatter'd trunk, and frequent flung,
Where seem'd the cliffs to meet on high,
His boughs athwart the narrow'd sky.
Highest of all, where white peaks glanced,
Where glist'ning streamers waved and danced,
The wanderer's eye could barely view
The summer heaven's delicious blue;
So wondrous wild, the whole might seem
The scenery of a fairy dream.

Sir Walter Scott

At a turn of the road Loch Achray is before you. Beyond expression beautiful is that smiling lake, mirroring the hills, whether bare and green or plumaged with woods from base to crest. Fair azure gem in a setting of mountains! – the traveller cannot but pause to drink in its fairy beauty . . . At every step the scenery grows wilder. Loch Achray disappears. High in upper air tower the summits of Ben-Aan and Ben-Venue. You pass through the gorge of the Trossachs, whose rocky walls, born in earthquake and fiery deluge, the fanciful summer has been dressing these thousand years, clothing their feet with drooping ferns and rods of foxglove bells, blackening their breasts with pines, feathering their pinnacles with airy birches, that dance in the breeze like plumage on a warrior's helm. The wind here becomes a musician. Echo sits babbling beneath the rock. The gorge, too, is but the prelude to a finer charm; for before you are aware, doubling her beauty with surprise, there breaks on the right the silver sheet of Loch Katrine, with a dozen woody islands, sleeping peacefully on their shadows.

Alexander Smith

June in the Hills

But it is in June, I think, that the mountain charm is most intoxicating. The airs are lightsome. The hill-mists are seldom heavy, and only on south-wind mornings do the lovely grey-white vapours linger among the climbing corries and overhanging scarps. Many of the slopes are blue, aerially delicate, from the incalculable myriad host of the blue-bells. The green of the bracken is more wonderful than at any other time. When the wind plays upon it the rise and fall is as the breathing of the green seas among the caverns of Mingulay or among the savage rock-pools of the Seven Hunters or where the Summer Isles lie in the churn of the Atlantic tides. Everything is alive in joy. The young broods exult. The air is vibrant with the eddies of many wings, great and small. The shadow-grass sways with the passage of the shrewmouse or the wing's-breath of the darting swallow. The stillest pool quivers, for among the shadows of breathless reeds the phantom javelin of the dragon-fly whirls for a second from silence to silence.

William Sharp: "Fiona Macleod"

The Beautiful City of Perth

Beautiful and ancient city of Perth,
One of the grandest upon the earth,
With your stately mansions and streets so clean,
And situated betwixt two Inches green,
Which are most magnificent to be seen.

The North Inch is beautiful to behold,
Where the daisies and butter-cups their petals unfold,
In the warm summer time of the year,
While the clear silvery Tay rolls by quite near,
And such a scene will your spirits cheer.

The South Inch is lovely, be it said,
And a splendid spot for military parade,
While along the highway there are some big trees,
Where the soldiers can rest or stand at ease,
Whichever way their commanders please.

The surrounding woodland scenery is very grand,
It cannot be surpassed in fair Scotland,
Especially the elegant Palace of Scone, in history renowned,
Where some of Scotland's kings were crowned.

And the Fair Maid of Perth's house is worthy to be seen,
Which is well worth visiting by Duke, Lord, or Queen;
The Fair Maid of Perth caused the battle on the North Inch
'Twixt the Clans Chattan and Kay, and neither of them did
flinch,
Until they were cut up inch by inch.

The scenery is lovely in the month of June,
When trees and flowers are in full bloom,
Especially near by the Palace of Scone,
Where the blackbird is heard whistling all day
While near by rolls on the clear silvery Tay.

Of all the cities in Scotland, beautiful Perth for me,
For it is the most elegant city that ever I did see,
With its beautiful woodland scenery along the river Tay,
Which would make the tourist's heart feel gay,
While fishing for trout on a fine summer day.

There, the angler, if he likes to resort
For a few day's fishing, can have excellent sport,
And while he is fishing during the day,
He will feel delighted with the scenery along the river Tay.
And the fish he catches will drive dull care away,
And his toil will be rewarded for the fatigues of the day.

Beautiful city of Perth, magnificent to be seen,
With your grand statues and Inches green,
And your lovely maidens fair and gay,
Which, in conclusion, I will venture to say,
You cannot be surpassed at the present day.

William McGonagall

Glencoe

In the Gaelic tongue, Glencoe signifies the Glen of Weeping; and in truth that pass is the most dreary and melancholy of all the Scottish passes – the very Valley of the Shadow of Death. Mists and storms brood over it through the greater part of the finest summer; and even on those rare days when the sun is bright, and when there is no cloud in the sky, the impression made by the landscape is sad and awful. The path lies along a stream which issues from the most sullen and gloomy of mountain-pools. Huge precipices of naked stone frown on both sides. Even in July the streaks of snow may often be discerned in the rifts near the summits. All down the sides of the crags heaps of ruin mark the headlong paths of the torrents. Mile after mile the traveller looks in vain for the smoke of one hut, or for one human form wrapped in a plaid, and listens in vain for the bark of a shepherd's dog, or the bleat of a lamb. Mile after mile the only sound that indicates life is the faint cry of a bird of prey from some storm-beaten pinnacle of rock. The progress of civilisation, which had turned so many wastes into fields yellow with harvests or gay with apple blossoms, has only made Glencoe more desolate. All the science and industry of a peaceful age can extract nothing valuable from that wilderness; but in an age of violence and rapine, the wilderness itself was valued on account of the shelter it afforded to the plunderer and his plunder.

Lord Macauley [1855]

Horseman of Iona

On this eve of big Michael
Do not linger by westering seas
Where lost years lie bleeding,
But spur your black stallion
To the necklet of stones
On our green high hill.
Here at the bouldered cairn,
Round hallowed quartz,
Turning, wheel your stallion's head
On the hub of this dying day
And dedicate him to the sun.

W. Gordon Smith

The man is little to be envied whose patriotism would not gain force upon the field of Marathon or whose piety would not grow warmer among the ruins of Iona.

Samuel Johnson

When I first visited Iona I had probably never heard the word piety and would not have understood what it meant. But I remember having a peculiar feeling as I walked up to the Abbey and on to the beach beyond. I subsequently attributed that feeling to the lie of the land, the very white sand, interspersed with pinkish rocks, and the colour of the surrounding sea, which really is "wine dark". Through some geological accident Iona is not composed of bogs and precipices, but is largely covered with a light, springy turf. To walk on this responsive surface, and to feel free to walk in any direction, was immensely exhilarating. But after repeated visits I began to realise that the purely physical qualities were not the whole reason for my devotion. There are places in the world where even someone as insensitive as I am must feel a vibration from the remote past, an exhalation, whether of good or evil: Delphi, Delos, Mycenae (very evil), Monte Oliveto, Avila, Cézanne's house beside the quarry of Bibemus. Among such places I would include Iona. . . .

Kenneth Clark

Over the Sea to Skye

On a fine morning there is not in the whole world a prettier sheet of water than Loch Eishart. Everything about it is wild, beautiful, and lonely. You drink a strange and unfamiliar air. You seem to be sailing out of the nineteenth century away back into the ninth. You are delighted, and there is no remembered delight with which you can compare the feeling. Over the Loch the Cuchuillins rise crested with tumult of golden mists; the shores are green behind; and away out, towards the horizon, the Island of Rum – ten miles long at the least – shoots up from the flat sea like a pointed flame. It is a granite mass, you know, firm as the foundations of the world; but as you gaze the magic of morning light makes it a glorious apparition – a mere crimson film or shadow . . . Beyond Rum, fifteen miles out yonder, the sea is smooth, and flushed with more varied hues than ever lived on the changing opal – dim azures, tender pinks, sleek emeralds. It is one sheet of mother-of-pearl. The hills are silent . . . But the sea, literally clad with birds, is vociferous.

Alexander Smith

St Andrews

St. Andrews by the Northern Sea,
A haunted town it is to me!
A little city, worn and grey,
    The grey North Ocean girds it round,
And o'er the rocks, and up the bay,
    The long sea-rollers surge and sound.
And still the thin and biting spray
    Drives down the melancholy street,
And still endure, and still decay,
    Towers that the salt winds vainly beat.
Ghost-like and shadowy they stand
Dim-mirrored in the wet sea-sand.

O, broken minster, looking forth
    Beyond the bay, above the town,
O, winter of the kindly North,
    O, college of the scarlet gown,

297

And shining sands beside the sea,
    And stretch of links beyond the sand,
Once more I watch you, and to me
    It is as if I touched a hand!

Andrew Lang

The Protestants avenged George Wishart. Cardinal Beaton, that Prince of the Roman Church and sire of so many bastards, was left to rot on his castle walls at St Andrews. He hung like a cross by an arm and a leg and a man called Guthrie pished in his mouth. It was a godly act!

John Knox

The Young Man of Montrose

There was a young man of Montrose
Who had pockets in none of his clothes.
    When asked by his lass
    Where he carried his brass
He said "Darling, I pay through the nose."

Arnold Bennett

The Aberdeen Tailor

The man from the islands, exiled in Aberdeen, had been sent a bolt of homespun Harris tweed from his family. He went to a tailor in Union Street and asked the assistant if he could have a suit made. The tailor measured the tweed and told the man it was an inch or two short; he couldn't make the suit. So the islander crossed the road to another tailor who agreed to take on the job. A month later, when the islander went to collect the suit he was surprised to see a small boy in the shop wearing a jacket made out of the family tweed. But his suit fitted perfectly and he was very pleased with it. As he was leaving the shop he asked the tailor how he had managed to cut the suit so well and have enough left over to make his son a jacket, yet the tailor across the road had declined the job on the grounds that the bolt was too short. The tailor laughed. "He has twa sons," he said.

The Bydand Myths

Breakfast in Caithness . . .

"Good Morning, Landlady," said Mr Innes: "we have a good mind to take Breakfast here if you can give us Tea?" She answered very briskly, "Pray, Sir, what kind of Tea do you desire to have?" Looking about to me, he winked, and said, "That's so far good, and promises well. Well, good woman, what kind of tea can you give us?" "Why, Sir, I can give you Green-Tea, Bohea-Tea, or Coffee." "Upon my Word, that is good sense truly," said Mr Innes. "Come, let us alight, and get a good Breakfast even in the Wilds of Caithness." And, indeed, this surprised us all greatly, and proved an agreeable Disappointment to us, particularly to myself, as I had been advised, yea, importuned by some, before setting out, to take . . . some good Bread, along with me, when entering into Caithness, being so poor and despicable a Country that I could have no good thing to eat in it.

Robert Forbes

Wick

The meanest of men's towns on the baldest of God's bays.

Robert Louis Stevenson

LONDON MAN: I suppose that when the Highland line is snowed up you may be cut off for a whole week and not know what is going on in London?

WICK MAN: Aye, that happens now and then. But then, ye see, the people in London are no better off. For a whole week they don't know what's going on in Wick.

The Bydand Myths

299

Dear Gordon:

I confess I find it difficult. Far from being a homogeneous race of people with your own singular culture, you seem to be a polyglot mish-mash of Celts, Picts, Norsemen, Angles, Saxons and God knows what else, speaking no fewer than three languages, two of which are very perplexing. Of course I recognise your countrymen's claims for the recognition of their separate national identity. But the more I try to simplify it for myself the more confused I become. Are there really *two* Scotlands, with the Gaelic-speaking Highlanders appearing to be *more* Scottish than the Lowlanders?

Dear Mortimer:

The fog in your mind is a whiff of Scotch mist or the beginnings of the Celtic twilight. Of course there are two Scotlands – if not four or five. We differ from each other in many ways, but in no one way more than we differ, all of us, from the English. That's not a complaint – just a fact. All Scots are different, but the Highlander, as you're about to see, is more different than others.

That Other Scotland

We were always in the habit of conversing with the Highlanders ...
The Prince highly appreciated the good-breeding, simplicity, and
intelligence which make it so pleasant, and even instructive to talk to
them.

Queen Victoria

Land of the Gaels

I am returned from Scotland charm'd with my expedition: it is of the Highlands I speak: the Lowlands are worth seeing once, but the Mountains are extatic, & ought to be visited in pilgrimage once a year. None but these monstrous creatures of God know how to join so much beauty with so much horror. A fig for your poets, Painters, Gardiners, & Clergymen, that have not been among them: their imagination can be made up of nothing but bowling-greens, flowering shrubs, horse-ponds, Fleet-ditches, shell-grottoes, & Chinee-rails.

Thomas Gray

The Model Peasant

Donald Gunn, one of the tightest and most active of Highlanders. Indeed, every possible element which entered into the structure of this man's mind, as well as into the size and make of his body, combined to constitute him the very model of a Highland peasant. He was exactly of the middle size, and well made, with just as much flesh on his bones as simply served to cover them, and no more. He had a face full of expression, which conveyed most unequivocally the shrewdness, cunning, acuteness, and caustic humour so strongly characteristic of his race. Donald Gunn surpassed his whole neighbourhood and, perhaps, the whole parish, in all rustic and athletic exercises. At a brawl, in which, however, he but seldom engaged, none could exceed him in the dexterity and rapidity with which he brandished his cudgel; and though many might exceed him in physical strength, his address and alert activity often proved him more than a match for an assailant of much greater weight and size. Then in dancing he was without a rival. With inimitable ease and natural grace he kept time, with eye and foot and fingers, to all the minute modulations of a Highland reel or Strathspey. He was also a good shot, a successful deer stalker, angler, smuggler, and poacher. Donald, however, with all these secular and peculiarly Highland recommendations was little better than a heathen. He was always under suspicion, and latterly made some hair-breadth escapes from the gallows, for he was, by habit and repute, a most notorious thief.

Donald Sage

303

Miraculous Air

The air of the Highlands is pure, and consequently healthy, insomuch that I have known such cures done by it as might be thought next to miracles – I mean in distemper of the lungs, as coughs, consumptions &c.

Edward Burt

Droit du Seigneur

Mr Baillie went to visit his friends in the Aird, and in the course of his researches was introduced to Lord Lovat, whose policy it was, on all occasions, to show great attentions to his neighbours and their children. The situation in which his lordship was found . . . was, if not quite unprecedented, nevertheless rather surprising. He was stretched out in bed between two Highland lasses, who, on being seen, affected out of modesty to hide their faces under the bedclothes. The old lord accounted for this strange scene by saying that his blood had become cold, and he was obliged to supply the want of heat by the application of animal warmth. It is said that he lay in bed for the most part of the two years preceding the Rebellion; till, hearing of Prince Charles's arrival in Arisaig, he roused himself with sudden vehemence, crying to an attendant: "Lassie, bring me my brogues – I'll rise *noo!*" One of his odd fancies was to send a retainer every day to Loch Ness, a distance of eight miles, for the water he drank.

Robert Chambers

An English lady . . . told me lately, that seeing a Highlander basking at the foot of a hill in his full dress, while his wife and her mother were hard at work in reaping the oats, she asked the old woman how she could be contented to see her daughter labour in that manner, while her husband was only an idle spectator? And to this the woman answered, that her son-in-law was a *gentleman*, and it would be a disparagement to him to do any such work, and that both she and her daughter too were sufficiently honoured by the alliance.

Edward Burt

Language of Eden

When Adam first his Eve did meet,
Shimmering bright as morning dew,
The first words he spoke to her
Were "Ciamar tha th'n daugh"
     ("How are you today?")

Anonymous

Mountain Maids

The young women of the mountains of Scotland are, in general, remark,
ably clean, when compared with our peasants. There is a charm in the
arrangement of their hair, and an ease and grace in their manner of
holding their head. Their short petticoat, commonly of a deep colour-
shows off the whiteness of their legs, which are admirably shaped,
though large and vigorous. They have the beauty of strength.

Charles Nodier

One thing I should have told you was intolerable, viz, the number of
Highlanders that attended a table, whose feet and foul linen, or woollen,
I don't know which, were more than a match for the odour of the
dishes.

Edward Burt

The Last Wolf

A poor woman, crossing the mountains with two children, was assailed
by the wolf, and her infants devoured, and she escaped with difficulty

305

to Moyhall. The chief of Mackintosh no sooner heard of the tragical fate of the babes, than, moved by pity and rage, he dispatched orders to his clan and vassals to assemble the next day at twelve o'clock, to proceed in a body to destroy the wolf. Pollochock was one of those vassals, and being then in the vigour of youth, and possessed of gigantic strength and determined courage, his appearance was eagerly looked for to take a lead in the enterprise. But the hour came and all were assembled except him to whom they most trusted. Unwilling to go without him, the impatient chief fretted and fumed through the hall, till at length, about an hour after the appointed time, in stalked Pollochock, dressed in his full Highland attire: "I am little used to wait thus for any man," exclaimed the chafed chieftain, "and still less for thee, Pollochock, especially when such game is afoot as we are boune after!" "What sort o' game are ye after, Mackintosh?" said Pollochock simply, and not quite understanding his allusion. "The wolf, sir," replied Mackintosh; "did not my messenger instruct you?" "Ou aye, that's true," answered Pollochock with a good-humoured smile; "troth I had forgotten. But an' that be a'," continued he, groping with his right hand among the ample folds of his plaid, "there's the wolf's head!" Exclamations of astonishment and admiration burst from chief and clansmen as he held out the grim and bloody head of the monster at arm's-length, for the gratification of those who crowded round him. "As I came through the slochk [gully], east the hill there," said he, as if talking of some every-day occurrence, "I forgathered with the beast. My long dog there turned him. I buckled wi' him, and dirkit him, and syne whuttled his craig, and brought awa' his countenance, for fear he might come alive again; for they are vera precarious creatures." "My noble Pollochock!" cried the chief in ecstasy "the deed was worthy of thee! In memorial of thy hardihood, I here bestow upon thee Seannachan, to yield meal for thy good grey hound in all time coming."

Sir Thomas Dick Lauder

The Clearances

Here you have a quiet, thoughtful, contented, religious people, suscep-tible of improvement, and willing to be improved. To transplant these people from their native mountain glens to the sea coast, and require them to become some cultivators, others fishermen, occupations to which they have never been accustomed, to expect a sudden and total

change of habits in the existing generation, instead of gradually pro-
ducing it in their children; to expel them by process of law from their
blackhouses, and if they demur in obeying the ejectment, to oust them
by setting fire to their combustible tenements – this sure is as little
defensible on the score of policy as of morals.

Robert Southey

Cracking the Nut

There lives in our neighbourhood, at a house (or castle) called Culloden,
a gentleman whose hospitality is almost without bounds. It is the custom
of that house, at the first visit or introduction, to take up your freedom
by cracking his nut (as he terms it), that is, a cocoa-shell, which holds
a pint, filled with champagne, or such other sort of wine as you shall
choose. You may guess by the introduction, at the contents of the
volume. Few go away sober at any time, and for the greatest part of his
guests, in the conclusion, they cannot go at all.

Edward Burt

Habit of Mind

The melancholy of the Highlands being far more morose, and having
no tendency to misanthropy, seems rather to be a habit of mind
produced by the combined effects of sensibility, solitude, and the
habitual contemplation of sublime scenery. Little employed in culti-
vating the ground, his mind is not fettered by minute attention to a
single spot; the range of his excursions is wide but it is lonely. In tending
his flocks he scales the lofty mountains, and traverses the extensive
moor or dusky forest, and has occasion from time to time to contemplate
the grandest objects in nature – the war of the elements – the impetuous
torrent sweeping everything before it – the thunder of heaven, reverberating, in repeated peals, among the mountains – the violence of the

307

winds, rendered furious, by being pent up in a deep and narrow valley – and snow coiled up in heaps, that interrupts for weeks the intercourse of a whole district. All these circumstances, alike unfavourable to frivolousness of thought, are well calculated to fix down the mind to habits of sober thinking, and to impress it with serious meditation on the vicissitudes of human affairs. Notwithstanding this general character of what may be called pensive susceptibility, which belongs to the Highlander, he is in the highest degree alive to joyous feelings. The Highlanders are fond of music and of dancing, with diversions of all kinds. In ancient times, when the hospitality of the chieftain furnished subsistence to his numerous dependents, it is remembered, in the traditions of the generation last passed, that the recitation of ancient Celtic poetry formed their favourite amusement; thus innocently did they twine the garland of poesy around dark Winter's brow.

Beriah Botfield [1829]

Burying the Dead

On the death of a Highlander, the corps being stretched on a board, and covered with a coarse linnen wrapper, the friends lay on the breast of the deceased a wooden platter, containing a small quantity of salt and earth, separate and unmixed; the earth, an emblem of the corruptible body; the salt an emblem of the immortal spirit. All fire is extinguished where the corps is kept; and it is reckoned so ominous for a dog or cat to pass over it, that the poor animal is killed without mercy.

The *Late-Wake* is a ceremony used at funerals. The evening after the death of any person, the relations and friends of the deceased meet at the house, attended by a bagpiper or a fiddle; the nearest of kin, be it wife, son, or daughter, opens a melancholy ball, dancing and greeting, i.e.

crying violently at the same time; and this continues till day-light; but with such gambols and frolicks among the younger part of the company, that the loss which occasioned them is often more than supplied by the consequences of that night. If the corps remains unburied for two nights, the same rites are renewed. Thus, *Scythian*-like, they rejoice at the deliverance of their friends out of this life of misery.

Thomas Pennant

Smooring the Fire

The ceremony of smooring the fire is artistic and symbolic, and is performed with loving care. The embers are evenly spread on the hearth – which is generally in the middle of the floor – and formed into a circle. This circle is then divided into three equal sections, a small boss being left in the middle. A peat is laid between each section, each peat touching the boss, which forms a common centre. The first peat is laid down in the name of the God of Life, the second in name of the God of Peace, the third name of the God of Grace. The centre is then covered over with ashes sufficient to subdue but not enough to extinguish the fire in name of the Three of Light. The heap slightly raised in the centre is called "Tulla nan Tri", the Hearth of the Three. When the smooring operation is complete the woman closes her eyes, stretches her hand, and softly intones one of the many formulae current for these occasions:

> The sacred Three
> To save,
> To shield,
> To surround
> The hearth,
> The house,
> The household
> This eve,
> This night,
> Oh this eve,
> This night,
> And every night
> Each single night.
> Amen.

Alexander Carmichael [1900]

309

The Fearless Fiennes

(The Fiennes were the traditional defenders of the Highlands from the sea pirates. Their chief, Fionn, had a remarkable tooth, a "wisdom" tooth, which, when pressed, would answer any question truly. His dog was the great Bran; his sword was called Mac an Luin, Son of Light. The Fiennes themselves were brave warriors, members of an elite band).

A canditate must give security that no revenge will be attempted for his death: must compose at least one song: be a perfect master of his weapon, a good runner and fighter. He must be able to hold out his weapon by the smaller end without a tremble: in the chase through wood and plain his hair must remain tied up; if it fell he was rejected. He must be light and swift so as not to break a rotten branch by standing on it, he must leap a tree as high as his forehead and get under a tree no higher than his knee: without stopping he must be able to draw a thorn from his foot: he must not refuse a woman without a dowry, must offer violence to no woman; be charitable to the poor and weak, and he must never refuse to fight nine men of any other race should they set upon him.

Martin Martin

Ossian's Tomb

In the centre of the "Sma' Glen", a stupendous pass of the Grampian Mountains, there is a huge stone of cubical form, designated Clach Ossian, or Ossian's Stone. It is believed to have formed the primitive memorial stone of the great Celtic bard. When General Wade was constructing in 1746 the Highland road which passes through the glen, his men ascertained that Ossian's Stone was resting on four large slab stones placed edgewise. On the removal of the formidable cover a chamber was discovered about two feet square, in which were contained the debris of bones and fragments of coins. The opening of the tomb caused the natives to assemble from vast distances. They took up the slabs, and the relics which they enclosed, and carried them in solemn procession to a sequestered spot among the hills, where they reinterred them amidst the sound of martial music.

Rev. Charles Rogers

The Captain's Orders

To Captain Robert Campbell of Glenlyon "For Their Majesties' Service".

Sir, – You are hereby ordered to fall upon the rebels, the M'Donalds, of Glencoe, and put all to the sword under seventy.

You are to have special care that the old fox and his sons doe upon no account escape your hands. You are to secure all the avenues, that no man escape. This you are to put in execution att five o'clock in the morning precisely, and by that time, or very shortly after it, I'll strive to be att you with a stronger party. If I doe not come to you att five, you are not to tarry for me, but to fall on. This is by the king's special command, for the good and safety of the country, that these miscreants be cutt off root and branch. See that this be putt in execution without feud or favour, else you may expect to be treated as not true to the king's government, nor a man fitt to carry a commission in the king's service. Expecting you will not faill in the fulfilling hereof as you love yourself, I subscribe these with my hand.

Robert Duncanson Ballocholis,
12th February, 1692

Roghefootide Scottis

Moreover, wherefor they call us in Scotland Reddshanckes, and in your Graces dominion of England roghefootide Scottis, pleas it your Maiestie to understande, that we of all people can tolleratt, suffir, and away best with colde, for boithe somer and wyntir, (excepte whene the froest is mooste vehement,) goyng alwaies bair leggide and bair footide, our delite and pleasure is not onely in huntynge of redd deir, wolfes, foxes, and graies whereof we abounde, and have great plentie, but also in rynninge, leapinge, swymynge, shootynge, and thrawinge of dartis therfor, in so moche as we use and delite so to go alwaies, the tendir delicatt gentillmen of Scotland call us Reddshanckes.

John Elder to King Henry VIII [1542]

To begin then with their shoes. The Highlander wears a sort of thin pump or brogue, so light that it does not in the least impede his activity in running; and from being constantly accustomed to these kind of shoes, they are able to advance or retreat with incredible swiftness, so that if they have the better in any engagement it is scarce possible to escape from them; and on the other hand, if they are over power'd they soon recover their hills, where it is impossible to reach them.

A Short History of the
Highland Regiment [1743]

The Warrior's Arms

Their arms were a broad sword, a dagger called a durk, a target, a musket and two pistols . . . In battle, they threw away the plaid and under garments [!], and fought in their jackets making thus their movements quicker, and their strokes more forcible. Their advance to battle was rapid, like the charge of dragoons. When near the enemy, they stopped a little, to draw breath and discharge their muskets, which they then dropped on the ground. Advancing, they fired their pistols, which they threw, almost at the same instant, at the heads of their opponents. They then rushed into their ranks with the broad sword, threatening, and shaking the sword as they ran on, so as to conquer the enemy's eye, while his body was yet unhurt.

John Dalrymple [1796]

Then . . .

The *Mattucashlash*, or arm-pit dagger, was worn there ready to be used on coming to close quarters.

Thomas Pennant [1769]

The Most Despicable Enemy

Edinburgh, 12th January, 1745–6. Sunday parole, Derby – Field-officer for the day; tomorrow, Major Wilson.

The manner of the Highlanders' way of fighting, which there is nothing so easy to resist, if officers and men are not prepossessed with the lyes and accounts which are told of them. They commonly form their front rank of what they call their best men, or true Highlanders, the number of which being always but few. When they form in battalions, they commonly form four deep, and these Highlanders form the front of the four, the rest being Lowlanders and arrant scum. When these battalions come within a large musket shott or three-score yards, this front rank gives their fire, and immediately throw down their firelocks and come down in a cluster with their swords and targets, making a noise and endeavouring to pierce the body or battalion before them, – becoming twelve or fourteen deep by the time they come up to the people they attack. The sure way to demolish them is, at three deep, to fire by ranks diagonally to the centre, where they come, the rear rank first, and even that rank not to fire till they are within ten or twelve paces; but if the fire is given at a distance, you probably will be broke, for you never get time to load a second cartridge, and, if you give way, you may give your foot for dead, for they being without a firelock, or any load, no man with his arms, accoutrements, etc., can escape them, and they give no quarter; but if you will but observe the above directions, they are the most despicable enemy that are.

Duke of Cumberland's Orderly Book

The White Cockade

My love was born in Aberdeen,
The bonniest lad that e'er was seen,
But now he maks my heart full sad,
He's ta'en the field wi' his white cockade.
    O he's a rantin' rovin' blade,
    O he's a brisk and bonnie lad,
    Betide what may, my heart is glad
    To see my lad wi' his white cockade.

Traditional Song

In the flight [from Culloden] I came up with a pretty young Highlander, who called out to me: "Hold your hand – I'm a Campbell." On which I asked him: "Where is your bonnet?" He replied "Somebody hath snatched it off my head." I only mention this to shew how we distinguished our loyal clans from the Rebels, they being dress'd and equipp'd all in one Way, except the Bonnet, – ours having a Red or Yellow Cross or Ribbon, theirs a white Cockade. He having neither of these distinctions, I desired him, if he was a Campbell, to follow me, which he promised; but on the first opportunity he gave me the slip.

James Ray [1749]

Highland Mafia

Contemporary with Rob Roy or his sons, there were a very few Highland gentlemen that kept bands of loose people, equally ready to rise in rebellion or to sweep away the cattle of an estate. Macdonald of Barrisdale also was a very noted character in his day, and is said to have drawn ten thousand merks a year in blackmail or contributions from the Lowlanders of the northern countries. So much was his protection valued, that even Lord President Forbes found it expedient to pay him blackmail, to prevent his tenants from being plundered and oppressed.

John Ramsay

Highland Election

X is the
Unknown
Factor,
But who's
The Laird?

W. Gordon Smith

The Demon Drink

With the Scots it was whisky or perish.
And how they have survived!

Lawton Mackall

The Demon Drink

Oh, thou demon Drink, thou fell destroyer;
Thou curse of society, and its greatest annoyer.
What hast thou done to society, let me think?
I answer thou hast caused the most of ills, thou demon Drink.

Thou causeth the mother to neglect her child,
Also the father to act as he were wild,
So that he neglects his loving wife and family dear,
By spending his earnings foolishly on whisky, rum, and beer.

And after spending his earnings foolishly he beats his wife –
The man that promised to protect her during life –
And so the man would if there was no drink in society,
For seldom a man beats his wife in a state of sobriety.

And if he does, perhaps he finds his wife fou',
Then that causes, no doubt, a great hullaballoo;
When he finds his wife drunk he begins to frown,
And in a fury of passion he knocks her down.

And in the knock down she fractures her head,
And perhaps the poor wife is killed dead,
Whereas, if there was no strong drink to be got,
To be killed wouldn't have been the poor wife's lot.

Then the unfortunate husband is arrested and cast into jail,
And sadly his fate he does bewail;
And he curses the hour that ever he was born,
And paces his cell up and down very forlorn.

And when the day of his trial draws near,
No doubt for the murdering of his wife he drops a tear,
And he exclaims, "Oh, thou demon Drink, through thee I
                                        must die,"
And on the scaffold he warns the people from drink to fly,

Because whenever a father or a mother takes to drink,
Step by step on in crime they do sink,
Until their children loses all affection for them,
And in justice we cannot their children condemn.

The man that gets drunk is little else than a fool,
And is in the habit, no doubt, of advocating for Home Rule;
But the best Home Rule for him, as far as I can understand,
Is the abolition of strong drink from the land.

And the men that get drunk in general wants Home Rule;
But such men, I rather think, should keep their heads cool
And try and learn more sense, I most earnestly do pray,
And help to get strong drink abolished without delay.

If drink was abolished how many peaceful homes would there be,
Just, for instance, in the beautiful town of Dundee;
Then this world would be a heaven, whereas it's a hell,
And the people would have more peace in it to dwell.

Alas! strong drink makes men and women fanatics,
And helps to fill our prisons and lunatics;
And if there was no strong drink such cases wouldn't be,
Which would be a very glad sight for all Christians to see.

I admit, a man may be a very good man,
But in my opinion he cannot be a true Christian
As long as he partakes of strong drink,
The more that he may differently think.

But, no matter what he thinks, I say nay,
For by taking it he helps to lead his brother astray,
Whereas, if he didn't drink, he would help to reform society,
And we would soon do away with all inebriety.

Then, for the sake of society and the Church of God,
Let each one try to abolish it at home and abroad;
Then poverty and crime would decrease and be at a stand,
And Christ's Kingdom would soon be established throughout
                                                    the land.

Therefore, brothers and sisters, pause and think,
And try to abolish the foul fiend, Drink.
Let such doctrine be taught in church and school,
That the abolition of strong drink is the only Home Rule.

                                        William McGonagall

The Water of Life

The word whisky derives from the Gaelic "uisge beatha" – water of life and so Scotland's unique aqua vitae or eau de vie progressed, like brandy and vodka, from peasant potion to very big business. Most proprietary Scotch whiskies are bottled blends of perhaps as many as a score of grain and malt whisky distillations from all over the country. Single malt whiskies, now more energetically marketed, are as a rule heavier, more distinctive, older and more expensive.

The most advanced systems of chemical analysis have failed to produce a satisfactory formula for synthesising Scotch whisky. Even the Japanese who, as imitators, often improve on the original, have so far failed to penetrate the final mystery of Scotch. There is such a substantial pot of gold at the end of this particular rainbow, however, that the hunt will continue.

Throughout the centuries whisky has been cursed and venerated, damned and blessed. Legends about its medicinal efficacy have always seemed far-fetched and no less euphemistic for being ancient.

Beying moderatelie taken, it sloweth age; it strengtheneth youthe; it helpeth digestion; it cutteth fleume; it abandoneth melancholie; it relisheth the harte; it lighteneth the mynde; it quickeneth the spirites; it cureth the hydropsis it healeth the strangury; it pounceth the stone; it repelleth grauel; it puffeth awaie ventositie; it kepyth and preserveth the head from whyrling – the eyes from dazelyng – the tongue from lispying – the mouth from snafflying – the teethe from chatteryng – the throte from ratlyng – the weasan from stieflyng – the stomach from wamblyng – the harte from swellyng – the bellie from wirthchyng – the guts from rumblyng – the hands from shiueryng – the sinowes from shrinkyng – the veynes from crumplyng – the bones from soakyng . . . trulie it is a soueraigne liquor.

Raphael Holinshed [1578]

Liking the Bite

When the men met in the morning they were supposed to have breakfasted at home, and perhaps had had their private dram, it being

cold work in a dark wintry dawn, to start over the moor for a walk of some miles to end in standing up to the knees in water; yet on collecting, whisky was always handed round; a lad with a small cask – a quarter anker – on his back, and a horn cup in his hands that held a gill, appeared three times a day among them ... When we were there the horn cup was offered first to us, and each of us took a sip to the health of our friends around us, who all stood up. Sometimes a floater's wife or bairn would come with a message; such messenger was always offered whisky. Aunt Mary had a story that one day a woman with a child in her arms, and another bit thing at her knee, came up among them; the horn cup was duly handed to her, she took a "gey guid drap" herself, and then gave a little to each of the babies. "My goodness, child," said my mother to the wee thing that was trotting by the mother's side, "doesn't it *bite* you?" "Ay, but I like the bite," replied the creature.

Elizabeth Grant

Drinkin' Drams

He ance was holy
An' melancholy,
Till he found the folly
  O' singin' psalms:
He's now as red's a rose,
And there's pimples on his nose,
And in size it daily grows
  By drinkin' drams.

He ance was weak,
An' couldnae eat a steak
Without gettin' sick
  An' takin' qualms;
But now he can eat
O' ony kind o' meat,
For he's got an appeteet
  By drinkin' drams.

He ance was thin,
Wi' a nose like a pen,
An' haunds like a hen,
  An' nae hams;
But now he's round and tight,
An' a deevil o' a wight,
For he's got himsel' put right
  By drinkin' drams.

He ance was saft as dirt,
An' as pale as ony shirt,
An' as useless as a cart
  Without the trams;
But now he'd race the deil,
Or swallow Jonah's whale –
He's as gleg's a puddock's tail
  Wi' drinkin' drams.

Oh! pale, pale, was his hue,
An' cauld, cauld was his broo,
An' he grumbled like a ewe
  'Mang libbit rams;
But noo his broo is bricht,
An' his een are orbs o' licht,
An' his nose is just a sicht
  Wi' drinkin' drams.

He studied mathematics,
Logic, ethics, hydrostatics,
Till he needed diuretics
  To lowse his dams;
But now, without a lee,
He could make anither sea,
For he's left philosophy
  An' taen to drams.

He found that learnin', fame,
Gas, philanthropy, an' steam,
Logic, loyalty, gude name,
  Were a' mere shams;

That the source o' joy below,
An' the antidote to woe,
An' the only proper go,
 Was drinkin' drams.

George Outram

Cheer-Upping

When the Lowlanders want to drink a cheer-upping cup, they go to the public-house, called the Change House, and call for a chopin of twopenny, which is a thin yeasty beverage, made of malt, not quite so strong as the table-beer of England. This is brought in a pewter stoup, shaped like a skittle; from whence it is emptied into a quaff, that is, a curious cup made of different pieces of wood, such as box and ebony, cut into little staves, joined alternately, and secured with delicate hoops, having two ears or handles, It holds about a gill, is sometimes tipt round the mouth with silver, and has a plate of the same metal at the bottom, with the landlord's cypher engraved.

The Highlanders, on the contrary, despise this liquor, and regale themselves with whisky, a malt spirit, as strong as geneva, which they swallow in great quantities, without any signs of inebriation: they are used to it from the cradle, and find it an excellent preservative against the winter cold, which must be extreme on these mountains – I am told that it is given with great success to infants, as a cordial, in the confluent small pox, when the eruption seems to flag, and the symptoms grow unfavourable.

Tobias Smollett [1771]

One Toast Leads . . .

Here's to you and yours,
No forgettin' us an' oors;

An' whenever you an' yours
Comes to see us an' oors,
Us an' oors'll be as guid
To you and yours,
As ever you an' yours
Was to us an' oors,
Whenever us an' oors
Cam to see you an' yours.

Anonymous

... To Another

Here's a bottle and an honest friend
    What wad ye wish for mair, man?
Wha kens, before his life may end,
    What his share may be o' care, man?

Then catch the moments as they fly,
    And use them as ye ought, man;
Believe me, happiness is shy,
    And comes no ay when sought, man!

Robert Burns

Riotous Excess

From the middle till the close of the eighteenth century, Scotland could lay no claim to religious superiority. The bulk of the people were uncultivated and rude. Licentiousness prevailed among all classes. Riotous excess became the characteristic of a gentleman.

The upper ranks dined early and sat late. When the substantial of dinner were consumed, the gentlewomen were expected to return to the spinet or the distaff. The punch-bowl, now copiously filled, was placed

before the host. There was a succession of public and family toasts and numerous sentiments, to all of which a glass of the potent liquor was drained off. The drinking-glasses of the period contained twice as much as those of the present-time. Special toasts were drunk with peculiar honours, – each guest mounting upon his chair, and resting his right foot upon the table, quaffed his liquor; he then raised his glass aloft in upturned fashion, and gave nine loud huzzas. On such occasions the overthrow of the table was not an unfrequent occurrence . . .

There were instances in which hard drinkers died in their chairs. A West country laird at one of these social meetings was seized with apoplexy and immediately expired. "The laird's looking unco gash," said the host, who had at last remarked the altered appearance of his guest. " 'Deed he is," answered a neighbour, "for he's been with his Maker this hour and mair. I didna like to spoil the fun by speaking o't."

Saturday dinner-parties were common; they were protracted till the Sunday had closed. Every guest expected to drink till he fell under the table. When all had reached this degrading position, the male attendants of the family entered and carried them to their chambers. When the apartments were insufficient for the number of guests, those who were unaccommodated with beds were extended on the floor, and covered, their neckcloths being loosened to prevent the risk of suffocation. The servants expected handsome gratuities from the guests as they departed.

Rev. Charles Rogers [1867]

323

The Bane of that Country

The whisky was a bad habit, there was certainly too much of it going. At every house it was offered, at every house it must be tasted or offence would be given, so we were taught to believe ... Whisky-drinking was and is the bane of that country, from early morning till late at night it went on. Decent gentlewomen began the day with a dram. In our house the bottle of whisky, with its accompaniment of a silver salver full of small glasses, was placed on the side-table with cold meat every morning. In the pantry a bottle of whisky was the allowance per day, with bread and cheese in any required quantity, for such messengers or visitors whose errands sent them in that direction. The very poorest cottages could offer whisky; all the men engaged in the wood manufacture drank it in goblets three times a day, yet except at merry-making we never saw any one tipsy.

Elizabeth Grant

I have been tempted to think that this spirit has in it, by infusion, the seeds of anger, revenge, and murder. This I confess is a little too poetical, but those who drink of it to any degree of excess behave, for the most part, like true barbarians, I think much beyond the effect of other liquors.

Edward Burt

To be fou' or, as he would put it, to have a drappie in his eye, is the Scotchman's notion of bigness and freedom and manly independence. He is a ranter and roarer in his cups, and on the whole much more distressing to meet drunk than sober – which is saying a great deal.

T. W. H. Crosland

Freedom and whisky gang thegither.

Robert Burns

Nearly all the bards have been poor – the children of misfortune. Some have brought discomfort upon themselves by that love of whisky which is so inherent in Scottish minstrels of the lowlier rank.

Rev. Charles Rogers

Blessing Utensils . . .

Towards the end of the dessert the ladies withdrew, in conformity with the custom of the country. The toasts then commenced, and a great number was drank with spirit and vivacity. The English [*sic*] provide for everything; and if the diuretic influence of the liquors is felt, there are certain utensils at hand, which are used without ceremony; and as the ladies here are extremely delicate, this may be the reason for their withdrawing before the toasts begin.

Faujas de Saint-Fond [1784]

. . . and a Wall

In this excellent country, you drink neat. I several times joined in fairly copious libations, but in particular I can never forget the white Lisbon of a certain doctor who proposed Royalist toasts that I could not possibly refuse to a degree that sent so much loyalty to my head that I was glad there was a wall on my way back to the inn.

The Chevalier de Latocnaye

A Parting Glass

"Jeanie," said the Duke, "you must have *doch an' dorroch*, or you will be unable to travel."

There was a salver with cake and wine on the table. He took up a glass, drank "to all true hearts that lo'ed Scotland", and offered a glass to his guest.

Jeanie, however, declined it, saying, "that she had never tasted wine in her life."

"How comes that, Jeanie?" said the Duke, – "wine maketh glad the heart, you know."

"Ay, sir, but my father is like Jonadab, the son of Rechab, who charged his children that they should drink no wine."

"I thought your father would have had more sense," said the Duke, "unless, he prefers brandy. But, however, Jeanie, if you will not drink, you must eat, to save the character of my house."

Sir Walter Scott

Advice from a Stutterer on the Evils of Drink

W
Wh
Whi
Whis
Whisk
Whisky

M M M M Maks ye

F
Fr
Fri
Fris
Frisk
Frisky

B B B B Bit

B
Br
Bra
Bran
Brand
Brandy

M M M M Maks ye

R
Ra
Ran
Rand
Randy

David Morrison

Utopia

The ale-houses (as indeed also private families) were but scantily provided with glasses, and I have seen a single glass go round a large company. Armstrong of Sorbie, a noted border toper, who died within my remembrance, lamenting in his latter days the degeneracy of the times, said, "that it was a better world when there were more bottles and fewer glasses."

Thomas Somerville

The Crookit Horn

("Ewie" is a euphemism for an illicit whisky still)

> Were I but able to rehearse
> My ewie's praise in proper verse,
> I'd sound it out as loud and fierce
> As ever piper's drone could blaw.
> > The ewie wi' the crookit horn,
> > A' that kent her might hae sworn
> > Sic a ewie was never born,
> > Hereabouts, nor far awa'.

Traditional Song

The Moonshiners

An adventure of a singular nature is said to have befallen a gentleman who was paying a visit to the Hebrides. While making some geological researches, he was induced to descend a precipice to examine the nature of the strata of a rock, and entering a cave that attracted his attention, he was astonished to hear the noise of persons, as if revelling at a banquet. Being fearful of danger he was about to retire, when he was accosted by a person inside and requested to advance. Considering compliance the best policy, and his curiosity being a good deal excited, he followed the individual into the cavern, and was no little astonished to find himself introduced to a number of persons seated on benches round a table, regaling themselves with as much apparent satisfaction as if in a palace. On looking round, he perceived a number of casks of spirits ranged as if in a cellar, with old swords and other weapons of defence, plainly indicating that he had fallen in with a party of smugglers. Apprehensive that he was an officer of the revenue, he was eyed with great distrust, and questioned most particularly as to his pursuits; but finding that his profession was of a different nature, they told him candidly what they were, treated him with much kindness, and, after enjoining secrecy, suffered him to depart, but not without partaking of a hearty glass, and a share of all the luxuries of their solitary grotto.

A person constructed a distillery so artfully, that it eluded the vigilance of the most expert officers of excise, though known to have long existed in the neighbourhood. A determined gentleman of this department resolved to find it out at all hazards, and, on one moonlight night, unaccompanied by any person, he followed a horse led by a peasant, having a sack across the back of the animal, which, he suspected contained materials for this mysterious manufactory. When the horse had arrived at a certain place, the sack was removed from his back, and suddenly disappeared. The officer made his observations, returned to his residence, and having procured military assistance, repaired to the place, where the horse had been unloaded, all was silent, the moon shone bright, the ground was unmarked by any peculiar appearance, and he was almost inclined (as well as those who accompanied him) to think that he laboured under a delusion. Perceiving, however, some brambles loosely scattered about the place, he proceeded to examine more minutely, and on their removal, discovered some loose sods, under which was found a trap door leading to a small cavern, at the bottom of which was a complete distillery at full work, supplied by a subterraneous stream, and the smoke conveyed from it through the windings of a tube that was made to communicate with the funnel of the chimney of the distillers' dwelling-house, situated at a considerable distance.

Contemporary Account, 1887

Flitting the Cellar

At the time we was removing the wine out of the seller in the town house to be sent to Abbotsford, Sir Walter cumes down to see how I was getting on.

"Have you any notion what quantity of wine there will be?"

"I cannot answer your question just now, Sir Walter, but I am keeping a correct account of the dozens as I pack them up."

"Verrey good, but you must not taste ower often, or then you will be apt to forget."

"Well, Sir Walter, I have packet up a good many dozens already, and I have not tasted yet, but as you are here, if you have no objections, we will have a tasting."

"No, no, I have no objections."

So drawing a bottle of white wine, and offering the furst of it, he just put it to his lips and said "it would be a very poor cellar if it could not afford a little to support you when you was working so hard."

I packet up three hundred and fifty dozens of wine, and thirty-six dozens of spirits, and never tasted until we was putting it past into Abbotsford cellars.

William Dalgleish
(butler to Sir Walter Scott)

Royal Favours

Lord Conyngham, the Chamberlain, was looking everywhere for pure Glenlivet whisky; the King [George IV] drank nothing else. It was not to be had out of the Highlands. My father sent word to me – I was the cellarer – to empty my pet bin, where was whisky long in wood, long in uncorked bottles, mild as milk, and the true contraband *goût* in it. Much as I grudged this treasure it made our fortunes afterwards, showing on what trifles great events depend. The whisky, and fifty brace of ptarmigan all shot by one man, went up to Holyrood House, and were graciously received and made much of, and a reminder of this attention at a proper moment by the gentlemanly Chamberlain ensured to my father the Italian judgeship.

Elizabeth Grant

Dear Mortimer.

That's it, then.

It's at this stage that the apologies usually begin – I should have included this or excluded that or tarted up yon or left well alone. Right at this moment, all these thousands of words later, I don't feel like apologising to anybody. Certainly not to the scholars and academics and hoodie-crow critics at whom such a book was not directed; certainly not to my fellow Scottish writers so many of whom, for the price of a dram, have generously allowed me to quote from their work; certainly not to the people of my country because most of them are big enough and ugly enough to get their own back in a thousand devious ways.

Up there in that heathery fastness, in this last quarter of a hellish century, it's like the end of the big sleep. To indulge the metaphor so dear to your heart – the game's gone into extra time, the Scots have the ball at their feet, and all they have to do is kick it into the back of an empty net instead of blootering it, as they usually do, over the bar.

So maybe Knox and the Reverend Macpherson and all the others were right. Maybe we are "the chosen" after all. But since "Jock" started all this, it's only right and proper that he should have the last word.

> See us? We're so pathetically unlucky, so pathologically committed to a horizontal position in the mud, that when the trumpet sounds on that great day when our ship finally comes in – *we'll* all be at the airport.

You'll have noticed my change of address.

By Way of Saying Thank You . . .

In some cases the following books have been of great assistance; in every case the following books deserve to be read as steps towards another view of Scotland. I acknowledge both debts.

ANDERSON, W. E. K. *The Journal of Sir Walter Scott*, Oxford University Press, 1972.

BRIDIE, James and MCLAREN, Moray. *A Small Stir: Letters on the English*, Hollis & Carter, 1949.

CAIRNS, J. B. *Bright and Early*, Cairns Brothers, Edinburgh, 1953.

CARSWELL, Donald & Catherine, *The Scots Week-End*, George Routledge & Sons Ltd., 1936.

CHAMBERS, Robert, *Traditions of Edinburgh*, W. & R. Chambers Ltd., 1824, reprinted 1868, 1912 and 1967.

CLARK, Kenneth, *Another Part of the Wood*, John Murray, 1974.

COLVIN, Sidney, *The Letters of Robert Louis Stevenson*, Vol 1, Methuen & Co., 1899.

DOUGLAS, Ronald Macdonald, *The Scots Book*, W. & R. Chambers Ltd., 1935.

FYFE, J. G. *Scottish Diaries and Memoirs, 1550–1746*, Eneas Mackay, Stirling.

GLOVER, Janet R. *The Story of Scotland*, Faber & Faber, 1960.

GRAY, W. Forbes, *Memorials of His Time*, Robert Grant & Son, 1946.

GUTHRIE, E. J. *Old Scottish Customs*, Hamilton, Adams & Co., 1885.

HENDERSON, T. F. *Old-World Scotland*, T. Fisher Unwin, 1893.

HOOD, Paxton, *Scottish Characteristics*, Hodder & Stoughton, 1883.

KING, Charles, *Twelve Modern Scottish Poets*, University of London Press Ltd., 1971.

LAFFIN, John, *Scotland The Brave*, Cassell & Co., 1963.

LINDSAY, Maurice, *Scotland: An Anthology*, Robert Hale & Co., 1974.

MACDIARMID, Hugh, *The Golden Treasury of Scottish Poetry*, Macmillan & Co., 1948.

MACKAY, Ian, *The Real Mackay*, News Chronicle Publications, 1953.

MACKIE, R. L. *A Book of Scottish Verse*, Oxford University Press, 1934.

MCNEILL, F. Marian, *The Scots Kitchen*, Blackie & Son, 1929.

MITCHISON, Rosalind, *A History of Scotland*, Methuen & Co., 1970.

ROGERS, Rev. Charles, *Traits and Stories of the Scottish People*, Houlston & Wright, 1867.

ROUGHEAD, William, *Burke and Hare*, William Hodge & Co. Ltd., 1921.

SCOTT, Tom, *The Penguin Book of Scottish Verse*, Penguin Books, 1970.

Scottish Women's Rural Institutes, *S.W.R.I. Cookery Book*, various editions.

SMOUT, T. C. *A History of the Scottish People, 1560–1830*, Collins, 1969.

STEVENSON, Robert Louis, *Edinburgh: Picturesque Notes*, Seeley & Co., 1889.

UNIVERSITY OF EDINBURGH PRESS, *Scottish Poetry*, Volumes I to V.

Acknowledgements

I am grateful to the literary executors of James Bridie, J. M. Caie, J. B. Cairns, Sir Alexander Gray, Ian Mackay, Neil Munro, Charles Murray, George Outram, and William Soutar for permission to quote from the works of these writers.

I am at least as grateful (a very Scottish way of putting it) to the living authors, poets, dramatists, and various other kinds of artists and craftsmen who have not only given permission for their work to be quoted, but who, in most cases, have gratuitously added expressions of affection and good will. Therefore my thanks and salutations to: Alan Bold (and the Hogarth Press); George Mackay Brown (and the Hogarth Press for the poem from *Fishermen With Ploughs*); Tom Buchan; Lord Clark; Alastair M. Dunnett; Cliff Hanley (from *Dancing in the Streets*); Harold Hobson; Alan Jackson; Tom Leonard (from *Poems*, E. & T. O'Brien, Dublin); Maurice Lindsay (*Selected Poems 1942–1972*, Robert Hale); Liz Lochhead (from *Memo for Spring*, Reprographia, Edinburgh); Norman MacCaig (various publications by Hogarth Press); Albert D. Mackie; Hugh MacDiarmid (Routledge and Kegan Paul, and Macmillan Publishing Co., Inc.); John MacGlashan; Alasdair Maclean; Roddy McMillan, Bruce Marshall; Edwin Morgan (from *The Second Life*, Edinburgh University Press); Margaret Morris (from *The Art of J. D. Fergusson*, Blackie); David Morrison (from *Hammer and Thistle*, Caithness Books); Stephen Mulrine; David Niven (from *The Moon's a Balloon*, Hamish Hamilton); Alexander Reid (from *Steps to a Viewpoint*, Andrew Dakers, 1947); Tom Scott (and *The Scotsman*); Alan Sharp; Iain Crichton Smith (from *The Law and the Grace*, Eyre and Spottiswoode); Gordon Williams.

I have received valuable help from Dundee Public Library, particularly with the works of William MacGonagall; from the Scottish National Library; and my forty-year-long indebtedness to every limb of Edinburgh's superb civic library system continues to deepen.

Brigadier Douglas Ross-Ewing, of Haughs of Benholm, kindly allowed me to examine and quote from his family papers, "The Bydand Myths", and has granted me the copyright.

My plays *Jock* and *Knox* and all other dramatic works are administered by Andrew Hewson of John Johnson, 51–54 Goschen Buildings, 12–13 Henrietta Street, London.

Finally, for the inevitable sins of omission, my apologies in advance.

W.G.S.   Edinburgh, 1976.

Index to Authors